NEW LOOKS AT ITALIAN OPERA

Essays in Honor of Donald J. Grout

Donald J. Grout

NEW LOOKS AT ITALIAN OPERA

Essays in Honor of

DONALD J. GROUT

by

Robert M. Adams   *   Dénes Bartha
Robert A. Hall, Jr.   *   William C. Holmes
Claude V. Palisca   *   Nino Pirrotta
Luigi Tagliavini   *   Jack Allan Westrup

Edited, with an Introduction, by

WILLIAM W. AUSTIN

CORNELL UNIVERSITY PRESS

Ithaca, New York

Contents

Illustrations

Preface

Not only the authors represented here, but also a huge, far-flung community of colleagues, friends, students, and readers, testify to the achievement of Donald Jay Grout, and all join in wishing him many years of freedom from administration and teaching, freedom to pursue further his scholarly work, both specialized and speculative. The range of his work in the past three decades or so is suggested, though not nearly matched, by the essays we present to him now. These essays express an anticipatory tribute to the work he has only lately embarked on—editing and publishing the operas of Alessandro Scarlatti—as well as admiring gratitude for all he has done so far.

Seventeenth-century operas, Italian, French, and German, were the subjects of Grout's first publications, in 1941, when he was teaching at Harvard. In 1947, Columbia University Press published his two-volume handbook, *A Short History of Opera*, which is often cited in our essays, as it has been since 1947 in most special studies of opera. Columbia brought out a second edition in 1965. Meanwhile Grout had written his *History of Western Music* (New York, 1960), which met to an unparalleled extent the needs of teachers and students. After leaving Harvard, he taught at the University of Texas, and in 1945 he came to Cornell University, where he is now Given Foundation Professor of Musicology. He served as editor of the *Journal of the American Musicological Society* and as president both of this society and of the International Musicological Society, accomplishing large and delicate tasks on behalf of his fellow scholars with a grace worthy of a Scarlatti or a Mozart.

In Grout's work there is a natural alternation of specialized research and broader humane concern. Though both accident and calculation affect this alternation, it is more like a musical rhythm, with many interacting levels of tension and relaxation. The strength of his big books depends partly on their including much concrete detail, studied afresh. The strength of his specialized work depends on the broad perspectives in which he views his subjects and the lucidity with which he writes. It is characteristic of him that even in the midst of the most pressing editorial or administrative work he has always found time to read and reread Dante, Mark Twain, Joyce, C. S. Lewis, and other favorites. Thus it is fitting that our essays include literary studies alongside the musical ones. We are confident that in the current phase of his work, which is perhaps a climax of specialization, broader concerns will by no means be neglected.

When his sixty-fifth birthday approached, Professor Grout asked the editor of this volume to "quash any suggestions of a *Festschrift*, if necessary." His friends agreed that a collection of many essays on miscellaneous topics would not constitute a proper celebration for him at this still early stage of his career. But we hope he will find this volume unusual enough to warrant its dedication. His Cornell colleagues, especially John Kirkpatrick, Harold Samuel, and Mary Cullen, though their names are absent from the Contents, have contributed to the project enthusiastically, each one characteristically. Above all, Mrs. Cullen worked with the skill, tact, speed, and patience that are familiar to Grout from many another project. In various phases of the editorial planning, William Holmes gave indispensable help, and in particular he made the translation of Professor Tagliavini's essay. Furthermore we were encouraged by advice from Professor Oliver Strunk of Princeton University, Professor Paul Lang of Columbia University, and Professor Friedrich Blume of

Kiel, three of Grout's closest associates and friends. All these friends share with the authors and the editor the responsibility for a broad interpretation of Grout's modest request.

The staff of Cornell University Press helped refine and realize our unusual project. They, like the authors, are only representatives of many more friends of Donald Grout at Cornell and around the world.

W. A.

Ithaca, New York
September 1967

Contributors

Robert M. Adams is Professor of English and member of the Department of Comparative Literature at Cornell University.

Dénes Bartha is Chairman of the Musicological Department at the Franz Liszt Academy of Music, Budapest. He was Visiting Professor of Music at Cornell in 1965-1966.

Robert A. Hall, Jr., is Professor of Linguistics and member of the Department of Romance Studies at Cornell.

William C. Holmes is Associate Professor of Music at Cornell.

Claude V. Palisca is Professor of Music at Yale University.

Nino Pirrotta is Professor of Music at Harvard University.

Luigi Tagliavini is Professor of Music at the University of Fribourg and teaches also at the Conservatory at Bologna. He has visited Cornell several times as lecturer and organ recitalist.

Sir Jack Westrup is Professor of Music at Oxford University. He lectured at Cornell in 1957.

NEW LOOKS AT ITALIAN OPERA

Essays in Honor of Donald J. Grout

Introduction

By WILLIAM W. AUSTIN

Italian opera in every land and every generation breeds both fanatic devotees and incredulous scoffers. Again and again, scoffers claim that devotees are out of date, but new, young devotees keep proving them mistaken. Italian opera may not win over any great proportion of the growing audiences of Beethoven's symphonies, or Bach's concertos, or Bartók's quartets, or Fellini's movies, or the Beatles' songs. But it survives as a grand international institution and inspires ever-new enthusiasms. Its specialized lore seems to thrive by itself, with little concern for the relation of opera to the rest of the world. If the devotees bother to answer the scoffers at all, they defend their grand institution for its own sake; their very devotion hinders their seeing opera in perspective. If they compromise to the extent of liking French opera, or German, or Russian, or Ukrainian, or American, or opera in translation, still what they like in any language is something as close as possible to Italian opera, the enduring international standard of singing and of composition for the theatre. Their opponents propose various new standards, or some vision of freedom from all standards. The arguments proceed at cross purposes.

Besides its devotees and scoffers, Italian opera has calmer, wiser friends, willing to let various other interests share their admiring concern in alternation with opera. They may be ready to see connections between opera and other interests which neither faction in the usual arguments can see clearly or steadily, for whoever sees enough of the interconnections must join, if he is not already one of them, the calmer, wiser friends. Readers of this book are naturally among them, as are all the writers and the dedicatee.

Connections exist in profusion, awaiting our study. One book is not enough to survey them systematically. Italian opera has influenced, and been influenced by, so many things in so many ways that a perspective view can be no more than a sketch, and a book has room for only a few samples studied in fresh detail. The detailed studies may confirm the sketchy view that is about to be put forward here. The sketch simply introduces and loosely links together the studies of particular works and influences, whose main values are their freshness and precision.

A broad international historical perspective is needed to bring into view the most important connections. Mere opera lore, as a background of the works well known today, does not satisfy the need. It is too short-sighted. The enduring repertory of Italian opera in performance extends from Rossini's *Barber of Seville* (1816) to Puccini's *Turandot* (1926). But, for musicians and music lovers, these names and dates call to mind Rossini's contemporaries Beethoven and Schubert and Puccini's contemporaries Debussy and Schoenberg; in the perspective where such composers tower, Rossini and Puccini may seem lowly and remote from the center of things—even Verdi may be overshadowed by Wagner. But, now, if we step back and bring Mozart into the picture, all the relations change. Though his native language was German, Mozart was an enlightened cosmopolitan, and though the Austrian emperor preferred the genuine Italian Salieri, we recognize in Mozart the supreme master of Italian opera. The repertory today makes a surer place than ever before for three of Mozart's Italian works, along with one or two of his German ones. Yet, at the same time, our concert repertories give him supremacy as inventor of the modern concerto, and perfecter, jointly with Haydn, of the symphony and quartet. He was the center of everything musical. Further, in depending on Mozart the symphonic tradition from Beethoven through Schoenberg depended on earlier Italian opera. This indirect dependence the composers took for granted. Only twentieth-century Americans, perhaps, with their abundance of orchestras and paucity of opera houses, could try to cultivate the symphonic tradition by itself and miss the indispensable central function of opera in the world of European music.

If we broaden our perspective further, to include what we call the Baroque period alongside the classics and Romantics, then Monteverdi appears as another central figure comparable to Mozart. And between Monteverdi and Mozart we may infer, though we are not yet sure of the details, that Italian opera constituted the main stream of music, feeding its innovations and its standardizations into other forms, provoking other national styles of opera, and absorbing again from the other forms and styles everything that developed in them. The rise of opera in the seventeenth century and its clear predominance in the eighteenth are naturally connected with every aspect of the art of music from that time onward. Our basic ideas about the orchestra, about keys and chords and modulations, about rhythms and forms and musical expression, were shaped by opera, and especially by the pace-setting Italian opera. The clarification of these ideas depends to a considerable extent on our extending and refining our knowledge of the thousands of Italian operas that led up to Mozart. Even though revivals of Monteverdi's works may always be special events—and revivals of Peri, Cesti, Scarlatti, or Gasparini very rare indeed—yet the careful study of these and many more is an urgent need, for the sake of the vital connections between Baroque opera and the rest of European music then and later.

Three of the essays presented here, like the current studies of Donald Grout himself, contribute to the fulfillment of this urgent need. Professor Pirrotta's long essay brings together a wealth of precise knowledge about the early seventeenth-century aria, in and out of opera, knowledge accumulated and interpreted only recently; what scholarly investigation of this topic up to the 1940's had achieved, as summed up in Grout's *Short History of Opera*, was so incomplete that it afforded no safe basis for generalization; many investigations of the 1950's contributed disconnected details, such as to make Grout's revised edition of 1963 even more cautious than the original in its general statements. (The changes from the original page 59 to the new page 49, and those from 83 to 77, are especially noteworthy and typical.) Pirrotta does not claim to have arrived at a final word on the subject here, but he has surely done much to advance the understanding of fellow specialists and other interested readers alike. Professor Holmes and Professor Westrup each present a concise study of a single opera, whose long-neglected music they have brought to vivid life, and whose place in history they have defined better than anyone could have done before. Each of these operas, Cesti's and Scarlatti's, has unique intrinsic values, and each of them can nourish our understanding of Monteverdi and Mozart by demonstrating something more of the continuity between them.

The importance of eighteenth-century Italian masters for Haydn and Mozart is shown here by the essays of Professors Tagliavini and Bartha. Tagliavini informs us of hitherto unknown manuscript evidence of one very concrete connection. Bartha brings up to date the astonishing record of Haydn as opera conductor, which first came to many people's attention in Bartha's book of 1960; the general implications of this record will be unfolding in many minds for a long time.

It was the instrumental music of Haydn, Mozart, and Beethoven that exemplified the essence of Romanticism for E. T. A. Hoffmann. And it was the Romantic attitude of Hoffmann and others toward such music, more than any thought of the great composers themselves, that entered and shaped the main stream of literary culture, and restored music to a place of honor in the wider world, which it had lost wherever a shallow rationalism

held sway. Italian opera in its heyday before Mozart never inspired men of letters with such utter reverence or even jealousy
as that with which symphonic music and Wagner's symphonic
music-drama inspired a long line of nineteenth-century writers.
Their attitude is still potent in the twentieth century. If we
accept or reject that attitude without reference to the older
tradition of opera, we miss much of the significance of any music
and some of the significance of much modern literature. If, on
the contrary, we connect nineteenth- and twentieth-century
music with Italian opera, our appreciation of Beethoven and of
Hoffmann may continue to grow, along with our appreciation
of Schoenberg and Stravinsky, Joyce and Brecht.

Beethoven himself was pupil and friend of Salieri; he continued occasional lessons with Salieri long after he had learned all
he could from Haydn and Albrechtsberger, from the violinist
Schuppanzigh and the quartet composer Förster. And Beethoven, we know, regarded Cherubini as his greatest contemporary.

Hoffmann himself, though we easily forget it if we hear of it
at all, was an opera composer and conductor before he became a
man of letters. And he never ceased to love and admire the old
arias of Leo and Durante, which he emulated more nearly than
he could Mozart or Beethoven. Hoffmann's Romanticism was
not yet so one-sided as the "absolute music" idolatry of the later
nineteenth century. For all his fresh emphasis on the romance of
the symphony, he would have assented to the argument advanced in 1937 at Cornell by E. J. Dent, that "opera, at any rate
for the Romantic period, is by far the most important of all
musical forms." Dent, with his unrivaled knowledge of Scarlatti
and Mozart, and probably more knowledge of Leo, Durante,
and the rest than Hoffmann could have had, traced the spirit and
techniques of music that he called "romantic" continuously from
Scarlatti to Bellini and Weber. Hoffmann's work, his compositions, his fictions, and his musical criticism should be seen more
often as Dent saw it, in the long perspective of Italian opera.

The metaphor of "the main stream of music" was elaborated in a famous essay by D. F. Tovey, with appropriate apologies for its limitations and risks. Tovey was a more conservative musician than his close contemporary Dent, whose historical researches were all intended to serve the cause of freedom for contemporary music and its listeners. Tovey was content to neglect Scarlatti, at least until Haydn's symphonies had been completely brought to light. He fully recognized the dramatic quality of the symphonies and sonatas that he put at the center of his world, and he could show warm respect for Salieri, but he was impatient with most opera and only grudgingly acknowledged that opera had contributed to that dramatic quality of "absolute music."

I find no difficulty in regarding opera of all kinds as in its integrity an ultimately pure form of music. The main practical difficulty with opera is that its historic progress has by no means been essentially the progress of good music. Opera has continually subsided with full popular and fashionable acclamation into dead conventionality and bottomless vulgarity; but, from the lowest depths, it has shown a capacity to rise almost as high as absolute music can rise.[1]

Tovey's main stream relegates most opera to the backwaters:

For me the main stream of music becomes navigable at the end of the fifteenth century with such composers as Josquin des Pres, and remains smoothly navigable throughout the sixteenth century. At the beginning of the seventeenth century, it enters into regions partly mountainous and partly desert, and becomes choked with weeds. In the eighteenth century, it is drastically cleared up by Bach and Handel, and drained off into various smaller channels by other composers. In the middle of the century, these channels unite and carry the main stream in another direction, represented by Haydn, Mozart, and Beethoven. . . . Having thus sketchily traced the main stream of music to what we may regard as the ocean of Wagner, I

[1] D. F. Tovey, *The Main Stream of Music, and Other Essays* (New York, 1949), p. 350.

can go no further. At the present day, all musicians feel more or less at sea, and not all of us are good sailors.[2]

Tovey does not claim that his "main stream" is a substitute for history, or a summary of it. His essay has room for many glances at the historically important "side channels." But he emphasizes the great composers' transcendence of history:

The musical composer is the most detached of all artists. For him, the time is either out of joint or irrelevant. . . . Art has an unlimited capacity for minding its own business, and history has so much business that not even the art of Thomas Hardy's *Dynasts* can wholly convince the mere musician that history has a mind at all.[3]

No twentieth-century historian is likely to side with Hardy against Tovey. But Tovey's "main stream," escaping history for his purposes, can very well be pumped back into historical studies like those that concern us here. His perspective view is naturally not quite ours, for we of a later generation or two are all farther out "at sea," to continue his metaphor. We have our own various perspectives. If we hope to stay afloat in the tides of today's music, we have additional motives for studying Italian opera, and we welcome opportunities to do so that were not yet available to Tovey.

The new music of our time, in its conspicuous contrast with the "common practice" that prevailed roughly from Cesti and Scarlatti to Puccini and Montemezzi, and also in its many new ways of collaborating with literature and drama, might seem to restrict the place of Italian opera even more than did Tovey's conservative view. Surely, the musical-theatrical experiments of John Cage, Karlheinz Stockhausen, Luciano Berio, and their rivals do not directly continue any musical "stream" from the past, main stream or undercurrent. But these experiments, and many others not quite so radical, reflect influences from modern literature that had absorbed something profound from earlier music. The perspective view that shows up this to-and-fro of

[2] *Ibid.*, pp. 333, 351.   [3] *Ibid.*, p. 347.

influences must be a lofty and vague one, but Italian opera by no means disappears in it. The last two essays here may indicate something of the allurement of this post-Joycean view.

Professor Hall's study of Fogazzaro shows music as both a concrete subject and a useful symbol, permeating the work of a sober and sympathetic novelist. Professor Adams shows the "operatic" literary work of another Italian, D'Annunzio, contributing an essential stimulus to Joyce, who was to surpass D'Annunzio and all others in the achievement of a new international musical art in words.

These two literary topics differ from each other as much as they differ from a musicological one. Together, the two suggest a whole spectrum of further connections between Italian opera and world literature, which will guarantee the perennial interest of opera in history, even if some day the institution should pass away like so many of its styles.

How opera began has been a fascinating question ever since it did begin, and will probably continue to occupy investigators as long as the perennial interest in opera lasts. Literary men as well as singers and composers have generally been credited with essential ideas and impulses. Perspective views back through the centuries to ancient Greek drama have been cited. But just how these views affected changing practices of musical drama, this is a web of history that can be unraveled indefinitely. New discoveries and a new interpretation of the relevance of the Greeks are the contribution here of Professor Palisca. He enables us to return to the beginning of opera with greater understanding than we have brought to it before. His interpretation emphasizes "prevailing trends" of the sixteenth century—not a main stream, but several strands of continuity. In this interpretation, as in his patient documentary study, Palisca can be seen as typical of our time. He connects his sixteenth-century theorists with us twentieth-century historians, through and around the whole history of opera.

The Alterati of Florence, Pioneers in the Theory of Dramatic Music[1]

By CLAUDE V. PALISCA

The potent mixture of a brilliant musical life and flourishing literary academies in late sixteenth-century Florence was bound to fuse into an amalgam of unique and splendid properties. No wonder that the musical pastorales of Ottavio Rinuccini and Jacopo Peri emerged there between 1598 and 1600. Given the ingredients and the climate, the compound seems almost inevitable.

Yet early historians of opera, who knew little of the climate, looked for a catalyst. They thought they found it in the Camerata of Count Giovanni Bardi. But they were deceived. What they called the Camerata was really two different and separate, indeed even opposed, social and intellectual circles. One, Bardi's Camerata, was oriented toward talking about learned topics, listening to music, and perhaps amateur music making. The later

[1] This essay is based on a paper read at a meeting of the Greater New York Chapter of the American Musicological Society at the New York Public Library on April 28, 1962. The author's research in Florence in 1960–1961 was made possible by a fellowship from the John Simon Guggenheim Memorial Foundation.

group, sponsored by Jacopo Corsi, was a kind of semi-professional musical and dramatic workshop, bent toward experimentation in theatrical productions. It was directly responsible for the first musical pastorales. The discussions in Bardi's Camerata undoubtely stimulated the experiments and gave them direction. However, the process of cause and effect here, as in most historic events, is an elusive and complex one.

Nino Pirrotta has shown that the set of beliefs that is usually associated with the Camerata evolved mainly outside it and that Florence at this time seethed with conflicts of esthetic principles and personalities.[2] Caccini and Peri were rivals, and so were their patrons Bardi and Corsi. Emilio de' Cavalieri, the boss of Florentine artistic enterprises under Grand Duke Ferdinand I, managed to alienate almost everyone, smooth diplomat though he was. The principal source of the ideology once attributed to Bardi and Galilei was actually in Rome in the person of an erudite classicist interested in ancient Greek musical theory—Girolamo Mei.[3] Furthermore, there were not only the Camerata and Corsi's workshop but four other academies interested in drama, and one of them, the Alterati, was full of musical amateurs. The overlapping of membership among all these groups, moreover, makes it hard to keep their contributions distinct. Of all the academies, the most poorly documented, because it was unofficial, is the Camerata. Beside the host Bardi, the only members of which we can be sure are Giulio Caccini, who acknowledged having frequented the circle and was the first to refer to it as the "Camerata"; Vincenzo Galilei, a protegé of Bardi who wrote a dialogue to instruct certain members of the circle in music theory; and

[2] Nino Pirrotta, "Temperaments and Tendencies in the Florentine Camerata," *Musical Quarterly*, XL (1954), 169–189. See also C. V. Palisca, "Musical Asides in the Diplomatic Correspondence of Emilio de' Cavalieri," *Musical Quarterly*, XLIX (1963), 339–355.

[3] See C. V. Palisca, ed., *Girolamo Mei: Letters on Ancient and Modern Music to Vincenzo Galilei and Giovanni Bardi* (American Institute of Musicology, 1960).

Pietro Strozzi, who with Bardi is one of the two interlocutors in the dialogue.[4]

By contrast to this informal academy, the official literary academies that were active in Florence in the second half of the sixteenth century are well documented. The one that contained the greatest number of musical amateurs was the Accademia degli Alterati. The records of this academy, from its first official meeting up to January 23, 1606, are preserved in the manuscript Ashburnham 558 of the Biblioteca Medicea Laurenziana of Florence. This is the "Diario dell'Accademia degli Alterati" in three volumes, bound in two.[5] The Academy, according to the record, was founded on February 17, 1568, Florentine style, or 1569 (all dates in this article will be converted to the modern calendar). Its founders were seven gentlemen, all but one already members of the Accademia Fiorentina. By 1571 it had twenty-one members and in that year acquired the name Alte-

---

[4] Giulio Caccini, "Ai lettori," in Le nuove musiche di Guilio Caccini detto Romano (Florence: Marescotti, 1602), trans. in Oliver Strunk, Source Readings in Music History (New York, 1950), p. 378. Galilei, in his Discorso intorno all'opere di messer Gioseffo Zarlino (Florence: Marescotti, 1589), pp. 51–52, says that it was mainly to instruct certain gentlemen with whom he was associated in some aspects of music theory that he wrote his Dialogo della musica antica et della moderna (Florence: Marescotti, 1581).

[5] Since the Diario is chronological, references to it will be by date rather than volume and folio. Dates are given in the Diario in Florentine style, which began the year on March 25, ab incarnatione. I have converted these to the modern calendar. Members' names are recorded only through their academic pseudonyms. I have translated these to their proper names with the help of the list of members in Domenico Maria Manni's history of the academy, Memorie della fiorentina famosa Accademia degli Alterati (Florence: Stecchi, 1748). The most extensive discussion of the Diario is Bernard Weinberg, "The Accademia degli Alterati and Literary Taste from 1570 to 1600," Italica, XXXI (1954), 207–214. Weinberg has also published extracts from the codex pertaining to literary matters in "Argomenti di discussione letteraria nell'Accademia degli Alterati (1570–1600)," Giornale storico della letteratura italiana, CXXXI (1954), 175–194.

rati. The academic pseudonyms of the members are given in the Appendix following this article.

The significance of the name was explained by its first "Reggente" or Regent, Giulio del Bene, in a discourse on the Academy's aims. It was dedicated, he said, to the "alteration" or improvement of its members through the cultivation of elegant speech, good conduct, and a knowledge of all the arts and sciences.[6] Thus it had a broader base than the older Accademia Fiorentina or the younger Accademia della Crusca, which was modeled on the Alterati. Both of these other academies were preoccupied with the study and spread of the Tuscan language and its literature.

The Alterati first met at the home of Tommaso del Nero. After his death on August 3, 1572, they used temporary quarters briefly before establishing their home in the palace of Giovanni Battista Strozzi the Younger, known as *il Cieco*. They ordinarily convened once or twice a week. Certain formalities through which their sessions were organized seem to have been original and peculiar to this academy. At the beginning of a regency—a term of six months—an amphora was formally opened with an oration. Into the amphora members were expected to drop original poems, essays, tragedies, comedies, translations, commentaries, and the like. At the end of a semester the accumulated writings were assigned to two censors and a defender, who prepared critiques of the works. The censures and defenses were then heard to determine whether each composition itself should be read. If a vote was favorable, the tragedy, poem, or discourse was read and discussed, and the author often modified it on the basis of the Academy's review. This collective criticism constituted an important though small part of the work of the Academy.

From around 1571 it became the custom to focus discussions

[6] Giulio del Bene, "Del convivio delli Alterati," Florence, Bibl. Naz. Cent., MS Magl. IX, 137, fol. 18v. According to the Diario, this was delivered on February 16, 1575.

around a subject or subjects chosen for his term by the regent. For example, in June 1573, Baccio Neroni decreed that questions related to the *Poetics* of Aristotle would occupy the academicians during his regency. After January 1574 it became customary for two academicians to be assigned each time to take the pros and cons of a particular aspect of the topic. On January 21, 1574, the proposition that poetry may be defined as an imitation made with words was argued, Antonio degli Albizzi taking the affirmative and Alessandro Rinuccini the negative. Beside these prepared debates, there were prepared and impromptu lectures and discussions. Some of the prepared lectures and more of the extemporaneous ones were penalties imposed on academicians found guilty of such misconduct as failure to appear when scheduled to speak or late arrival. Mere absence was not considered sufficient cause for punishment.

No reigning philosophy can be attributed to the Alterati such as characterized the Accademia Platonica of the fifteenth century. There were certainly some neo-Platonists still around, but the dominant tone of the discourses that survive is anti-Platonic. A good index of the Alterati's temper is their attitude toward love. This was a favorite topic of earlier academies, particularly the relationship between earthly and divine love. The attitude of the Alterati toward love is pertinent to our interest in the Academy as a force in the development of attitudes toward music, because love is a key to the esthetic theories of the early Renaissance. Through loving the beauty of earthly things and artistic products, it was believed, one rises by steps to the true love of the divine. One of the Alterati's leading thinkers, Lorenzo Giacomini de' Tebalducci Malespini, raised the question whether love was a suitable subject for academic discussion. Much of what the interlocutors of Plato's *Symposium* say about love and beauty, he declared, is either said in jest or is vain, sophistic, and plainly incredible. Giacomini proposed a more realistic view. He who is enamoured "greatly loves and wishes well a beautiful person, and hoping to be loved in return, seeks with all means possible to attain this end as the most delightful thing and as a cause of many other delights." [7] Love to Giacomini was simply one of the affections, along with such others as hate, anger, pleasure, and friendship. Thus stripped of such concepts dear to Platonists as desire for immortality, union with the divine, and intuition of divine beauty, love was admissible in academic forums only if investigated through natural science and ethics. This changed outlook on love is an important sign of the philosophical orientation of the generation that founded the Alterati.

Some of the barriers that effectively excluded music from some of the earlier academies were now cut down. Giulio del Bene, in enumerating the liberal arts, takes music out of the quadrivium, in which it was a traditional partner of geometry, arithmetic, and astronomy, and places it beside the disciplines of the old trivium, grammar, dialectic, and rhetoric, to which he adds poetics. [8] He thus arrives at five liberal arts: grammar, rhetoric, music, poetics, and dialectics. Music, poetry, and rhetoric

---

[7] "Ragionamento d'amore," Florence, Bibl. Riccardiana, MS 2437, fol. 3v: "colui diciamo esser innamorato il quale grandemente ama et vuol bene à persone bella; et sperando essersi amato cerca con tutti i mezzi à lui possibili conseguire questo fine, come cosa dilettevolissima, et come cagione di molti altri diletti." A somewhat edited version of this lecture is in Prose fiorentine raccolte dallo Smarrito [Carlo Dati] accademico della Crusca (Florence: Santi Franchi, 1716-1745), Pt. II, Vol. V (1730), pp. 116-152. Quotations in these footnotes, on the contrary, preserve the archaic and inconsistent orthography of the original writers.

[8] "Del convivio delli Alterati," fols. 18v-19r. We study the liberal arts, Del Bene says, "à fine che noi possiamo, per la gramatica bene et correttamente ragionare, non havendo noi questo da natura, per la retorica persuadere, et tirare la volunta delli huomini dove ci pare, et per la musica imparare ad essere ordinati et composti bene nel animo nostro, et a movere gli affetti non meno che si faccia la retorica et per delettarsi et sollevarci dalle fatiche che nelle operatione humane ogni giorno supportiamo. et finalmente della poesia accio che possiamo descrivere et dimostrare col imitare lationi delli huomini quasi lidea delle virtu et de virtu de gli eccelenti huomini, et id il verso, nel quale è opinione che sia il parlare delli dei exprimere inoltre concetti et imitare gli affetti et i costumi altrui, e delettare et giovare l'uno laltro per questa cosi piacevole et bella arte."

are further linked in that they all serve to move or express the affections. Del Bene betrays his dependence on Aristotle's *Politics* when he cites as the other uses of music its capacity to order and repose the soul and to provide pleasure and solace from workaday burdens. The tendency to look to Aristotle as the guide runs throughout the deliberations of the academy. But there is also a pronounced desire to improve on Aristotle, to find solutions that better answered contemporary needs.

The Alterati's interest in music and its importance was not limited to the group's avowed concern with esthetic principles. Many of the members themselves had noteworthy musical connections.

The man who deserves to be mentioned first is Giovanni Bardi. His attendance was recorded as early as June 3, 1574, when he improvised a sonnet, and he was a frequent participant from then on. Perhaps it was deemed wiser to have him in the group than not, for on January 14, 1573, the Diario reports that the regent, Cosimo Rucellai, failed to appear at a meeting and gave as his excuse that he had gone "a far musica" at the house of Monsignor Bardi.[9] The Alterati present were so indignant they resolved to stay away next time so that Rucellai would find himself alone. Bardi must have been initiated around December 1574, for on the thirtieth he was instructed to submit his academic pseudonym and *impresa*, or device. He adopted the name *il Puro* and a device showing a flask used for distilling brandy and the motto *Alterato, io raffino* (Altered, I refine).[10] All but the earliest devices of the Alterati had some connection with wine, because the device of the Academy represented a vat for pressing wine heaped up with grapes bearing the motto *Quid non designat* [*ebrietas*] from Horace. Bardi was introduced, as was the custom, by another academician, whose oration in Bardi's behalf survives.

[9] This may be the earliest record of a meeting of the Camerata, Diario, Vol. II, fol. 3v.

[10] Giovanni Maria Mazzuchelli, *Gli scrittori d'Italia* (Brescia: Bossini, 1753–1763), II, 333.

After praising Bardi's military and literary accomplishments, his great skill in Greek, Latin, and Tuscan, his understanding of mathematics, of both judicial and cosmic astrology, of many useful and liberal sciences, the anonymous orator finally extolled Bardi's dedication to poetry and music:

It is evident that everyone loves those things that are in keeping with and proportioned to his condition. For this reason the person of Irate [temperament] desires contests, the Sanguine enjoys pleasing and cheerful things, the Melancholic loves solitude, and the Phlegmatic above all tranquility and quiet. It is not surprising that our Signor Giovanni, altogether well proportioned in soul and body, has always borne a singular affection for the suave and delectable harmony of music, the art of the ancient Greeks, among whom flourished all the noble arts and virtues to such a degree that whoever was not versed and practiced in music was looked upon as ill bred and vulgar. In music he has produced such artful compositions that he has surpassed many who pursue music as a profession.[11]

Another member, Piero del Nero, who had a keen interest in ancient music, was initiated on February 12, 1572. In 1602, he published Girolamo Mei's *Discorso sopra la musica antica e moderna*. This he dedicated to Baccio Valori, another of the Alterati.[12] The del Nero family was prominent among the early members; the Academy met at first in the house of Tommaso del Nero.[13] Another member of the family who figures in the history of music is Nero del Nero, brother of Tommaso and twice regent of the Alterati. At his house in Rome early in the 1590's, Caccini

[11] Florence, Bibl. Medicea Laurenziana, MS Ashburnham 559, item 24. The reference to Bardi's compositions is interesting, because no music of Bardi's is known earlier than "Lauro ohimè, lauro," printed in *Il lauro secco* (Ferrara: Baldini, 1582).

[12] Baccio and his son Filippo Valori are not listed as members by Manni, but Michele Maylender does include them in *Storia delle accademie d'Italia* (Bologna, 1926–1930), I, 154–160.

[13] He was one of the founding members along with Giulio del Bene, Renato de' Pazzi, Vincenzio Acciaiuoli, Lorenzo Corbinelli, Alessandro Canigiani, and Antonio degli Albizzi, according to Salvino Salvini, *Fasti consolari dell'Accademia Fiorentina* (Florence: Tartini, 1717), p. 203.

sang some of the airs and madrigals which he had previously sung in Bardi's Camerata and which were later printed in *Le nuove musiche*.[14] Agostino del Nero, son of Tommaso, was an accomplished amateur singer and player and was also interested in ancient music. A long letter addressed to him on that subject by Girolamo Mei found its way to a later Alterato, Giovanni Battista Doni, who credited it with stimulating his researches into Greek music.[15]

Two Rinuccini brothers were Alterati. The older, Alessandro, was a noted poet and senator and three times regent of the Academy. He spoke on the choruses of the Greek drama in January 1575.[16] Ottavio, the librettist of *Euridice, Dafne,* and *Arianna*, was not proposed as a member until March 28, 1586, and was formally admitted on September 4 of that year.

One of the most scholarly members of the Academy was Lorenzo Giacomini. Although his main field was poetic theory, a manuscript attributed to him in the Riccardiana Library shows that he was learned also in ancient music. A translation of the musical section of Aristotle's *Problems* into Italian, it is the first known translation into the vernacular.[17] Giacomini may have been an amateur musician too, for Giorgio Bartoli, who often acted as his amanuensis and secretary, wrote him from Venice on May 24, 1572, that he had finally sent him his harpsichord.[18]

---

[14] Caccini, foreword to *Le nuove musiche*, trans. in Strunk, *Source Readings*, p. 379.

[15] Palisca, *Girolamo Mei*, p. 10. Francesco Nori, who delivered an oration on the death of Agostino at the age of twenty-one, praised his musical ability in *Delle lodi del Barone Agostino del Nero*, printed in *Prose fiorentine*, Pt. I, Vol. IV (1731), pp. 58–92. He is not listed anywhere as a member, but he probably was one, since members' sons were admitted as soon as they came of age. On June 1, 1587, Agostino del Nero founded an academy, known as the Desiosi, said to have been interested in music and drama.

[16] This information is not found in the Diario, but in a letter dated Jan. 22, 1574 (1575), from Giorgio Bartoli to Lorenzo Giacomini in Bibl. Riccardiana, MS 2438 bis, Pt. III, no. 60 (my numbering).

[17] Bibl. Riccardiana, MS 1612.

[18] Bibl. riccardiana, MS 2438 bis, Pt. III, letter no. 24.

The only man honored with nonresident membership during the Academy's first twenty years was Girolamo Mei. Although Florentine by birth and a founding member of the Accademia Fiorentina, he lived most of his life outside Florence. His writings on music and Tuscan prose and poetry circulated widely among the literary circles of his native city. Few spoke of the ancient drama without citing his authority. He was elected *in absentia* on September 2, 1585, and Piero del Nero was assigned the duty of advising him of this. Mei, then in his sixty-sixth year, replied on September 20, 1585, from Rome:

Signal Sirs:
If the favor with which Your Lordships have honored my old age by desiring me with such amicable and universal affection to be of your number could alter that old age and make it regain the vigor of years gone by, I might then acquire the means to give you thanks, if not equal to my desire, at least sufficiently to succeed in persuading you of how much I consider myself obligated.

He went on with similar rhetorical flowers, closing with regrets about the distance that would prevent him from enjoying "the fruit of presence in a company after my own heart." In replying, Vincenzo Martelli asked Mei to send some "recent or older offspring of his noble genius" for their review.[19] Mei sent a tragedy, one of the four that he once acknowledged writing to test Aristotle's poetic theories. In the entry of the Diario for August 11, 1589, we read that Alessandro Rinuccini was sentenced for having been absent when he was due to lecture—to censure Mei's tragedy.

Another late entrant was Jacopo Corsi, harpsichordist, composer with Peri of Rinuccini's *Dafne*, and sponsor of Peri's and Rinuccini's *Euridice*. He was initiated September 4, 1586.

Two men whose names have not previously been associated with music remain to be mentioned: Antonio degli Albizzi and

---

[19] Mei's letter and Martelli's reply are given in an appendix to the Diario, Vol. III, fols. 172v–173v.

Cosimo Rucellai, both among the earliest regents. They are credited in the *Diario* with pronouncing lessons on music.[20]

The only other members who can be connected with music are the poets whose verses were set by numerous composers. Most notable of these are Gabriello Chiabrera and Giovanni Battista Strozzi. The latter was author of the fourth intermezzo of the 1589 festivities produced by Emilio de' Cavalieri and directed by Giovanni Bardi. Prince Giovanni de' Medici, who staged Caccini's *Rapimento di Cefalo* in 1600, was another member.

Professional musicians are completely absent from the Academy's records, as is any trace of music making. Perhaps the only occasions for music were the annual symposia held to celebrate the founding of the Alterati on the so-called "Nativity" day, February 17. This called for a sumptuous banquet. At the Riccardiana Library there is a large folded folio that documents this side of the Academy's activity. It is an itemized statement of expenses for one such annual feast: "Spese fatte nel simposio." [21] Some of the items listed below will give an indication of the academicians' taste for the good things of life, as well as of the degree of inflation of the lira over the years. The total expenditure was 205 lire, 3 soldi.

10 lbs. grapes	1 lire	13 soldi	4 denari
150 prunes	3	15	
81 lbs. strawberries	1	26	8
48 large pears and others for cooking	2	18	8
peaches for the gelatin and others	4		
15 lbs. cake flour (*fior di farina*)	4	10	

. . .

[20] Albizzi was the author of a masque staged by Giovanni Bardi at the carnival of 1574 called *Mascherata del piacere e del sentimento* that cost the considerable sum of 4000 scudi (Bartoli letters dated Feb. 20 and 27, 1573 (1574), Bibl. Riccardiana, MS 2438 bis, Pt. III, nos. 57 and 51. Albizzi remained active as an amateur musician until his old age, which he spent in Kempten. See *Dizionario biografico degli Italiani* (Rome, 1960), II, 21-22.

[21] Bibl. Riccardiana, MS 2471, fol. 98.

6 legs of veal	4 lire		
. . .			
1 bottle milk	1		
6 turkeys	27		
3 capons	15		
24 tortolotte [turtle-doves?]	20		
. . .			
21 bottles red wine	25	10	
3 bottles greco di chianti	4	5	soldi
78 lbs. snow [to cool the gelatin?]	7	16	
10 large 2-lb. candles	5	12	
. . .			

If the table was set, as I estimate, for about twenty-four people, the banquet enjoyed much better attendance by far than any of the weekly meetings, when an average of eight and sometimes only two turned up. Although music was probably an ornament to the banquets, it is never mentioned and no record of payments to professional musicians is preserved.

Lectures on music, orations in praise of it, and discussions of musical topics are recorded in the Diario at a number of points. The records are sketchy and uneven, however, and must contain only a partial accounting of the place music occupied in the Alterati's deliberations. On November 19, 1573, with only four present, Antonio degli Albizzi gave a lesson on music. The Diario tells no more about it and it cannot be traced among the papers of the Academy. This is unfortunate because his other contributions reveal a deep and independent thinker.[22] On November 25, 1574, Cosimo Rucellai delivered an oration in praise of music. He was the one who once was absent during his own regency to go to Bardi's "to make music." On December 10, 1574, an extemporaneous discussion was held on the proposition

[22] See Bernard Weinberg, *A History of Literary Criticism in the Italian Renaissance* (Chicago, 1961), II, 838 ff.

"that music is better than conversation with friends." Bernardo Davanzati took the affirmative and Carlo Rucellai the negative. The main significance of these items is that music should be on the agenda at all, as most of the literary academies ignored it.

The most revealing and relevant statements about music are found in discourses on literary and philosophical topics. The definition of poetry and of its various genres and the nature of poetic creation were frequently recurring themes. What is said about poetry was either applied by the speaker himself to other arts or has such obvious general implications that these statements reveal better even than the musical writings of the period the basis of the changing artistic taste.

Several entire semesters were given over to poetic theory. The discussions were usually focused on specific areas, such as the theory of imitation, which occupied the period between December 1573 and February 1574. Sometimes the publication of a new commentary on Aristotle's *Poetics* or a new treatise on the subject occasioned the discussion.

Francesco Patrizi provided such a stimulus in 1584, two years before his *Poetics* was published. In June, Bardi returned from a trip to Mantua and Ferrara, where he had seen Patrizi, then working on his monumental treatise.[23] Bardi reported to the Academy on June 12 the titles of the parts and chapters of this work, and these were discussed. The first chapter of Part II, the "Deca disputata," bears the title "Del furore poetico," and it may have prompted Lorenzo Giacomini's lecture on July 10 on the question: "Whether divine furor is the efficient cause of poetry and whether in the poet art is more important than nature." Patrizi's fondness for the Platonic concept of divine madness was bound to incite opposition among the predominately Aristotelian Alterati. Apparently Giacomini revised his lecture after Patrizi's first two volumes appeared in 1586, for the version that has been

[23] Francesco Patrizi, *Della poetica* (Ferrara: Baldini, 1586).

published was delivered in 1587 under the title "Del furor poetico." [24]

Plato's theory [25] that poets composed during seizures of divine furor or madness was generally accepted by early Renaissance poetic theorists. Lorenzo Giacomini considered in his lecture all the arguments raised by Plato, Plutarch, Cicero, Seneca, and others in support of this theory and found them all insufficient. Giacomini asked if what these writers called *furor poeticus* was not rather "an internal disposition that is often hidden from our knowledge." [26]

The problem had come up on two previous occasions. On January 28, 1584, Ruberto degli Albizzi was "condemned" to defend the necessity of madness for the poet, while Francesco Guicciardini spoke against the proposition. Giovanni Battista Strozzi resolved the matter by redefining the term as "a faculty and disposition to transform oneself into anything." So understood, he concluded, furor was necessary to the poet. Alessandro Rinuccini agreed, but added that art too was necessary. Farther back in the Diario we learn that on March 18, 1574, it was decided to argue the proposition that "poetry derives from furor, not art," and eleven days later Baccio Neroni lectured on this topic. The Alterati evidently had been searching for a new determination of the roles of inspiration and art in the creation of poetry.

Although declining to recognize divine furor, Giacomini acknowledges that the poet must be gifted with several natural qualities: *ingegno, giudicio, docilità,* and *memoria* (genius, judgment, docility, and memory). A unique natural combination of

---

[24] "Del furor poetico: Discorso fatto da L. G. Tebalducci Malespini nel Academia de gli Alterati nel anno 1587," in Giacomini, *Orationi e discorsi* (Florence: Semartelli, 1597), pp. 53–73. What appears to be an earlier version of this is in Bibl. Naz. Cent., MS Magl. IX, 124, no. 21, fols. 168r–186v.

[25] *Phaedrus,* 244; *Ion,* 533.

[26] Page 65: "l'interna dispositione; la quale molte volte ci è ascosa."

all these gives the poet the capacity to enter into an affection through "a concentration of the imagination" (*la fissa imaginazione*). In this state he composes not artificially and coldly but almost from the heart. For a genuine affection awakens the conceits that will express it and move others to the same affection. Thus what some regard as furor comes from the poet's capacity to transform himself into one possessed of a certain affection. After the poet has composed in the heat of a simulated affection, he must resort to judgment to correct the fruits of this rapt state, removing inappropriate conceits after examining his work as if it were that of another.

The affections are crucial to Giacomini's conception of the creative process. Once they were considered pertinent mainly to the arts of rhetoric and oratory. But in the last quarter of the sixteenth century, theorizing about the affections burgeoned in every area of criticism and philosophy. A symptom of this preoccupation is the naming of one of the masques of the carnival of 1574 *Gli affetti.*[27] The agenda of the Alterati reflect this obsession with the passions. On February 28, 1572, the question was "whether the movement of the affections is outside the art of rhetoric," Tommaso del Nero taking the affirmative, Lorenzo Gabrielli the negative. The next five meetings were all on the passions in oratory. Years later the subject came up again (March 1584), with poetry now contrasted to rhetoric in their power to move the affections. Giacomini showed that poetry had greater means for moving the passions, while rhetoric was more apt for persuading.

It was on the question of the purgation of the affections in tragedy that poetics and musical esthetics met in the Alterati's deliberations. This link was already established by Aristotle. In speaking of music in the *Politics* he observed that certain melodies cured persons seized with a form of madness as if they had

---

[27] Bartoli, letters dated Feb. 20 and 27, 1573 (1574), Bibl. Riccardiana, MS 2438 bis, Pt. III, nos. 57 and 51.

undergone a purgative treatment.[28] He added that he would explain more fully what he meant by this catharsis of the passions in his treatise on poetics. But either the section is lost or he failed to keep his promise, for catharsis is not clearly explained there. Indeed, it is barely mentioned in the definition of tragedy: "Tragedy is an imitation of an action . . . through pity and fear affecting the proper catharsis, or purgation, of these emotions." [29] Commentators have had to elucidate this application of the term *catharsis* through Aristotle's views on music.

The nature of purgation in the tragedy was probed in several sessions of the Alterati. On December 22, 1583, Filippo Strozzi defended the proposition "that tragedy through pity and fear purges us of the same passions," while Giulio del Bene took the negative side. Giacomini made a formal exposition on the subject in 1586 in a discourse entitled "De la purgatione de la tragedia" that is rich in implications for music.[30]

Giacomini recognizes at the outset that several interpretations of what Aristotle meant by catharsis are possible. The tragedy purges compassion and fear by making men experience these same passions; or it purges not the passions represented on the stage but the opposite; or it shows us the vanity of things acquired through good fortune and therefore moderates love, desire, hope, and joy. Giacomini finds no substance in the last two. Catharsis, clinically speaking, denotes a medication that moves humors of the body that fail to move on their own. Such medications are homeopathic, that is, similar to the humors being purged. For example rhubarb, aloe, and black hellebore are used because they have a natural affinity to the choleric, phlegmatic, and melancholic humors. Consequently catharsis of an affection is brought about by the representation of a similar affection. In

---

[28] *Politics*, viii, 7, 1342a.   [29] *Poetics*, vi, 2, 1449b.

[30] Giacomini, *Orationi*, pp. 29–52, reprinted in *Prose fiorentine*, Pt. II, Vol. IV (1729), pp. 212–250. Baxter Hathaway has recently recognized this essay as one of major importance in the history of the interpretation of the concept of purgation (*The Age of Criticism: The Late Renaissance in Italy* [Ithaca, 1962], pp. 251–260).

experiencing the passion of the protagonist on stage the spectator is relieved of his own.

To drive this point home, Giacomini examines the nature and mechanics of the affections. He defines an affection as "a spiritual movement or operation of the mind in which it is attracted or repelled by an object it has come to know." [31] He declines to agree either with Aristotle, who said the seat of the affections is the heart, or with Galen, who located it in the brain, for Giacomini regards its central place as immaterial. People vary in their disposition toward particular affections, depending on the balance and diversity of spirits in their bodies. An abundance of agile and thin spirits disposes a person toward joyous affections, while many torpid and impure vapors prepare the way for sorrow and fear. When the soul is in a sad affection, a great quantity of spirits evaporates and rises to the head. The vapors go particularly to the anterior part of the head, stimulating the seat of fantasy. Condensation of these vapors causes the face to contract and tears to flow. This contraction in turn affects the quality of the voice. Giacomini's elaboration of this last point has particular significance for musical esthetics.

From the same cause arise cries of lamentation, expelled by Nature through a natural instinct without our awareness to remove thus the bad disposition that afflicts the sensitive part of the soul, contracting it and weighting it down, and especially the heart, which, full of spirits and heat, suffers most. Therefore the heart moves to shake off its pain and expand and liberate itself of anguish. The lungs and other organs of the voice are set in motion and emit shrieks and groans if not impeded by the intellect. In this way the soul, weighted down by sorrow, lightens itself and gives birth to sad conceits and liberates the passionateness that was in it. Having delivered itself of these, the soul remains free and unburdened. So, even if it should want to cry some more, it cannot, because the vapors that

[31] Giacomini, *Orationi*, p. 38: "altro non è affetto che seguitamento o fuga del anima di alcuna cosa appressa da lei, o come convenevole, o come disconvenevole."

filled the head and are the substance of tears have been consumed. They remain scarce until the mind returns to its original disposition because of some internal alteration of the vapors, or through some active qualities, sad imaginings, or an external incident.[32]

This process, Giacomini explains, produces a natural cure. The principle of catharsis, which Aristotle probably meant to apply metaphorically to describe the effect of a tragic stage action, is reduced by Giacomini to mechanical terms. The mechanics of the affections as analyzed by Giacomini bear a strong resemblance to those later described by Descartes.[33]

Now Giacomini applies his theory to music. As a point of departure, he cites Aristotle's classification of songs into moral, active, and enthusiastic.[34] Aristotle's view that all these kinds of music should be cultivated appealed to Giacomini more than that of Plato, who allowed only ethical music. For ethical music was not capable of effecting purgation, because melodies analogous to the ancient Dorian, an ethical mode, were not suited to this purpose. Rather most apt to achieve purgation was music like the ancient Phrygian and Mixolydian tunes and those of the aulos, which were not used in the moral training of youth.

From harmonies that serve to waken the affections like the Phrygian and Mixolydian, which had the property of making the soul con-

[32] *Ibid.*, pp. 39–40: "Da la medesima cagione derivano le voci lamentevoli per naturale instinto senza nostro accorgimento da la Natura procacciate; per rimuovere cioè la mala dispositione, che affligge ristringendo & aggravando la parte sensitiva, e'l cuore principalmente, che come pieno di spiriti, e di calore, piu patisce. onde per scuotere il dolore, e per allargarsi, e liberarsi dal affanno, si muoue, e muouesi il polmone, e gli altri organi de la voce, e fansi strida, e gemiti, se dal intelletto non sono impediti. Per queste vie l'anima gravida di mestizia si sgrava, e partorisce i dolorosi concetti, e gli appassionamenti, che erano in lei, i quali partoriti, resta libera, e scarica, si che quando il bramasse, piu non potrebbe piagnere, essendo consumati quei vapori materia del pianto, che riempievano il capo, fino a che o per altra interna alterazione di vapori, o da qualità attive, o per trista imaginatione o per accidente esterno non ritorna a la primiera dispositione."

[33] René Descartes, *Les passions de l'âme* (Paris: le Gras, 1649).

[34] *Politics*, viii, 7, 1341b.

tracted and somewhat saddened, and from purgative songs that are in keeping with these modes, persons who are quickly moved to sorrow, pity and fear, as well as people in general, receive a purgation, alleviation, and relief that not only is not injurious but is delightfully salutary.[35]

Affections, then, are not evil in themselves, as Cicero implied, but quite useful. Only when passions are uncontrolled and misguided, Giacomini argues, are they evil perturbations.

Giacomini reflected in his thinking an important trend in contemporary music. No longer did the composer seek only to soothe and moderate emotions for ethical ends, but he aimed to move listeners to the strongest passions, perhaps thereby to purge them. The passions could be evoked only through vivid conceits and by exploiting the more exciting instrumental and vocal effects, melodic successions, and harmonies. The better a composer learned to sustain an affection, the more thoroughly could he induce purgation through a simulated passion.

The main purpose of Giacomini's essay was not, however, to deal with music but to illuminate the process of purgation in tragedy. By inducing pity and fear in the spectators, tragedy purged them of these emotions. This, he maintains, is what Aristotle meant in the *Poetics*. The most enlightened commentators, he says, are of this opinion, including Giovanni della Casa [36] and Girolamo Mei. Concerning the latter, he addresses the Alterati: "You must add the opinion of this fellow academician, whose authority among you and among scholarly men in general is rightfully greatly esteemed. Mei, I say, understands purgation in

[35] Giacomini, *Orationi*, p. 42: "tanto coloro, i quali sono gagliardamente volti a la mestizia, a la compassione, & al timore, quanto universalmente tutti gli huomini, ricevon da le armonie che vagliono a destare affetti, quale è la Frigia, e la Mixolidia, di cui era proprio render l'anima ristretta, e per poco addolorata, e da canzoni purganti conformi a le armonie, ricever dico, purgatione, sfogamento, & allegiamento non dannoso, anzi salutevole con diletto."

[36] Giovanni della Casa, *Il Galateo ovvero de' costumi*, trans. R. S. Pine-Coffin (Penguin ed., 1958), p. 41.

the tragedy in this sense." [37] The reference is probably to Mei's "De modis musicis antiquorum" (1573), of which the fourth book contains an extended commentary on the phenomenon of catharsis and its musical and medical significance.[38]

Having resolved the main issue of his essay, Giacomini now considers the elements in tragedy that aim at pleasure. Here are adumbrated many of the ingredients that were compounded into the Roman and Venetian operas of the seventeenth century. The tragedy delights the spectator, he states, by means of the following (my numbering):

(1) by teaching him about the action represented, for learning is naturally enjoyable; (2) the marvelous, which shows incredible things actually happening; (3) the recognition of things imitated; (4) the loftiness of the conceits, the beauty of the metaphors; (5) the sweetness of the verse; (6) the sweetness of the music; (7) the festiveness of the dance; (8) the magnificence of the apparatus or machinery and the sumptuousness of the regal costumes; (9) the artfulness of the poet's arrangement of the plot—through digressions, recognitions, reversals of fortune. (10) There are also pleasures accessory to the cathartic process. Since compassion is a virtuous act, we are happy in feeling virtuous. Fearful adventures cause pleasure by making us realize we are free of them. We delight in knowing kings and princes suffer calamities, because this shows that material possessions are no help in achieving virtue and immortality, the only true goals, which are accessible to all.[39]

These pleasures more than compensate for the small discomfort caused by the spectacle of painful, though unreal, objects. It is evident, Giacomini concludes, that the four goals assigned by

[37] Giacomini, Orationi, p. 44: "Aggiugnete il giudicio di Academico vostro la cui autorità appresso voi, & appresso gli huomini scienziati è meritamente di molta stima, il Mei dico, che in questo sentimento prende la purgatione de la Tragedia."

[38] Rome, Vatican Library, MS vat. lat. 5323, Bk. IV, pp. 35 ff. There is evidence that Giacomini was already reading this and other writings of Mei in 1577. See notes 47 and 48 below.

[39] Giacomini, Orationi, pp. 46–47.

Aristotle to music—purgation, moral training, relaxation of the mind, and esthetic contemplation—should also be considered the ends of tragedy.

Although fundamentally a commentary upon Aristotle's *Poetics* in the light of the philosopher's remarks about music in the *Politics*, Giacomini's essay is less a faithful elucidation of the text than a document of the prevailing taste. This was a taste that demanded of the stage not true tragedy but a mixed genre that adds to the emotionally purgative experience a feast of the senses and the mind.[40]

The form of the tragedy was also a subject of discussion at the Alterati. On May 29, 1580, the Diario relates that the academy

argued about many things concerning tragedy, and it was resolved that to tragedy are appropriate the line of eleven syllables without rhyme, not excluding the use of seven syllables for certain purposes; and for the chorus one should compose *canzonette*. That the style in a tragedy should be magnificent and forceful. That the persons of the tragedy should be sought in history from as close to our times as possible, and failing to find these some action about a historical personage should be made up.[41]

Ottavio Rinuccini, who was not yet a member, did not follow this prescription, for in *Dafne*, *Euridice*, and *Arianna*, eleven- and seven-syllable lines are mixed in various rhyme schemes for the speeches of the characters, while the choruses only occasion-

[40] Francesco Bonciani, another accademico Alterato, in two discourses on imitation addressed to the Accademia Fiorentina in 1578, concentrated on the art of the masque, which he said was particularly popular "in our times and in our city." Visual ornament, he said, was more essential here than Aristotle conceded in the *Poetics*. Bonciani dwelt on the *meraviglia* (wonder) aroused by imitating—he clung to the word tenaciously—false and unlikely things, such as manlike gods; virtues, arts, sciences, or cities represented as human beings; and the personification of animals, plants, stones, and even the elements (Bibl. Riccardiana, MS 2237, fols. 96r–138r). The attribution to Bonciani was made by Bernard Weinberg in "Nuove attribuzioni di manoscritti di critica letteraria del Cinquecento," *Rinascimento*, III (1952), 249–250.

[41] Italian text in Weinberg, "Argomenti," p. 183.

ally have the strict strophic forms and uniform lines and rhymes of canzonets. As regards subject matter, the Alterati were well in advance of the earliest opera librettists, who relied upon Greek mythology, Roman history, and medieval romance to the exclusion of anything more contemporary.

Several other discussions betray a preoccupation with modern rather than ancient practice. On December 30, 1582, Torquato Malaspina contended that tragedy must have a happy ending, while Francesco Bonciani took the opposite view. On April 13, 1589, Marcello Adriani maintained that prologues should be linked to the action of the drama. Giacomini disagreed, explaining that in modern times they are detached from the play. Both Bonciani and the Regent seemed to side with Giacomini. Whether the tragedy should be divided into five parts came under examination on January 28, 1584, with Giulio del Bene taking the affirmative and Marcello Adriani the negative. Carlo Rucellai and the current regent, Alessandro Rinuccini, supported the five-act division.

In this connection it should be recalled that Guarini's *tragicommedia pastorale*, *Il pastor fido*, completed in 1585 and published in 1590, is in five acts, mixes lines of seven and eleven syllables in blank verse, and uses rhymed stanzas for choruses, as the Alterati recommended. Guarini's poem was read to the Academy before publication, and their opinion was to have been communicated to the poet by Matteo Botti. So Leonardo Salviati reported to Guarini in a letter of October 8, 1586, in which he added that from talking to five or six of the Alterati he gathered that *Il pastor fido* left them quite confused though full of admiration.[42] Rinuccini's *Euridice*, on the other hand, lacks the five-act division, being rather in six scenes; Striggio's later *Orfeo* does have the five acts.

The function of the chorus in the tragedy and the character of

[42] Salviati's letter is printed in Vittorio Rossi, *Battista Guarini ed Il pastor fido: Studio biografico-critico con documenti inediti* (Turin, 1886), pp. 299–300.

its music came up at least once in the discussions of the Alterati. Although the Diario is silent on these matters, there is evidence in a letter from Giorgio Bartoli to Lorenzo Giacomini. On January 23, 1575, according to Bartoli, Alessandro Rinuccini read a paper on the choruses of the tragedies and comedies. Bartoli, a member of the Accademia Fiorentina but not the Alterati, may have attended as an alternate for Giacomini, for he reported that "the purpose for which he [Rinuccini] argued choruses were introduced in the tragedies was to leave the actors free to negotiate among themselves." [43] The question had come up earlier in Bartoli's correspondence with Giacomini, when the latter was in Ancona taking part in a performance of the tragedy *Orbecche*. The author is not named, but what is said fits Giraldi Cinthio's tragedy of that name. Bartoli suggests that one chorus in the play should represent citizens coming to the palace on various business errands, and these should sit quietly except to make speeches. Another chorus of young people should enter singing and dancing, and he added "I believe these may sing anything they like, although it would be better to sing something related to the story of the tragedy, as Aristotle prefers, so that the entire tragedy would be as much as possible a single action." [44] Two weeks later he revised his opinion. The chorus is important because it serves as an audience for those who relate messages. Some of the chorus members make individual speeches, while others sing.

[43] Bartoli, undated letter of around the end of January 1575, Bibl. Riccardiana, MS 2438 bis, Pt. III, no. 37: "il fine per il quale disse che si introduceva il coro ne le tragedie cio è per dare agio à gli istrioni di negoziare." He had written in the letter dated Jan. 22, 1574 (1575), no. 60: "Domani legge ne l'accademia il Rinucino, intendo che trattera de' cori de le tragedie e comedie."

[44] Bartoli, letter dated Dec. 26, 1573, Bibl. Riccardiana, MS 2438 bis, Pt. III, no. 11, fol. 1 verso: "Pero penso che questi possino cantare qualunque cosa vogliono, benche sia meglio cantar cose appartenenti à la favola de la tragedia, come vuole Aristotile, per fare quanto è possibile che sia tutta la tragedia una azzione."

Those who sing music, I should think, could imitate those who go around the city making feasts and masquerades, and one member may sing alone as well as many together and dance at the same time. And I do not believe it would be out of place if they sang interpolated songs as Aristotle calls them,[45] although he does not sanction these but prefers that they sing things pertaining to the tragedy to make it so far as possible a single action. . . . The ancient choruses, I believe, were performed in the following manner. A single person sang to the accompaniment of an instrument, reciting one verse. Then the others responded with the same air, their voices tuned in consonance. He who sang alone was called the Master of the Chorus, I believe. This is the procedure followed in singing litanies, but the music is not the same.[46]

Bartoli's argument provides some justification for the mixture of styles displayed in the *Euridice* scores of Peri and Caccini and in Monteverdi's *Orfeo,* where songs in villanella style are introduced amidst passages of severe recitative. Since such choral

---

[45] *Poetics*, xix, 7, 1456a.

[46] Bartoli, letter dated Jan. 9, 1573 (1574), MS 2438 bis, Pt. III, no. 16, fol. 2r: "quegli che cantano in Musica crederei che potessino imitar coloro che vanno per la città facendo feste et mascherate et che possi cantare et un solo et molti et ballare ancora. et non mi par inconveniente che cantino fra messi come chiama Aristotile benche non gli accetti, ma vorebbe che cantassero cose appartenenti à la tragedia per farla una azzione quanto piu è possibile. . . . Il canto de cori antichi credo che fusse in questo modo cantava un solo accompagnato dal suono et diceva un verso, poj gli altri tutti rispondevano con la medesima aria con le voci accordate. et quello che cantava solo credo che si chiamasse maestro del coro. tal ordine si tiene in cantar le letanie, ma la musica non è la medesima." Bartoli's implication that some interventions of the chorus are part of the action and should be spoken by individuals while others are choral songs anticipates interpretations of later commentators on Aristotle: Alessandro Piccolomini (Venice, 1575) and Antonio Riccoboni (Padua, 1587) and the theories of Angelo Ingegneri, *Della poesia rappresentativa & del modo di rappresentare le favole sceniche* (Ferrara, 1598). See the quotations and discussion in Donald Jay Grout, "The Chorus in Early Opera" in Anna Amalie Abert and Wilhelm Pfannkuch, eds., *Festschrift Friedrich Blume* (Kassel, 1963), pp. 151–161.

songs would be natural to participants in carnival feasts and masquerades, this kind of writing preserves verisimilitude by not demanding of the simple people represented in the chorus a music more sophisticated than they would ordinarily sing in real life. Bartoli also suggests a humanistic pretext for the method used both in the intermezzi and the early musical pastorales of having one member of a group, such as a single shepherd, sing a strophe, followed by the entire group singing the same air, but in harmony, on one or more strophes, with perhaps further alternation between soloists and chorus in subsequent strophes.

As for the nonchoral parts of a tragedy, Bartoli was not sure how much of the poetry of the dramatic roles was sung in ancient times. He believed that at least some of it was, as he wrote to Giacomini on November 9, 1577. Giacomini had apparently asked Bartoli his opinion of Girolamo Mei's theories concerning the music of the tragedy.[47] Mei believed, as many in Florence knew, that the ancient practice was to sing both the choral and solo parts of the tragedies.[48] Bartoli replied that

---

[47] Some notes, probably in Giacomini's hand, on the back of Bartoli's letter of Nov. 2, 1577 in Bibl. Riccardiana, MS 2438 bis, Pt. III, no. 5, seem to be jottings of questions Giacomini intended to ask Bartoli concerning Mei's views: how the voice is produced; whether music is necessary to comedy and tragedy; whether the acute accent had the same effect in music [as in speech]; whether there are shorts and longs in the Tuscan language; if in Tuscan verse only this pleases; and two other questions that are not fully decipherable pertaining to purgation and the monochord. These questions suggest that Giacomini was reading not only Mei's "De modis musicis antiquorum" but also his treatise "Del verso toscano," of which there are copies in Bibl. Riccardiana, MSS 2597, 2598, and Paris, Bibl. Nat., lat. 7209³.

[48] This theory was expounded mainly in Book IV of "De modis musicis antiquorum," which Mei sent to Piero Vettori in 1573, encouraging him to pass it around his circle, which included Giacomini. It may have been Giacomini's interest in Mei's writings that prompted Bartoli to copy six of the letters Mei wrote to Galilei and Bardi between 1572 and 1581. Bartoli apparently made these copies—the only ones extant—which are in the Vatican Library, MS Regina lat. 2021, between 1578 and 1582. See the four-page insert of addenda in Palisca, *Girolamo Mei,* under p. 82.

though he admired Mei's learning and partook of his distrust of secondary sources, he was not entirely convinced.

I believe that what he told you is the truth, particularly concerning ancient music and also about the manner of reciting speeches and dialogue in the tragedies. But perhaps this was not done universally, and what is more important it is not acceptable as the most perfect manner [of performance] if we follow the doctrine of Aristotle, for in the *Rhetorics* he gives tacit precepts . . . cautioning that speeches should not be made rhythmic, so that the listener would not become preoccupied with the voice of the speaker, as happened with the public crier who wished to communicate nothing when he chanted in this way. Now the theatres were built so that a great multitude of people could hear, and not everyone had the capacity to speak to large numbers, no more than Isocrates, but a naturally strong chest was required, which could be augmented by exercise. In short, that someone should have used a song-like delivery when reciting poems as well as speeches, this may stand; whether this is the best way is open to question.[49]

Bartoli's skepticism was not unusual. Most literary critics assumed that only the choruses were sung.

What kind of poetry should be set to music, and in what manner, ought to have been a vital subject for an academy strong in literary men who were sensitive to music. Yet all that has

[49] Bartoli, letter, Nov. 9, 1577, Bibl. Riccardiana, MS 2438 bis, Pt. III, no. 19: "Credo che dica il vero di quanto v'ha detto et massime de la Musica antica. et ancora del modo del recitare l'orazioni e parlare ne le tragedie ma forse non era fatto universalmente: et quello che è pju importante non acettabile per modo perfetto per la dottrina d'Aristotile, poiche ne la Retorica da tasiti precetti . . . advertendo di non far l'orazione numerosa accioche l'uditore non vadi a preocupando la voce del dicitore come avviene del banditore per il che non voleva dir niente quando ci diceva tali cose. et à la moltitudine si riparava con far i Teatri accioche tutti sentissero. et à la moltitudine ogniuno non era atto à parlare come ne anche Isocrate. ma bisognava forza di petto per natura, et per esercizio s'acquistava l'augumento. Insomma che qualcuno usasse pronunziare à modo di canto cosi il recittar li poemi come anche l'orazioni puo stare, ma è da advertire se è l'ottimo in tal modo facendo."

survived along these lines is an interesting comment by Giovanni Bardi in a lecture, "In difesa dell'Ariosto," delivered to the Alterati on February 24, 1583. Bardi defended Ariosto's *Orlando furioso* against the criticism made by Francesco Bonciani in the Accademia Fiorentina, to which they both belonged. One of the proofs of the poem's excellence, Bardi said, was its popularity. This in turn was largely explained by the aptness of Ariosto's verses for musical setting. Ariosto's poem is sung in taverns and barber shops as well as by people of learning and nobility and has been set to music by professional musicians like Domenico da Nola. Poetry is written in verse to make it singable. "Those verses will be best that have the best rhythm and the best sound. Consequently they will be the most musical, hence the most singable." [50] Bardi's other remarks in this lecture leaned heavily on Aristotle. Yet he was conscious of a standard aside from rules, measured by sensuous appeal and *sensus communis*.

These excerpts from the records and papers of the Alterati help us to reconstruct the intellectual environment out of which the early musical pastorales emerged. The treatises, discourses, and letters of Mei, Bardi, and Galilei, read against the background of surviving music, strike the scholar as iconoclastic. But it is evident from what survives of the discussions of the Alterati that the ideas circulating in Bardi's Camerata were equally at home at Giovanni Battista Strozzi's, that indeed they were characteristic of the milieu of humanist musical amateurs. Though amateurs of music, Bardi, Giacomini, and other leading Alterati cannot be dismissed as fatuous dilettantes. Some of them possessed a knowledge of the classics that later only professors of Greek and Latin could match. The humanist amateurs who first experimented with the musical pastorale were not innocent, chartless adventurers who discovered music drama while searching to revive Greek tragedy. Rinuccini and his circle were too

[50] Quoted and translated in Weinberg, *A History*, II, 985.

steeped in the classics to believe that *Dafne* or *Euridice* realized a rebirth of ancient tragedy, though they were conscious of certain parallels between these and the ancient tragedies and comedies. If any misunderstanding of Greek drama was a factor in the experiments it was that inherent in the theory proposed by Mei, that the tragedies were sung in their entirety. To this, as we have seen, not everyone subscribed. The other classicistic features of the musical pastorales were mainly already familiar on the Florentine stage.

The desire to imitate the ancients was still a powerful motive, but no longer the foremost one. The ancients were read as much in search of justification for prevailing trends as to find solutions and models to imitate. Aristotle, the most explicit of the philosophers about artistic matters and also the most sympathetic, bolstered the humanists' confidence in the rightness of what they were doing. As they interpreted the *Poetics* and *Rhetorics*, the proper goal of the creative artist is to move the affections through the imitation of human actions and feelings. This demands of the artist not so much a divine madness through which to seize the heavenly harmony and truth as the exercise of the imagination. The artist must awaken in himself the emotional state he wants to express and to call forth the images and forms that will awaken it in others. The late sixteenth-century interpreters of Aristotle understood enough of the cultural context of his thought to know that the ancient genres and standards could not be transplanted into the modern world. Recent traditions and possibilities demanded new solutions. The knowledge that many differences of opinion existed among the classical authors also forced the humanists to recognize their own freedom and responsibility to make a choice. This choice, moreover, was not entirely rational. It could not help being influenced by the tastes of a leisure class that cared more for visible and audible marvels than for good drama. The battery of classical citations deployed in the academic discourses defended a pragmatic eclecticism. A

head full of classical poetics but an ear to the ground was at this
moment a good recipe for public success.

APPENDIX

The pseudonyms, dates, and principal occupations of the
members of the Alterati mentioned in this article are listed below
in alphabetical order.

Adriani, Marcello, *il Torbido* (1562–1604), professor of classics.

Albizzi, Antonio degli, *il Vario* (1547–1626), after 1576 mainly
in Rome and Germany in service of Cardinal Andreas of
Augsburg.

Bardi, Giovanni de', *il Puro* (1534–1612), admitted June 30,
1574, poet, amateur composer, patron. (Florentine usage includes *de'* meaning "of the family of the" in the name. Elsewhere, the particle is spelled *dei*, or is omitted, as has been the
practice throughout this book.)

Bardi, Pietro de', *l'Avvinato* (before 1570–after 1643), son of
Giovanni, admitted July 22, 1599, one of leaders of Accademia della Crusca.

Bonciani, Francesco, for two years *il Dubbioso*, later *l'Aspro*,
admitted Aug. 4, 1572, literary critic, Archbishop of Pisa.

Chiabrera, Gabriello (1538–1612), poet.

Corsi, Jacopo (d. 1604), patron, amateur musician.

Davanzati, Bernardo, *il Silente* (1529–1606), translator and editor of the works of Tacitus.

Del Bene, Giulio, *il Desioso*, a founder.

Del Nero, Agostino (c.1570–c.1591), son of Tommaso, amateur
musician.

Del Nero, Nero, *l'Orrido*, brother of Tommaso, one of first
admitted after founding.

Del Nero, Tommaso, *lo Sconcio* (1544–1572), a founder, first
host.

Doni, Giovanni Battista (1594–1647), Secretary of the Sacred College, author of works on ancient music.

Gabrielli, Lorenzo, *l'Agevole*.

Giacomini (de' Tebalducci Malespini), Lorenzo, *il Mesto* (1552–1598), admitted July 8, 1583, classicist, literary critic.

Guicciardini, Francesco, *lo Smemorato*.

Malaspina, Torquato, *il Tardo*.

Medici, Don Giovanni de', *il Saldo*, son of Duke Cosimo I.

Mei, Girolamo, *il Pianigiano* (1519–1594), classicist, literary critic.

Neroni, Baccio, *il Grave*.

Rinuccini, Alessandro, *l'Ardito* (1555–1621), poet, senator, three times regent.

Rinuccini, Ottavio, *il Sonnacchioso* (1562–1621), brother of Alessandro, admitted Sept. 4, 1586, poet.

Rucellai, Carlo, *lo Sdegnoso*.

Rucellai, Cosimo, *il Travagliato*.

Rucellai, Piero, *l'Umido* (d. c.1625).

Strozzi, Filippo, *lo Svegliato*.

Strozzi, Giovanni Battista the Younger, *il Tenero* (1551–1634), poet, host to Alterati after c.1572, four times regent.

Valori, Baccio (1535–1606), senator, connoisseur of arts.

Valori, Filippo (d. 1606), son of Baccio, admitted July 29, 1599, President of University of Pisa.

Vettori, Piero, *l'Assicurato* (1499–1585), senator, professor of moral philosophy and Greek and Latin rhetoric, inactive in Alterati.

Early Opera and Aria

By NINO PIRROTTA

Few other genres have their beginnings as precisely determined as opera. Its landmark is the first performance of *Euridice,* with music by Jacopo Peri on a text by Ottavio Rinuccini, which took place on the evening of October 6, 1600, in the Pitti palace in Florence in the apartment of Don Antonio dei Medici,[1] a half brother of Maria dei Medici, the future queen of France. We must dismiss any proposal to consider *Dafne,* music by Jacopo Corsi and Jacopo Peri on a text also by Rinuccini, as the starting point, not because the dates of its various performances are uncertain and a complete score missing, but because both the text and the few surviving fragments of the music [2] make this

---

[1] The best possible reference for the antecedents and early history of opera is, of course, Donald J. Grout, *A Short History of Opera* (2d ed.; New York, 1965), chs. 4–7, and its comprehensive bibliography (particularly sects. 2 and 3). Antonio dei Medici, born in 1576, was recognized by Francesco I dei Medici as his natural son by Bianca Capello, although it would seem that the whole affair of her pregnancy had been a pretense, for she could bear no child. Antonio grew up in the Medici family and escorted Maria dei Medici to Paris after her wedding.

[2] For the dates of *Dafne* and its surviving fragments see now William V. Porter, "Peri and Corsi's *Dafne:* Some New Discoveries and Observations," *Journal of the American Musicological Society* (*JAMS*), XVII (1965), 170–196. The earliest available text is a libretto printed in 1600; it is reported, however, that every new performance since 1597 (i.e., 1598—see the note on calendars, page 11, n. 5) had brought modifications and improvements of both text and music. The former

work seem immature and preliminary compared to the full-fledged vitality of *Euridice*. Also to be dismissed is the challenge coming from *Il rapimento di Cefalo*, text by Gabriello Chiabrera and music for the greatest part by Giulio Caccini, which was performed three days later than *Euridice*, on October 9, but which was given in the huge Sala delle Commedie of the Uffizi palace as the major spectacle (offered by Grand Duke Ferdinand I himself) in the series of events celebrating the marriage of Maria dei Medici to Henry IV of France and Navarre.[3] *Euridice* had been merely the homage paid to the new Queen by a private citizen, Cavaliere Jacopo Corsi; yet *Il rapimento* was practically forgotten soon after its performance,[4] while *Euridice* had the most extraordinary success in print among the early operatic scores, rivaled only by Monteverdi's *Orfeo*.[5]

I. BORN UNDER THE SIGN OF DISCORD

Even if the printed scores of Peri's *Euridice* were not available to us, a clue to its importance would be provided by the storm of

---

was once more revised for the performance in Mantua in 1608 with completely new music written for the occasion by Marco da Gagliano.

[3] The performance lasted five hours, required more than one thousand men for the handling of the stage machinery, and cost 60,000 scudi; see Angelo Solerti, *Musica, ballo e drammatica alla corte medicea dal 1600 al 1637* (Florence, 1905), p. 26. Alois M. Nagler, *Theatre Festivals of the Medici* (New Haven, 1964), pp. 96–100, gives a detailed description of the spectacle, and, on p. 95, a much shorter one of *Euridice*. The title of Nagler's fifth chapter, "Opening of the Uffizi Theatre," is misleading; the Sala delle Commedie was so called because it was occasionally used as a theatre, but was never a permanent one. It was part of the theatrical game of the time to create anew on each occasion the arrangement and decoration of the large hall or courtyard selected for the performance. This probably also applies later to the so-called Barberini theatres in Rome.

[4] Only the final chorus remains, included in *Le nuove musiche di Guilio Caccini detto Romano* (Florence: Marescotti, 1602).

[5] Peri's opera appeared in two editions—the one of 1600 (1601) mentioned below, p. 42, and a second one printed in Venice in 1608—even before the first of the two editions of *L'Orfeo* were published.

polemical gestures and documents that accompanied and followed its performance. The performance itself was intruded upon by Caccini, who was able to replace part of Peri's music with his own under the pretext that singers who were his pupils could sing only the music written for them by their master. Yet his having disrupted the artistic unity of the work we consider as the first real opera, and having imposed on Peri the same kind of artistic promiscuity (most usual at the time) to which *Il rapimento* was being subjected,[6] was not enough for Caccini, who swiftly proceeded to claim exclusive authorship for his own profit. Shortly after the Florentine nuptials were over, he had already composed and published a complete score of *L'Euridice posta in musica in stile rappresentativo da Giulio Caccini detto Romano* (Florence, Marescotti, 1600), which he was able to dedicate to his former patron, Giovanni Bardi, Count of Vernio, on December 20, 1600.[7] Nowhere in the print is Rinuccini named, or the existence and recent performance of Peri's score hinted at, or the fact acknowledged that "favole in musica" had already been composed and staged in Florence since 1591 by Emilio dei Cavalieri. Instead, a reference to certain conversations on musical matters that had been held at a much earlier time in the house of Bardi—in the so-called Camerata—flatters the dedicatee and lends support to Caccini's contention that he had been writing "such manner" of music for at least fifteen years, a claim

---

[6] Caccini was in charge of all the solo parts—that is, practically the basic play—plus the final chorus; at least three other composers wrote the other choruses, which, combined with spectacular changes of scenery taking place under the very eyes of the audience, formed the *intermedi*, imbedded, so to speak, in the main action.

[7] Caccini had even been Bardi's secretary about 1592; see my "Caccini," *Enciclopedia dello spettacolo*, Vol. II (Rome, 1954), col. 1447. A modern edition of the first three episodes of *Euridice* is included in Robert Eitner, ed., *Die Oper von ihren ersten Anfängen bis zur Mitte des 18. Jahrhunderts*, I (Leipzig, 1881), 35–76; an English translation of its foreword is given by Oliver Strunk, *Source Readings in Music History* (New York, 1950), pp. 370–372.

that he was soon to restate at greater length, if not as forcefully, in the foreword of *Le nuove musiche.*[8]

Meanwhile Peri had reacted by having *Le musiche di Jacopo Peri . . . sopra l'Euridice del signor Ottavio Rinuccini* (Florence, Marescotti, 1600 [1601]) published.[9] The modesty displayed in this title is an evident rebuke of Caccini's impudence as well as an acknowledgment of Rinuccini's merit. Also stressed—on the title page, in the dedication to the new queen (dated February 6, 1600 [1601]), and in the customary address to the reader—were the facts and occasion of the October performance. Finally, and again in pointed contrast to Caccini's bad manners, Peri makes a graceful bow to both his opponents, Cavalieri and Caccini.

There was indeed a third party to the dispute. Emilio de' Cavalieri was a Roman gentleman whom the Grand Duke had brought with him from Rome at the time of his accession to the rule of Florence and had entrusted in 1588 with the supervision of all artistic activities of the Florentine court.[10] Cavalieri had first checked and then superseded the authority of Count Bardi on matters of theatre and music. More recently, however, Cavalieri had found occasion to get away from Florence and to revert to Rome, although his ties with the Florentine court had never been severed, nor his superintendence revoked.[11] Cavalieri's grand manners had prevented him from seeking publicity by having the musical pastorales printed which he had composed for Florence during the nineties. In 1600, however, he was actually

---

[8] English translation in Strunk, *Source Readings,* pp. 377–392. For *Le nuove musiche* and its contents, see below, p. 51.

[9] Facsimile edition edited by Enrico Magni Dufflocq (Rome, 1934). An English translation of the foreword is given in Strunk, *Source Readings,* pp. 373–376.

[10] Biographical information is given in my "Cavalieri," *Enciclopedia dello spettacolo,* Vol. III (Rome, 1956), cols. 256–258, and, more recently, in C. V. Palisca, "Musical Asides in the Diplomatic Correspondence of Emilio de' Cavalieri," *Musical Quarterly,* XLIX (1963), 339–355.

[11] Palisca, "Musical Asides," pp. 343–347.

the one who started the printing race by permitting, in his aristocratic high-handed way, an obscure editor to give to the printer *La rappresentatione di anima, et di corpo novamente posta in musica dal sig. Emilio del Cavaliere per recitar cantando* (Rome, Mutii, 1600).[12] The work had been performed in February in the oratory of the Chiesa Nuova in Rome, but the dedication of the print to Cardinal Aldobrandini was dated by Alessandro Guidotti, the appointed editor, on September 3, 1600, the very moment at which the Florentine spectacles for the wedding were being rehearsed.[13] The timing qualifies the print as an unspoken reproach to the Grand Duke, who on the occasion of the royal wedding had forsaken Cavalieri's merits as an old friend and faithful servant; among these merits were the plays he had conceived, written the music for, and staged in Florence in 1591 and 1595, insistently mentioned in both the dedication and the address to the reader.

Cavalieri attended the Florentine wedding and possibly helped with the staging of *Euridice*,[14] but left for Rome shortly there-

[12] Facsimile edition edited by Francesco Mantica (Rome, 1912) with preface by Domenico Alaleona; dedication and foreword are reprinted by Angelo Solerti, *Le origini del melodramma* (Turin, 1903), pp. 1–12.

[13] There are no extant letters in Cavalieri's correspondence between Easter and November 1600; so Palisca conjectures ("Musical Asides," p. 344) that "he must have been busy in Florence with the preparations for the wedding." It seems to me that the preparation of the printing of *La rappresentatione* must have kept him in Rome; he probably expected to be recalled to Florence to take charge of the nuptial spectacles, but was too proud to make the first move. Hence, his silence and his later complaints that the Grand Duke had forgotten his past services in the field of theatre and neglected to take advantage of his experienced advice. Cavalieri was only commissioned to write the music for Giovanni Battista Guarini's elegant but perfunctory *Dialogo di Giunone e Minerva*, a laudatory piece involving the descent of the two goddesses on flying machines, performed on October 5 during the official banquet.

[14] Palisca, "Musical Asides," p. 350. It seems to me that the stage decor and action, and possibly some details of instrumentation, are the matters in which Cavalieri is most likely to have helped; it is strange, however, that Peri, with all his ostentatious good manners, does not mention Cavalieri's contributions in his foreword.

after. It would have been inconceivable for him to become involved in a public argument with such commoners as Caccini, Peri, or even Rinuccini, but he continued to express his dismay in a series of letters he addressed from Rome to Marcello Accolti, the secretary of the Grand Duke. The contents of these letters have recently been made available.[15] His Highness had neglected Cavalieri's proven theatrical experience to avail himself of unexperienced advice—namely that of his half-brother, Don Giovanni dei Medici; as a result, not only had he had his money practically wasted, but also had "lost that reputation that Florence had always had in such things."[16] However, a new element of bitterness comes to the foreground, stemming from Rinuccini's dedication of the printed libretto of *Euridice* (Florence, Giunti, 1600). Cavalieri complains (November 10, 1600) that "he [Rinuccini] acts . . . as if he had been the inventor of this way of representing [action] in music"; but "this was invented by me, and everyone knows this, and I find myself having said so in print [in the foreword of *La rappresentatione*, of which Cavalieri thus acknowledges himself the real author]. Now whoever sees the libretto of Little Frog [Ranocchino, for Rinuccini] will consider me a liar."[17]

Milder, though equally contemptuous, are Cavalieri's reactions to the printing of Caccini's *Euridice*, which he had already received in Rome on January 20, 1601, when he writes: "I find nothing in it that annoys me. For my *rappresentatione*, which is printed, having been printed three and a half months earlier, settles all the contentions."[18] Cavalieri must have realized, however, that Caccini's point was not to claim priority in the writing of "rappresentationi in musica," but to assert that such "rappresentationi" were in a style that he, Caccini, had invented. In turn,

[15] Palisca, "Musical Asides."

[16] *Ibid.*, pp. 351–352. In Palisca's opinion the undated postscript belongs to a letter of November 24, 1600.

[17] Translated by Palisca, *ibid.*, pp. 353–354.

[18] Translated by Palisca, *ibid.*, p. 354.

Peri also claimed to have invented and applied to *Euridice* an impassioned style of singing never heard before. To these claims, if my interpretation is correct, Cavalieri gave an oblique answer by encouraging the publication of Luzzasco Luzzaschi's *Madrigali . . . per cantare, et sonare a uno, doi, e tre soprani* (Rome, Verovio, 1601).[19] Luzzaschi's arrival in Rome in the retinue of Cardinal Aldobrandini is reported by Cavalieri on April 6, 1601; and in May, in another letter in which he is critical of Caccini, Cavalieri mentioned having discussed the recent musical events with Claudio Merulo and with Luzzaschi.[20] The latter's belated decision to release some samples of the "reserved" soloistic repertory of the famous singing ladies of Ferrara seems to me an intimation—cognate to Cavalieri's thinking, and possibly suggested by him—that a refined style of soloistic song had long been in existence, independent of Caccini. In turn, Luzzaschi's publication may have prompted Caccini to restate his claims with the printing of *Le nuove musiche*.

The gist of the whole story seems to be that each contestant was deeply convinced of his own right to the priority he claimed and either failed to see the differences between his accomplishments and those of his rivals or else was afraid that the slightly different claims made by others might dim his own precious personal glory. Among those not directly involved in the dispute, the general feeling was of a fundamental unity of the Florentine style of singing. This style in turn was considered not too different from the style of soloistic singing practiced in other

---

[19] I have not yet seen the modern edition published by Adriano Cavicchi in *Monumenti di musica italiana*, 2d ser., Vol. II (Brescia and Kassel, 1966).

[20] Palisca, "Musical Asides," p. 353 and n. 54. Cardinal Aldobrandini, to whom both Cavalieri's *Rappresentatione* and Luzzaschi's *Madrigali . . . per cantare, et sonare* were dedicated, had taken possession of Ferrara after the death of Duke Alfonso II d'Este and ruled there as a papal legate. It would seem that he had also inherited some of the Este musicians and the critical attitude of the Ferrarese court toward the exploits of its Florentine rival.

parts of Italy, yet different enough to justify the reluctant admission, about 1628, by an unbiased Roman observer, that Caccini had been, after all, "almost the inventor of a new manner of singing." [21] Whatever differences existed among the opposing claims, and no matter how strongly these differences were felt by the various claimants, they found them difficult to define precisely in words. We may be in a better position from the vantage point of our historical knowledge of later developments; we must be careful, however, not to apply indiscriminately to the music of the early seventeenth century such criteria as are suggested to us by the manifestations of later periods.

II. "RECITAR CANTANDO" VERSUS "CANTAR RECITANDO"

"Recitar cantando," generally considered a typical expression of the so-called Florentine Camerata, stems from Cavalieri, who might well never have attended any of the musical conversations in Bardi's drawing room.[22] Cavalieri himself used the term most casually, as, for instance, in the title of La rappresentatione ("posta in musica . . . per recitar cantando"), with no other meaning than that of a play to be acted in singing; and indeed all he claimed was to have been the first to devise and bring to the stage such dramatic actions as could be developed completely in songs and music, contrary to the previous theatrical use of music as an incidental element.[23] It is true that the preface of La

[21] Vincenzo Giustiniani, "Discorso sopra la musica de' suoi tempi," in Solerti, Le origini, p. 116.

[22] Bardi left Florence for Rome in 1592, but the years between 1588 and his departure had been a time of veiled but strong animosity between himself and Cavalieri. Anyway, the time of most intense musical activity of his "camerata" had been the late seventies and early eighties, when Galilei was preparing his Dialogo della musica antica e della moderna (Florence: Marescotti, 1581).

[23] All things considered, even the music of the very elaborate intermedi of 1589, Bardi's foremost accomplishment, is incidental with respect to the main action of the comedies with which they were performed. They have been published in D. P. Walker, ed., Musique des intermèdes de "La pellegrina" (Paris, 1963).

rappresentatione elaborates on the means by which "this manner of music, which he [Cavalieri] has restored, may move [listeners] to different emotions, such as pity and joy, tears and laughing"; [24] these words, however, were written by Guidotti, or dictated by Cavalieri, under the influence of the news arriving from Florence about the spectacles being prepared there and of much discussion going on in this connection about the emotional power of music. Even so, the blurb puts the accent more on variety and contrast of emotions than on their intensity; nor does Cavalieri claim to have found a special style for expressing them. On the contrary, the mention of one scene of *La disperatione di Fileno,* in which the singing of Vittoria Archilei "wonderfully brought on tears, while the *person* of Fileno provoked laughter," [25] hints of mimicry as one of the means of expression. Great emphasis is placed by Guidotti (or Cavalieri) on the "adornments," particularly dances, that must enliven such "rappresentationi" and must not be incidental additions to the plot. For "there will be more elegance and novelty if they can be made to appear different from normal dances; as would be the case of a *moresca* representing a fight, or a dance originating from sporting games." [26] As an example of the first, a scene of *La*

[24] "Volendo rappresentare in palco la presente opera, o vero altre simili, . . . e far sì, che questa sorte di Musica da lui rinovata commova à diversi affetti, come à pietà, & à giubilo; à pianto, & à riso, & ad altri simili, come s'è con effetto veduto in una scena moderna della Disperatione di Fileno, da lui composta: nella quale recitando la Signora Vittoria Archilei . . . mosse maravigliosamente à lagrime, in quel mentre, che la persona di Fileno movea à riso: volendola dico rappresentare, par necessario, che ogni cosa debba essere in eccellenza" (third unnumbered page in the original edition and in the facsimile; p. 5 in Solerti, *Le origini*).

[25] See n. 24.

[26] The passage reads as follows in the original: "Quando si è cantato un poco à solo, è bene far cantar i Chori, & variare spesso i tuoni; e che canti hora Soprano, hora Basso, hora Contralto, hora Tenore: & che l'Arie, e le Musiche non sijno simili, ma variate con molte proportioni, . . . & adornate di Echi, e d'inventioni più che si può, come in particolare di Balli, che avvivano al possibile queste Rappresentationi, sì

disperatione di Fileno is mentioned, in which "three satyrs come to blows, and with this pretext perform their fight singing and dancing to a tune of a *moresca*"; to the second type belongs the central scene of *Il giuoco della cieca*, in which "four nymphs dance and sing, while they encircle and tease blindfolded Amarilli according to the rules of the game" (the "giuoco della cieca" was similar to blindman's buff).[27]

The latter example is an obvious derivation from Guarini's *Pastor fido*, Act III, scenes 2 and 3. Cavalieri and Laura Guidiccioni, his dedicated friend who provided texts for the *rappresentationi* of 1591 and 1595, proclaimed themselves followers of the pastoral style of the poets of Ferrara, though the latter were violently opposed by the Florentine Accademia della Crusca of which Bardi was one of the founders.[28] Whether the products of the collaboration between Cavalieri and Guidiccioni had any artistic originality or were merely imitations of famous models is impossible to say because both the texts and music seem to be irreparably lost. They must have been in line, however, with the conception of an artificial, idealized pastoral life, to which conception elegance, ingenuity, and a mild sentimentalism somewhat tinged with sensuousness were more essential than the realistic

---

come in effetto è stato giudicato da tutti gli spettatori; i quali Balli, overo Moresche se si faranno apparir fuori dell'uso commune havrà piu del vago, e del nuovo: come per essempio, la Moresca per combattimento, & il Ballo in occasione di giuoco, e scherzo: sì come nella Pastorale di Fileno tre Satiri vengono à battaglia, e con questa occasione fanno il combattimento cantando, e ballando sopra un'aria di Moresca. Et nel giuoco della Cieca ballano, e cantano quattro Ninfe, mentre scherzano intorno ad Amarilli bendata, ubidendo al giuoco della Cieca" (see above, n. 24). For Cavalieri's skill as a choreographer, see D. P. Walker, *Musique des intermèdes*, pp. xxvii–xxix and liv–lviii.

[27] See n. 26.

[28] Tasso's visit to Florence in 1590 and the performance there of his *Aminta* in 1590 (1591) are in sharp contrast to the harsh criticism that had been addressed to him in prior years by the members of the Crusca Academy (founded in 1582 for the purpose of "sifting" good from bad linguistic usage), and particularly by Bastiano dei Rossi, the author of the printed description of the spectacles organized by Bardi in 1589.

poignancy of human passions and sorrows. Judging from Cavalieri's sparse written hints and from the score of his late spiritual
allegory, which attempts to bring the style up to date with
features rather clumsily derived from Peri and Caccini,[29] we can
agree with Giovanni Battista Doni's opinion of his music: "*Ariette* including many artful devices, repetitions, echo effects, and
similar things, that have nothing to do with the good and true
theatrical music." [30] Cavalieri was nevertheless correct in claim-
ing that he had created a new theatrical genre—all in music—and had been the first to make it public with the printing of
La rappresentatione. His invention, or quasi-invention, expanded the already strong musical component of the literary
pastorale, and accentuated its tendency toward a formal organization, while reducing and simplifying this pastorale form to
adjust it to the particular exigencies and slower pace of a musical
performance. The results, however, though significant when
compared with the stiff progress and almost symbolic gestures of
the cumbersome "courtly" *intermedi*,[31] must have been nearer to
what we would call a ballet or a pantomime than to an opera.

   While Cavalieri's claims centered on genre, Caccini and Peri

---

[29] This is no place for a stylistic analysis and evaluation of Cavalieri's
work; what I am concerned with is his contribution to the formulation
of the new style, which I consider rather slim. Even the alleged greater
sophistication of Cavalieri's continuo figuring (see Frank T. Arnold,
The Art of Accompaniment from a Thorough-Bass [London, 1931], pp.
35 and 49) is a consequence of the fact that he had in mind a fully
realized, multilinear accompaniment, probably conceived on and for a
keyboard instrument. (Arnold too, p. 47, mentions his sparse use of
stringed instruments for the realization of the continuo.) He, therefore,
simulated the external features of continuo writing but missed its
"recitative flexibility and chordal, rather than contrapuntal, meaning"
(for which see below, pp. 54 ff.).

[30] From Doni's "Trattato della musica scenica," ch. 9, in Solerti, *Le
origini*, p. 208.

[31] For the practice of what I call "courtly," most elaborate, *intermedi*,
see my "Intermedium," Friedrich Blume, ed., *Musik in Geschichte und
Gegenwart* (Kassel, 1949–), Vol. VI, cols. 310–326. The encyclopedia
will be referred to hereafter as *MGG*.

insisted on the style of singing. This is borne out most clearly by Peri, who, having acknowledged that Cavalieri, "before any other of whom I know, enabled us with marvelous invention to hear our kind of music upon the stage," immediately adds that "nonetheless as early as 1594, it pleased the Signori Jacopo Corsi and Ottavio Rinuccini that I should employ it *in another guise.*" [32] It may have been part of Cavalieri's earlier polemics with Bardi to prove that "our" modern music was as apt as the ancient for the stage; but Corsi and Rinuccini went further to show, with Peri's help, that modern music could be effective on stage even in a genre of dramatic intensity *comparable* to that of ancient tragedy. The evidence of this is grudgingly given by one of Cavalieri's letters reporting the opinion expressed in Rome by Bardi that "they [the Florentines, including the Grand Duke] should not have gone into *tragic* texts and objectionable subjects." [33] The old rivals were at least temporarily reconciled in their common distaste for the newest trends of music in Florence.

The revival of the ancient tragedy was to be attempted eight years later in Mantua by Rinuccini and Monteverdi. [34] In 1600, nobody knew better than Rinuccini that *Euridice* was no tragedy; yet, in a pastoral frame, the death of Euridice and Orpheus' despair have a poignant directness of tragic pathos, and even the less emotional moments of the action refuse to submit for the sake of music to the cunning engineering and formalistic procedures that seem to have characterized Cavalieri's works. Accordingly, Peri's "recitar cantando" (although he never used the expression) is "a harmony surpassing that of ordinary speech but falling so far below the melody of song as to take an intermediate

[32] Translated by Strunk, *Source Readings*, p. 373 (italics mine).

[33] Translated by Palisca in "Musical Asides," p. 352; to have represented the mythological loves of Aurora and Cefalo was deemed objectionable by Bardi.

[34] On the title page of the printed libretto of *Arianna* the word "Tragedia" is set symptomatically in a larger type than the title and Rinuccini's name.

form," [35] that is, a style of singing normally ruled (we shall later
mention the exceptions) by the accent and expression of the text
and by the needs of the action rather than by principles of
musical organization. Cavalieri's solution had been a stylization
and formalization of plots and dialogues to fit the exigencies of
dance music and song; Peri's is the opposite and can be described
as realistic insofar as it modifies the singing to bring it nearer to
speech, either ordinary and unemotional or, preferably, heightened by the urgency of vehement passions.

To my knowledge, neither Bardi's group nor Caccini had ever
considered the problem of "recitar cantando" before 1600. But
in that year Caccini's words were as swift as his actions; having
stated in the very first sentence of the dedication of his *Euridice*
that he had composed it "in music *in stile rappresentativo*," he
quickly added that this was "that style which, as Your Lordship
[Bardi] knows, I used on other occasions, many years ago, in the
eclogue of Sannazaro *Iten'all'ombra degli ameni faggi*, and in
other madrigals of mine from that time." [36] The eclogue is missing, but the others are pieces that later became part of Caccini's
Nuove musiche (1601 [1602]), in the foreword of which the
sequence is inverted but the sentence the same: "those fruits of
my music studies . . . , my compositions of airs, composed by me
at different times . . . [are] in that very style which later served
me for the fables which were *represented in song* in Florence." [37]
I have underlined the words corresponding to Cavalieri's "recitar
cantando." Caccini contended, however, that his own distinctive achievement was nothing else than the application to the
stage of a style he had previously used for pieces that we would
classify as chamber music. For the sake of distinction, not to
invent a new term, I shall call it here a "cantar recitando."
Caccini's other implication was, of course, that Peri had merely
followed his, Caccini's, path.

[35] Translated by Strunk in *Source Readings*, p. 374.
[36] Translated in *ibid.*, pp. 370–371.
[37] Translated in *ibid.*, pp. 377 and 379.

We may be surprised at the use of the term "stile rappresenta-tivo" for chamber pieces, yet there are other instances of it, independent of Caccini. "Stile rappresentativo" and "stile recita-tivo," the former even more common than the latter, soon spread as fashionable and practically synonymous terms, for to "recite" a play is commonly used in contemporary sources in the sense of "representing" one.[38] Both terms covered the full range of nu-ances between the extremes that we now call recitative and aria, as well as, when applied to a theatrical score, choruses, dances, and instrumental pieces. But their actual application to a stage work was a rare occurrence, depending on circumstances of court life over which the composers had little control. Far more frequent was the case of works, conceived for performance in a concert or "recital," that projected on an ideal stage either a dramatic scene or the affective reactions of a character to a dramatic situation.[39] This direction was most congenial to Cac-cini, for there can be no doubt that his *Nuove musiche* of 1602 and 1615 and the pieces in his *Fuggilotio musicale* of 1613(?) were songs—admittedly with a "recitative" or "representative" quality—composed by a consummate singer and voice teacher in such way that no audience could ever forget that their perform-ance was the exploit of a singer, that is, "cantar recitando."

[38] Indeed most title pages of the time use more cautious expressions, such as, for instance, "a voce sola per cantare sul chitarrone." However, Monteverdi's continuo madrigals of 1605 were shortly thereafter styled as "musica rappresentativa" according to Jack A. Westrup, "Rezita-tive," *MGG*, Vol. XI, col. 356. Monteverdi himself described his *Lettera amorosa* as being "in genere rappresentativo." On the other hand, Severo Bonini's *Lamento d'Arianna cavato dalla tragedia del Signor Ottavio Rinuccini* (Venice: Magni, 1613) contains considerably more excerpts from Rinuccini's theatrical work than the *lamento* indicated in the title, but terms them to be "in stile recitativo."

[39] The same idea was already present in many a polyphonic madrigal of the second half of the sixteenth century, although it was contended that polyphony lacked the directness necessary for such a kind of dramatic projection; it was soon to become the basic principle under-lying the seventeenth-century cantata.

We may, then, oppose Caccini, as a master of "cantar recitando," to the champions of "recitar cantando," Cavalieri and
Peri. We must keep in mind, however, that from another point
of view the eminently singable quality of Caccini's music is
nearer to Cavalieri's *ariette* than to the realistic eloquence of
Peri's style "half-way between song and speech." And finally, a
common expressive tendency makes Caccini and Peri into the
earliest representatives (if I may use the word) of the new
"representative" or "recitative" style, from which we must ex-
clude Cavalieri, in spite of his eleventh-hour effort in the score of
La rappresentatione.

III. THE ESTHETIC PROBLEMS OF THE NEW STYLE

"Stile rappresentativo" and "stile recitativo" both point to a
mode of performance, be it called a representation or a recita-
tion; and indeed the essential novelty of the new style, whether
we consider it from Caccini's or from Peri's point of view,
centers on the moment of communication with the audience.
Caccini described his own brand of the new style as "a noble
manner of singing," which, he asserted, was intended not only to
give pleasure, but also to capture the audience with its "grace"
and "to move the passion of the mind." [40] Related to the aim of
communication are the two technical features which both he and
Peri point out as being most distinctive of their works, *sprezzatura* and continuo accompaniment.

It is impossible to determine which one of the two composers
first introduced these two terms, which they both use in more or
less the same way. Regardless of who first put them in print, they
must have evolved their peculiar meaning during the previous
phase of verbal polemic exchanges of which we have no record.
Sprezzatura, whether or not used first by Caccini for a musical
purpose, fits perfectly the Platonistic veneer with which he liked
to substantiate his adherence to, and reliance on, the classicistic

---

[40] Translated by Strunk in *Source Readings*, p. 383.

ideals of Bardi and his group. The word had enjoyed a certain vogue since the first quarter of the sixteenth century, when it had been adopted by Baldassare Castiglione, in his classic and substantially Platonistic treatise on aristocratic manners and accomplishments, to describe the apparently inborn spontaneity and relaxed self-confidence that must characterize the performance of the perfect courtier, no matter how difficult his task.[41] Parallel to Castiglione's meaning, *sprezzatura* had been used during the same century to designate the ease and poise of the consummate dancer.[42] Caccini, too, takes the position that complete mastery of the most refined vocal techniques is an essential element of his style, but not the only one. The goal of the singer is to attain whatever spirit there is beyond the letter of music— that is, of Caccini's music—which goal can be reached through the *sprezzatura*, that is, through the intangible elements of rhythmic buoyancy and dynamic flexibility of the performance.

To the same purpose is aimed the reduction of the polyphonic accompaniment to an essential lineal minimum, the continuo, allowing a maximum of flexibility also to the accompanist and insuring expressive predominance and freedom to the singing voice. According to Caccini, the ideal situation would have been that of a singer who could accompany himself and thus exert a unified control on both vocal *sprezzatura* and instrumental ac-

[41] The following is Castiglione's text in *The Book of the Courtier*, translated by Charles S. Singleton (New York, 1959), p. 43: "But having thought many times already about how this grace is acquired (leaving aside those who have it from the stars), I have found quite a universal rule . . . : and that is to avoid affectation in every way possible . . . ; and (to pronounce a new word perhaps) to practice in all things a certain *sprezzatura* [nonchalance], so as to conceal all art and make whatever is done or said appear to be without effort and almost without any thought about it." Notice the relationship with the "grace" that some have from the stars. At least one modern dictionary, Policarpo Petrocchi, *Nòvo dizionàrio universale della lingua italiana* (Milan, 1887–1891), still explains *sprezzatura* as a "manner full of masterly neglect."

[42] Transferring the concept of *sprezzatura* to dance and music is made easy by suggestions offered by Castiglione, *Book of the Courtier*, Bk. II.

companiment—he explicitly mentions the practice of "singing on the theorbo or other stringed instrument." [43] This could not agree more with the ideas of Peri, who was himself highly praised as an extraordinary self-accompanying singer.[44] Were such a unified performance not possible, it was the task of the skilled accompanist not only to adhere as strictly as possible to the performance of the vocalist, but also to use his good judgment concerning the best way and the precise extent to which the continuo line should be integrated by "playing the inner voices on an instrument for the expression of some passion, these [inner voices] being of no use for any other purpose." [45]

[43] Strunk, *Source Readings*, pp. 381 and 392; the original has "chitarrone."

[44] Severo Bonini, usually biased in favor of Caccini, had this to say of Peri: "A much learned singer and composer was Signor Jacopo Peri, . . . who would have moved and brought to tears the hardest heart by singing his works, composed with greatest artfulness, for they were in a tearful style [concetto], his own specialty. . . . I shall only say that, in addition to being most gentle in his singing and experienced in the art of composing in the new style, he was elegant and artful in the art of playing keyboard instruments, and absolutely unique in the accompaniment of the singing voice with the middle parts" (translated from Solerti, *Le origini*, p. 137). In the *intermedi* of 1589, Peri sang on the *chitarrone*, impersonating nobody less than Arion.

[45] Translated by Strunk, *Source Readings*, p. 378. In the original, "con le parti di mezzo tocche dall'instrumento per esprimere qualche affetto" has an intimation of levity and restraint that is difficult to incorporate in a translation; I suggest as a freer alternative: "with the middle parts lightly touched by the instrumentalist to express some passion." In another passage, Caccini explains that he has tied some notes of the continuo "in order that, after the [full] chord, only the written note be struck again, it being the one most necessary." Again, I am suggesting a free interpretative alternate to the translation by John Playford followed by Strunk, *Source Readings*, p. 392; the original has "perchè dopo la consonanza si ripercuota solo la nota segnata, essendo ella la più necessaria . . . nella propria posta del chitarrone." I do not know whether "posta" refers to the *role* of the chitarrone or to some technical feature such as its open strings. The sentence immediately following is one more appeal made by Caccini to the discretion and understanding of the accompanist.

The last clause is worth noting not only for its thrust against counterpoint, but also for the implicit admission that the addition of the inner parts was ad libitum, justified only by special expressive aims; for the two main lines, voice and continuo, tended to form by themselves a self-sufficient texture. Our musical training and performing habits lead us, when we realize a continuo, to seek for two or three added parts that maintain a smooth linear conduct in spite of their basically harmonic function. This was probably also Cavalieri's approach, stemming from his greater familiarity with keyboard than with plucked string instruments. On the contrary, Caccini and Peri, like all musicians of the time who were used to realizing the continuo on the *chitarrone*, theorbo, or lute, must have thought of a supporting bass line discontinuously colored by chords, whose size and disposition were conditioned by both the expressive needs of the accompaniment and the fingering of the instrument.

Caccini's "basso continovato" (Florentine for "continuato" or "continuo") may resemble on paper the "basso seguente" practiced by keyboard players who were in charge of accompanying either sacred or secular polyphonic pieces. It actually owes its name to this resemblance,[46] increased by the fact that the older continuo also may have had figures occasionally added to the bass as a guide to the accompanist wherever more than one harmonization was possible. The two procedures, however, are basically different from the compositional point of view. The

[46] Once more, our distinction between "basso continuo" and "seguente" is based on later practices; however, we should remember that "continuo," "continuato," "seguito," and "seguente" were originally equivalent. An organ player accompanying a polyphonic piece on his instrument could use a score or intabulation, or else a bass line formed with the vocal bass or whatever other part happened to assume temporarily the function of a bass part. This new line was properly said to be "seguente" because it always doubled one or another of the vocal parts; at the same time, it had no rests, even though the vocal parts it followed came occasionally to a halt, and thus was properly said to be *continuous*. For the older continuo, see Arnold, *The Art of Accompaniment*, pp. 6–9.

old continuo or *seguente* was nothing more than a shorthand notation (replacing a full score or an intabulation) of harmonic successions arrived at as the result of contrapuntal considerations; while the new continuo is a line composed *ad hoc* in view of the rhythmic, harmonic, and expressive needs of the upper part. To put it in the language of the time, the new continuo and its harmonic implications—whether or not indicated by figures, and whether or not fully realized as chords by the accompanist— were entirely subservient to the "aria" of the vocal part.

We touch here a momentous term, which had been used by musicians at least since the early fourteenth century,[47] but which actually became a key word of the musical language during the sixteenth and seventeenth centuries. Nothing is more puzzling than its ubiquitousness and its oscillation between generic and specialized meanings. It might help in untangling them to realize that in spite of its coincidence in form and sound with the word indicating the atmospheric milieu in which we live, "aria" has a different basic meaning [48] which we may try to render by drawing a parallel with the English "countenance." As "countenance" can be taken to indicate the features that give a visage its individual physiognomy, thus, "aria" may be used to indicate the features that characterize a particular melody, and may be, therefore, the equivalent of "tune." But "countenance" also means the behavior of a person, determined by his intrinsic nature and acquired habits; and similarly "aria," applied to any musical entity (although preferably to a melodic one), indicates the quality it appears to possess as being, as it were, precisely determined and inflected on an unavoidable course—no matter whether such unavoidability stems from tradition, repetition, and habit or from an inner sense of coherence and finality.

As a rule, there was felt to be a strong contradiction between

---

[47] See my "Una arcaica descrizione trecentesca del madrigale," *Festschrift Heinrich Besseler* (Leipzig, 1962), pp. 157–158.

[48] It has also a different, though not too clearly determined, origin (*ibid.*, p.160, n. 20).

the nature and qualities of an aria and the melodic qualities of the many lines of a polyphonic composition; for in the latter it was the task of the composer to draw, spin, and weave together at his will a number of melodic lines, each of which could be plausible in itself but usually lacked an aria, that is, a sense of self-possessed determination. In the process, whatever melodic character the individual lines might have had initially—usually more strongly asserted at such climactic points as the entrance or re-entrance of a voice part—soon faded away in the less distinctive function of providing a background or even a contrast to the emergence of other parts. Thus, although the word is seldom mentioned, the concept of aria is deeply imbedded in the foundations of the persistent and manifold sixteenth-century criticism against polyphony.

When every extramusical element is discarded from this criticism, be it the desire for church reform or the dream of reviving a classical art, a constant residuum is the deep dissatisfaction with the fact that polyphony could soothe the ear with soft consonances or smoothly managed dissonances, could elicit admiration for the skill of the singers and the ingenuity of the composer, but lacked the power of captivating and moving its audience. Two explanations were usually given for this state of affairs. According to the first of them, both the structure and the ways of performing polyphonic music hindered the understanding of the text, with which the esthetic conceptions of the time identified the emotional message of the composition. Although this criticism was still repeated even by those who, like Caccini, inclined toward the second explanation, matters were not improved by the adoption of such soloistic methods of performance as the one indicated by the phrase "per cantare e sonare," or any other of those types of performance for which the term "pseudomonody" has been coined. Thus, the second and more classicistic explanation would seem to have been more to the point, according to which the simultaneous sounding of many melodic lines had the result of neutralizing the expressive message, the ethos that each one of them taken singularly might have conveyed. The latter view is expressed most clearly, to my knowledge, in a letter dated February 16, 1549, by one Bernardino Cirillo, an archpriest of the Santa Casa in Loreto, later the commander of the hospital of Santo Spirito in Saxia in Rome, and also a friend of Cardinal Marcello Cervini (later Pope Marcellus II). Cirillo finally advocated a reform of church music reinstating the practice of monophonic plain chant.[49]

It was one of the many merits of Girolamo Mei, the real mentor of the so-called Camerata, to have perceived that no ethos was possible even for each one of the single lines as long as they were determined by the polyphonist's combinatory criteria and not by their inner coherence to a mode.[50] We have only to replace the word "mode" by "aria" (and its ethos) to go back to our starting point. For mode in the sixteenth century had long since ceased to be a force that could influence the formulation of a melody, except, to a very limited extent, in the perfunctory observance of intermediate cadences and final goals. Nor could the vanished church modes be replaced by the restoration of the long-forgotten scales and tunings of the ancients, for, in spite of a number of attempted revivals (including Vicentino's and Vincenzo Galilei's), their musical meaning was, then as in our day, elusive. The only available concept was the rather vague one of

---

[49] I am not in a position to provide a precise quotation because the source (Paolo Manuzio, ed., *Lettere volgari di diversi nobilissimi huomini . . .*, Bk. III [Venice, 1567], pp. 216–224) is not presently available to me. Another version of the letter, from an authoritative manuscript source, is given by Pietro De Angelis, *Musica e musicisti nell'Arciospedale di Santo Spirito in Saxia* (Rome, 1950), to which, too, I have no access at the present time. In a second letter, written some twenty-five years later (and also reproduced by De Angelis), Cirillo mentions having discussed the same problems with Cardinal Marcello Cervini.

[50] C. V. Palisca, ed., *Girolamo Mei: Letters on Ancient and Modern Music to Vincenzo Galilei and Giovanni Bardi* (American Institute of Musicology, 1960), pp. 70–75; see also Palisca's "Girolamo Mei, Mentor to the Florentine Camerata," *Musical Quarterly*, XL (1954), 1–20.

an aria; certain melodies were felt and said to possess an aria, while it was denied to others (particularly to the lines of a polyphonic composition) on the basis of intuitive criteria whose validity was not diminished by the lack of a verbal definition.

We now begin to discern more in Caccini's *sprezzatura* and continuo than just their most obvious aspects connected with the moment of performance.[51] *Sprezzatura* is not only the self-assurance of the accomplished performer, but also the unrestricted and undiverted naturalness of the melody itself, its "air" of being entirely self-determined or self-propelled. Once more, Caccini's Platonistic orientation prompts him to use an expression that is not less suggestive for being philosophically amateurish; his music embodies in sounds "that complete grace which I hear in my mind," [52] stipulating, as it were, for each melody the necessity of a course predetermined by a model in the world of Platonic ideas. From its side, the continuo contributes to the esthetic aim insofar as it limits its own melodic definition to a minimum that, far from interfering with the free course (the aria) of the vocal part, supports and enhances it. In so doing the continuo exercises a *sprezzatura* of its own. Caccini has already referred to this aspect, in which *sprezzatura* becomes a harmonic quality of the continuo, in the preface of *Euridice:* "The notes of the bass I have sometimes tied in order that, in the passing of the many dissonances that occur, the note may not be struck again and the ear offended." [53] Even more definitely he relates *sprezzatura* and harmonic procedures in the blurb of *Le nuove musiche*, where he claims to have used "a certain noble neglect [*sprezzatura*] of the song, passing now and then through certain

---

[51] See above, pp. 53–57.

[52] Strunk, *Source Readings*, p. 378. Caccini's insistence on grace—here of inspiration, elsewhere of performance—makes the reference to Castiglione obvious (see above, n. 41); he probably considered himself as one of "those who have it from the stars."

[53] Strunk, *Source Readings*, p. 371.

dissonances, holding the bass note firm, except when I wished to observe the common practice." [54]

Attempts to free melodic invention from the strictures of polyphonic writing had been made long before Caccini and Peri. The custom goes back to the first half of the sixteenth century of trying to fill the modal gap with such substitutes of mode as a Paduan, Bergamasque, or Neapolitan aria; the results, however, were, above all, too tinged with local color and humorous overtones to be able to transcend the level of entertainment and become universal criteria of artistic practice. Particularly instructive in this regard is the history of the "canzone villanesca alla napoletana," or "aria napoletana." [55] Initially composed by real Neapolitan composers who set to recapture in its upper line the manners and mannerisms of popular singers, the *napoletana* developed into a widely recognized genre, more and more frequently practiced by composers from all over Italy and even by foreigners. In the process, both its peculiar southern flavor and its popular character became gradually attenuated; the name itself acquired a gentler sound as "villanella alla napoletana," and then was often replaced by "villanella" *tout court*, or "canzonetta." Finally, the genre merged with the generalized vogue of the so-called "musiche ariose," which came to affect the madri-

---

[54] *Ibid.*, p. 378; but Strunk, following Playford, has "except when I did not wish to observe the common practice." The original reads: "eccetto che quando io me ne volea servire all'uso comune." The "common usage" is that of polyphony and counterpoint, of which Caccini intended to avail himself whenever convenient.

[55] "Canzoni villanesche" (with or without "alla napoletana") is used in all collections known to us up to 1565, in which year "villanelle alla napoletana" and "villotte alla napoletana" make their first appearance. Reference to the peasant element is completely eliminated in such titles as "canzoni [or "canzonette"] alla napoletana" or just simply "napoletane," used during the seventies; thereafter, most titles are variations of "villanelle et arie alla Napoletana," or even, particularly in the seventeenth century, "villanelle." See Werner Scheer, *Die Frühgeschichte der italienischen Villanella* (Nördlingen, 1936), pp. 11–13.

gal itself, whether or not its printed collections were explicitly labeled as "madrigali ariosi." [56] The constant feature throughout this process is the presence of a straightforward (although by no means dancelike) rhythmic drive, and of simple, well-designed melodic contours of the upper part, minimally affected by contrapuntal upsurges of the lower voices. [57]

Even in the "musiche ariose," however, the composers' habit of thinking in the traditional terms of contrapuntal procedures (the "prima pratica") reasserted itself in the observance at all times of precisely determined intervallic relationships between the parts. The resulting thorough harmonization of every single note, eventually with repeated notes to accommodate the text in the lower parts, [58] is strongly objected to by Peri in a passage that parallels Caccini's remarks on harmonic *sprezzatura*. Peri, too, affirms that he has held his bass *"firm through the false and true proportions"*; and this he has done "in order that the flow of the discourse might not distress the ear (as though stumbling among the repeated notes [brought about] by the greater frequence of chords) and in order that it might not seem in a way to dance to the movement of the bass." [59]

[56] The oldest example, to my knowledge, is the *Primo libro delle muse a quattro voci di Ant. Barre et altri diversi autori* (Rome and Venice, Gardane, 1555), which had many reprints. Also cf. *Madrigaletti et napolitane a sei voci* in two collections by Giovanni de Macque (Venice, Gardane, 1581 and 1582), the first of which had a reprint in Antwerp in 1600.

[57] In "Tragédie et comédie dans la Camerata Fiorentina," *Musique et poésie au XVIᵉ siècle* (Paris, 1954), p. 202, I suggested that the parallel thirds and fifths of the *napoletane* might be the imitation of popular accompaniments on string instruments. One added reason may have been to avoid contrapuntal motions that might interfere with the aria of the upper part.

[58] To a great extent, the madrigal provides the model of the repeated-note monodic recitative—one more instance of revolutionary change depending on tradition. In both, repeated notes served effects of contrast beside being expedient as carriers of the text.

[59] Italics mine; once more, I introduce a few interpretive modifications in the translation offered by Strunk, *Source Readings,* p. 374.

Caccini acknowledged his indebtedness to the previous literature of "musiche ariose"—after all, Scipione del Palla, whom he repeatedly refers to as his famous teacher and alleged model, is known to us as a composer of pieces in that category. Most of Caccini's long-winded discourses, however, refer to a particular development of that genre, in which the lighter texts, dialectal or popular, tended to be discarded, while more and more attention was given to lavish, improvised coloratura.[60] At this point the modern critic is faced with the problem whether or not he should take at face value Caccini's insistence in describing coloratura as an essential expressive element of his music. I am personally inclined to admit the sincerity of his utterances, taking into account on one hand the vividness that could be added to "those long winding points, simple and double, that is redoubled or intertwined one with the other," [61] by an effective performance, and on the other hand the reactions of an audience conditioned by traditions, habits, and mental associations different from ours. Furthermore, it needs to be seen what Caccini's expressive intents were and precisely what he meant when he spoke of "moving the mind" of his audience.

Caccini's choice of texts—with the exception of *Euridice*, which he set about to compose for evident polemic reasons—is usually a very moderate one from the point of view of emotional intensity. Even more moderate is his treatment of them. As a rule, he establishes a restrained affective mood with a recitative beginning of the musical phrase (recitative in a modern sense), which is then prolonged and sensuously inflected toward a cadence by large, subsiding waves of coloratura. In spite of his dramatic attempts of 1600, Caccini seems to have been as much opposed as Cavalieri and Bardi to the "tragic" passional outbursts

[60] Pirrotta, "Tragédie et comédie dans la Camerata Fiorentina," pp. 290–291; the collection which includes the only known piece by Scipione del Palla has the significant title *Aeri raccolti insieme con altri bellissimi aggionti di diversi dove si cantano sonetti, stanze, et terze rime* (Naples, Cacchio dall'Aquila, 1577).

[61] Strunk, *Source Readings*, p. 377.

of Peri's *Euridice*, which he kept slandering for years, describing them as monotonous and, at best, "funereal." [62] We may sum up his esthetic goals as, on one hand, a "recitative" vividness of performance in the sense described above and, on the other hand, a participation of the audience based on a mild sentimental involvement and, even more essentially, on the *elation of expectations fulfilled by the aria of his music.*

One last point, although a minor one, needs to be made about Caccini. His involvement with vocal coloratura by no means represents the beginning of an era of luxuriant vocal improvisation, which had already been practiced for some decades. On the contrary, Caccini is strongly and outspokenly opposed to the whims of singers; he considers his *passaggi* as one of the most important vehicles of musical expression and makes them his own concern, the concern of the composer. It clearly emerges from his writings that, while some freedom was left to the performers in the application of a few vocal ornaments—such as *intonazione, trillo,* and *groppo,* which, however, assumed a dynamic, more than melodic, significance in his descriptions [63]— Caccini required that only such *passaggi* be performed as he, the composer, had provided as an intrinsic part of the aria of the composition. He violently opposed the "maiming and spoiling" of his music by the singers through ill use of ornamentation. [64] Peri's party, from its side, even criticized Caccini for his insistence on vocal embellishments. [65] It is hard to believe that either criticism

---

[62] See, for instance, Severo Bonini's text quoted above, n. 44. Peri's party retaliated by ridiculing Caccini's abuse of coloratura and comparing him to a certain painter, an expert in painting cypresses, who put them everywhere (see Gagliano, in Solerti, *Le origine,* p. 79).

[63] Concerning *intonazione,* Caccini dismisses the habit of touching first the lower third before coming to the correct pitch; he prefers instead "to tune the first note in its proper pitch, diminishing it [in intensity]" (Strunk, *Source Readings,* p. 382) and thus assimilating it to another of Caccini's favorite idioms, the *esclamazione;* this is halfway between ornamentation and dynamic effects, as are *groppo* (the equivalent of our trill) and *trillo* (a trill on a single repeated note).

[64] Strunk, *Source Readings,* p. 377.   [65] See above, n. 62.

could have suddenly halted the habit of ad libitum ornamentation by the singers; it was, however, in the nature of the new style to oppose unwelcomed interpolations and to subordinate vocal virtuosity to the expressive requirements of the music as conceived by the composer.[66]

It is difficult to determine to which extent the solutions given by Caccini to the problems of an expressive style of singing were exclusively his own. Peri, although somewhat younger, could match with Caccini much of the same musical background and the experience of a professional singer, to whom, as we are going to see, a soloistic style of "cantar recitando" had no less appeal than to Caccini. As the striking parallelism of both artists' utterances on such matters as *sprezzatura* and continuo is probably the result of competitive interaction, it is conceivable that they affected each other in other matters also during the rapid, but by no means sudden, process of their stylistic evolution.

The differences stem mainly from differences of temperament—Caccini's more lyrical, Peri's more dramatic—and, dependent on this, from the tasks each composer set out to accomplish. As far as we know, Peri, with the exception of an echo-madrigal he had composed and performed for the *intermedi* of 1589,[67] first came to the foreground as a composer with *Dafne*, which is said to have been started in 1594.[68] Accordingly, his problems were from the beginning more strictly representative,

[66] I am strongly opposed to any addition of vocal embellishments to the written scores of most seventeenth-century composers, except for some trills (possibly of the repeated-note type) and, later, for some appoggiaturas. The fact is that most composers wrote out ornaments wherever the situation required them.

[67] Included in Walker, *Musique des intermèdes*, pp. 98–106; the use of coloratura in this piece (often repeated by a "double echo") is more impressive and refined than in Caccini's "aria" of the fourth *intermedio* (*ibid.*, p. 156). The latter was omitted in the printing of 1591, which had been prepared by Cristoforo Malvezzi following instructions given to him by Cavalieri.

[68] Thus, even if we do not consider the echo piece of 1589, the two composers had at least five years during which they competed with, and influenced, each other.

centering on the need to give dramatic evidence to a text. He was led to overstress this point, however, in order to distinguish his own from Caccini's accomplishments; as a result, his "imitation of speech in song," obtained by means of "a harmony surpassing that of an ordinary speech but falling so far below the melody of songs as to take an intermediate form," [69] has come to be construed as a *dry* recitative, to which the composer himself allegedly pleaded guilty. Actually, even in this statement from the preface to *Euridice*, the extent to which Peri's music falls "so far below the melody of an ordinary song" is qualified and restricted by the words that follow that statement; furthermore, we have to remember that an obsession with text was the symptom of the sixteenth-century concern for expression.

Peri's music is quite often even richer than Caccini's in melody, the main difference, which Peri found difficult to put into words, lying in the larger scope and open continuity of his monologues and dialogues, compared with the narrower definition of a set piece that is an end in itself. Caccini from his side was affected as much as Peri by the need for declamatory evidence of the text, which he, too, overemphasized in his prefaces (even in places where other elements are the obvious determining factors),[70] not only because one of the esthetic axioms of the time was that the text was the carrier of the emotional contents, but also because he usually received inspiration from the text for the initial motion of his melodic phrases. Rhythm and accentuation of the words thus became, too, an intrinsic part of the aria (Example 1). Like Caccini's, Peri's melody also incorporates the rhythm, accentuation, and dynamics of the text in its aria, but faces different problems of development. The use of coloratura to expand an initial gesture into a melodic phrase is usually

[69] Strunk, *Source Readings*, p. 374. The word "dry" should be avoided because of the precise eighteenth-century technical meaning of "recitativo secco," indicating a recitative with continuo accompaniment (as opposed to recitatives "con strumenti obbligati" or "recitativi obbligati"), but not necessarily lacking melody.

[70] Strunk, *Source Readings*, pp. 385–391.

Example 1. Giulio Caccini, *Le nuove musiche*, beginning of Madrigal XI

precluded by him, as is textual repetition; melodic repetition is also a rare occurrence, needing to be justified by either text or action. At cadences the sense of enhanced finality rounding up the conclusion of set pieces must usually be avoided; on the contrary, new ways must be always found to stress continuity and to inject a new momentum wherever the flow of the dialogue tends to become stagnant. The ways in which Peri copes with these problems are manifold. To obtain a faster delivery of often lengthy texts, the supporting harmonies of the continuo tend to become more widely spaced and to extend the harmonic *sprezzatura* not only, as in Caccini's music, to passing notes of coloratura, but to notes accented by syllables (Example 2). Thus the continuo tends to lose all vestiges of linear conduct, reserving that for the moments of heightened lyrical interest. Its increased harmonic significance tends to avoid cadential successions (although we may feel they are still too frequent); instead, unexpected harmonies, or unexpected shifts of the tonal plane are often used to create diversions and to indicate new moods. Conceding that there are also moments of lesser interest, one

Example 2. Jacopo Peri, *Le musiche . . . sopra l'Euridice,* p. 30

nevertheless has to admire Peri's resourcefulness in adhering to his text and yet attaining a definite melodic coherence, resulting in a line endowed with aria (Example 3). Finally, the most impressive display of unusual and daring harmonies, often resulting from very unorthodox procedures, is brought about by the "tragic" moment of most impassioned pathos; and yet this display may lend itself (as in the well-known example of Orpheus's song at the gates of Hell) to a formal organization that is not the less remarkable for its obvious derivation from procedures familiar in madrigals.

Caccini contented himself with establishing an affective mood and letting it permeate the short span of his pieces, like a slow, sweet poison flowing through the veins of his coloratura. Peri, more nearly like Gesualdo and Monteverdi, seeks to depict more forceful passions, and feels the urge to plunge into their stream, to follow their meanderings, to explore their depths and shallows. To express not only passion but the dialectics of passion, the mere intelligibility of the text is not enough; a give and take is needed, in which music enhances the meaning and accentua-

Example 3. Jacopo Peri, *Le musiche . . . sopra l'Euridice*, pp. 2–3

Example 3 (cont.)

tion of the words and has its blind forcefulness motivated and guided by them. In this way the rhythmic formulation of the dramatic text and its various degrees of emphasis become the criteria of naturalness and necessity, that is, the aria, of the dramatic melody.

❧⁂❧

What I have said of Caccini's and Peri's works has been meant to indicate how they stem from, and diverge from, the common ground of musical and esthetic tendencies of their time, and also to help our further investigation of the dramaturgy of opera. For the sake of completeness, we may add that, in addition to the elements of style listed above, many others were present at the moment of an operatic performance that are not indicated in the scores we possess. They go farther than the "recitative" *sprezzatura* of the singers with which we have become familiar. These elements include changes of tempi, changes of texture and instrumental color of the continuo,[71] and possibly also linear interventions of other instruments beyond the basic continuo accompaniment.[72] The fact that these elements were not recorded, and could vary from one performance to the other, does not mean that they were not carefully weighted for a calculated effect. Even the simplest "rappresentatione per musica" was rehearsed for weeks or even months before its official presentation;[73] we

[71] See the instrumental indications given by Monteverdi on pages 36 and 38 of the original score of *Orfeo;* as I have often remarked, such indications were given as a record of what had been done in the original performance and as a guide, but not necessarily a rule, to future performances.

[72] I am referring to the intervention of those instruments that are said by Agostino Agazzari to "serve for ornament"; see his *Del sonare sopra il basso* (Siena, Falcini, 1607), translated by Strunk, *Source Readings*, pp. 424 ff.

[73] The Florentine spectacles of October 1600 were being rehearsed every morning as early as August 29 (Solerti, *Musica, ballo e drammatica*, p. 23). Similarly, *Arianna* was already under rehearsal in March of 1608, although the performance took place on May 28. For the long

delude ourselves, then, when we speak of these elements as being improvised at the moment of performance. Indeed, they were so thoroughly rehearsed and agreed upon that they come near to another characteristic trend of the music of the time, that of "stile concertato." [74]

IV. THE PASTORAL AURA

It may seem paradoxical that aria, if only as an indefinite quality and esthetic goal, should have been an important factor in the initial formulation of a style which we are accustomed to consider chiefly as recitative. The paradox, however, stems from our habits of thought more than from the factual situation. We still think of the early "stile rappresentativo" too much in terms of the later recitative. (This also, possibly, we think of too exclusively as mere non-aria.) To be sure, there are some barriers that need to be overcome to gain access to a musical idiom whose values were explicitly meant to come alive at the moment of performance. The difficulties are compounded by an unfamiliar notation, in which long notes often demand short values, and the modern reader is given little indication of where expressive and rhythmic stresses need to be placed.[75] Yet by giving indiscrimi-

---

preparations in Parma, see Irving Lavin, "Lettres de Parma (1618, 1627–28) et débuts du théatre baroque," Jean Jacquot, ed., *Le lieu théatrale à la Renaissance* (Paris, 1964), pp. 105 ff.

[74] See above, n. 69. Too much credit has been given to the etymology of "concerto" and "concertato" from the Latin *concertare*, "to contend or dispute"; but, also, the etymology from *conserere*, "to connect or bring together," given as the basic one by Franz Giegling, "Concerto," and Hans Engel, "Concerto grosso," both in *MGG*, Vol. II, cols. 1600 and 1604, is a half truth. Many elements and words of similar sound concur in the final meaning of *concerto*, but to an Italian of the fourteenth century (Boccaccio), as to those of the sixteenth and twentieth, the main meaning of *concertare* was "to make sure," "to reach an agreement."

[75] For works in this category, more than for any other style, I am opposed to modern editions that merely strive to reproduce the original notation, adding bars that correspond to the beat but not to the rhythm of music. Such editions avoid, not error, but taking responsibility for it

nate credit to all that was written or said in Florence at the turn of the century, and by magnifying it into the myth of a quarter of a century of ineffectual theorizing, we have made it all too easy to fall back on an erroneous condemnation of sterile intellectualism.

The discrepancy between verbal statements and actual deeds is borne out by Caccini himself in the foreword to his *Nuove musiche* of 1601 (1602). Having previously quoted Plato to the effect that music should follow, not precede, speech and rhythm,[76] he finds himself committed to giving embarrassed justifications for the pieces in this collection that he calls *arie*—ten of them, as distinguished from the twelve "madrigali." For not only do most of these *arie* apply the same music to the various verses of a polystrophic text (thus contradicting the fashionable Platonic slogan), but they even include some light pieces— ariette, in a frottola-like rhythm—for instance, those numbered as sixth, eighth, and ninth *arie*, which strongly resemble Orpheus' canzonetta "Ecco pur ch'a' voi ritorno" at the beginning of Act II of Monteverdi's *Orfeo*.[77] The fact is that aria in this more specific sense is also present in all Caccini's printed collections, and its purpose, in spite of solemn esthetic preambles, is to

---

and, above all, the process of trial and error through which a deeper knowledge of the music should be gained.

[76] Caccini's declared intent (see the unnumbered folio A2 verso of the facsimile edition) is to observe "quella maniera contanto lodata da Platone, & altri Filosofi, che affermarono la musica altro non essere che la favella [i.e., speech], e'l rithmo, & il suono per ultimo, e non per lo contrario, à volere che ella possa penetrare nell'altrui intelletto, e fare quei mirabili effetti, che ammirano gli Scrittori, e che non potevano farsi per il contrappunto nelle moderne musiche."

[77] See the modern edition of *Le nuove musiche* by Carlo Perinello (Milan, 1919; due to the peculiar format of the edition, page numbers would only be confusing). I do not agree with every detail of Perinello's rhythmic interpretation, yet a comparison with the facsimile, pp. 33–37, will bear out the point made above, n. 75. In favor of rhythmic interpretation is a recent and, I am afraid, not too convincing book by Putnam Aldrich, *Rhythm in Seventeenth-Century Italian Monody* (New York, 1966).

provide entertainment.[78] Nor is the musical quality of the madrigals much different; we may speak of them as unavowed non-strophic *arie*, having only internal repetitions brought about by repetition of text.

We would be mistaken again if we assumed that Caccini's melic temperament was the reason for an exceptional use of aria.[79] A quick glance at the two *Euridici, Orfeo,* or any of the extant early operatic scores will show that, far from being a continuous series of open recitatives, each of them includes a number of self-contained pieces. Limiting ourselves, for the moment, to Peri's opera, we may list in the first place its prologue, with seven strophes each followed by a short instrumental ritornello (only the bass line is given), and the five choruses, most of them including solo verses, that mark the end of the five episodes.[80] Also strophic, with two verses each, are the songs of Tirsi in the second episode and of Orpheus in the last one, "Nel puro

[78] "The thought also came to me that I should compose some canzonets in the form of arias, to be used in a consort of several stringed instruments, for the relief of depressed spirits," says Caccini, again in the foreword to *Le nuove musiche* (see the unnumbered folio B1 recto of the facsimile).

[79] Jan Racek, *Stilprobleme der italienischen Monodie* (Prague, 1965), which reached my desk too late for a profitable perusal, seems at first glance to place due emphasis on Caccini and on the literature of chamber songs depending on him, but to overstress the importance of his statements without putting them in their polemic context. Racek's work goes against Caccini's expressed opinion by completely disregarding dramatic monody.

[80] The first episode (rejoicing around Euridice; pp. 2–8 of the facsimile) is concluded by the chorus "Al canto, al ballo"; the second (arrival of Orpheus and friends, announcement of Euridice's death; pp. 8–21) by the responsorial threnody "Cruda morte"; the third (description of Orpheus' grief; pp. 21–28) by "Se de boschi i verdi onori," a chorus of thanks for the celestial solace descended on Orpheus; the fourth (short dialogue with Venus, followed by Orpheus' singing and pleading until Euridice is given back to him; pp. 28–40) by "Poi che gli eterni imperi," a chorus of infernal spirits celebrating human daring; the fifth (joyous return of the couple, general singing and dancing; pp. 41–52) by a chorus alternating with an instrumental ritornello. A change of stage setting, required by the fourth episode, is indicated on p. 28, and the re-establishment of the original setting on p. 41.

ardor" and "Gioite al canto mio." [81] "Antri ch'a' miei lamenti" (Example 4), sung by Orpheus upon his arrival on stage in the second episode, and his rondolike invocation at the gates of hell, "Funeste piagge," [82] resemble Caccini's monostrophic madrigals, although both span a wider range of emotions than any of Caccini's pieces. Finally, a number of shorter passages have a distinctive songlike quality. One such passage is Orpheus' triumphal exclamation, "O fortunati miei dolci sospiri" (Example 5) in the fourth episode.[83]

The fact needs to be stressed at this point that the protagonists, though not the title roles, of both of Rinuccini's operatic libretti are musicians: Apollo, the god of music, and Orpheus, the legendary singer, who, at least in the version of the myth followed by Rinuccini, is the son of Apollo and the Muse Calliope. That their common musical talent was no mere coincidence is indicated by subsequent operas. The title role of Agostino Agazzari's *Eumelio*, performed in Rome in 1606, is of an allegoric youth who is torn between the enticements of pleasure and vice and the appeals of reason and virtue, but who is also—quite unnecessarily from the point of view of the moral example he is called to give—an accomplished singer.[84] In the following year, 1607, Monteverdi and Alessandro Striggio the younger gave in Mantua another version of the Orpheus myth, which to a great extent parallels the one presented in Florence with Peri's and Caccini's music.[85] Also in Mantua, Apollo was brought back on stage in

---

[81] Pp. 11–12 and 46–47 of the facsimile.

[82] *Ibid.*, pp. 8–9 and 29–32.   [83] *Ibid.*, p. 38.

[84] This score deserves attention not as much for its intrinsic value as for its attempt at musical characterization; each character is given a kind of head-motif, which is repeated with most of his utterances. Like Rinuccini and Peri, Agazzari justified "recitar cantando" as a procedure that had been applied in classic times; he further justified strophic repetition of music by doubting that "the ancients" had felt obliged to give each strophe new music.

[85] Strong similarities and verbal reminiscences indicate that Striggio had the text of *Euridice* in mind when he wrote his libretto. I even believe that some divergences were suggested by Monteverdi in order

Example 4. Jacopo Peri, *Le musiche . . . sopra l'Euridice*, pp. 8–9

Example 4 (cont.)

Example 4 (cont.)

1608, when Marco da Gagliano reset to music Rinuccini's *Dafne*. There can be no doubt that all authors deliberately sought to justify singing of songs—"cantar recitando"—by choosing for protagonists such musical figures around whom other singers gather quite naturally.

Example 5. Jacopo Peri, *Le musiche . . . sopra l'Euridice*, p. 38

This way of justifying song is in line with an established tradition of the Italian theatre, according to which the exhibition on stage of one or more characters shown in the act of singing, playing instruments, or dancing was an accepted practice and a gratifying element of variety. We may even add that in no other genre had such a habit been as prominent as in the dramatic pastorale or tragicomedy, in which category, according to the rather rigorous classifications of dramatic genres prevailing during the late Renaissance period, we need not hesitate to place the early operatic libretti.[86] Yet, its obvious intensification in the

---

to avoid either dramatic situations that had proved their weakness or too obvious repetition of the most successful ones.

[86] The distinction between tragedy and comedy was based on the station of their characters as well as on the tragic or comic nature of the events they described. The tragic fate of highborn persons brought grief to those subject to their rule; the misfortunes of the common

new-born opera, and the lack of an equally obvious stylistic distinction between the pieces that represent "cantar recitando" and the rest of the score betray the qualms of the creators of the new brand of "recitar cantando" concerning the legitimacy of their creature.

I have previously described Rinuccini's and Peri's approaches to "recitar cantando" as realistic, as opposed to the formalistic approach of Cavalieri. This statement now needs further qualification, for it is evident that no departure from reality could be more conspicuous in a play than the systematic "imitation of speech in songs." There is, however, a realism of some sort in Rinuccini's and Peri's concern to provide a justification for their departure from reality, a justification which never before had been felt to be needed by the organizers of the spectacular symbolic *intermedi,* or by Cavalieri for his dancing and singing figurines. The justification given by both of them in the prefatory remarks to the libretto and the score of *Euridice,* namely, that continuous singing had been used by the ancients in their tragedies, was undoubtedly fashionable, but too simple and also, they probably knew, difficult to maintain. It was evidently intended to forestall the most superficial criticism with an *ipsi fecerunt.* More effective in the long run was the built-in defense which gave "recitar cantando" a motivation by endowing the

---

people affected only them, with the result that their despair could be laughed at. Concerning the pastorale, its theorist, Guarini, has this to say about its characters (after having "very well and sufficiently demonstrated" its being "a mixed story of tragic and comic elements"): "E, per intenderle meglio, hassi a sapere che gli antichi pastori non furono, in quel primiero secolo che i poeti chiamaron 'd'oro', con quella differenza distinti dalle persone di conto, che oggi sono i villani da' cittadini, perciocchè tutti erano ben pastori" ("To understand these things better, one has to know that the ancient shepherds of that primal age, called 'golden' by the poets, were not as sharply distinct from people of importance as peasants are nowadays divided from citizens, insofar as they were all shepherds"); from "Il compendio della poesia tragicomica" in G. B. Guarini, *Il pastor fido,* ed. G. Brognoligo (Bari, 1914), p. 268.

protagonists of opera with the most exceptional gifts for music and by placing them in the very special climate of the pastorale.

As pastorales the early operatic libretti are rather unusual in their pronounced reliance on mythological legends and characters. Yet a mythological quality had always been present in the pastorale even when no particular myth was referred to, for the world of the pastorale was that of a legendary Golden Age, vaguely located in an imaginary pre-historic Arcadia or Thessaly. In that Utopia-Uchronia, still unspoiled by the artificial needs and rules of social life and still blessed with innocence, naturalness, and freedom, men and women—that is, shepherds and nymphs—were not only happier than in the world we know, but also endowed with a spontaneous feeling for beauty and a natural gift for artistic expression, poetry, and music. The nostalgic dream of a utopia of perfect happiness thus becomes the esthetic vision of an idealized world, the imitation of which leads not to crude realism but to a more refined, and also more malleable, *vraisemblance*.

Gods and demigods are not too often present in the pastorale; yet they are always around the corner, and whenever they decide to intervene among the humans, their sudden appearance produces awe but no surprise. Nor is any logical fault found in their descending or ascending on wings, flying chariots, or soft puffs of clouds. At other times their invisible presence is made evident either mystically through the cryptic verdicts of oracles or, more poetically, through complacent echo answers—a trick that had already attracted the attention of musicians. Finally, and here is our main point, there is no breach of *vraisemblance* in the fact that the gods are exquisite singers; indeed, to all the characters of the pastoral landscape, the gift is given to express themselves in verse and in a language that has "a harmony surpassing that of ordinary speech." This is clearly stated by Guarini in his defense of his pastoral play: "It is no marvel that the Arcadian shepherds, noblest of all, embellished their speeches with poetic ornaments, being as they were more than any other people in the greatest intimacy with the Muses." He then goes on to quote Polybius to the effect "that all the Arcadians were poets; that their principal study, and their principal activity was in the music; that they learned it as children; that their laws required them to do so"; and so on.[87]

Such ideas may have been only vaguely in the minds of Rinuccini and Peri—after all, the combination of drama and music is a recurrent urge in all kinds of historical and geographical situations. Nonetheless, Guarini's ideas were in the air, particularly in Florence, which Guarini had visited first in 1588 and again more than once in 1599–1601, when he was, at least nominally, attached to the Medicean court; his *Compendio della poesia tragicomica*, from which I have quoted, although printed in 1602, was already known in manuscript in Florence in 1599.[88] In my opinion, one result of the strong influence exerted by the theories of pastoral poetry on the early "stile rappresentativo" and opera was a lack of a clear distinction between enhanced speech and song, a lack that once more reaffirms the catholic conception of the style itself, embracing, as it does, the full range of nuances from the most prosaic and matter-of-fact utterances to the most lyrical and even florid outbursts. To be sure, there are songs that are definitely songs—"cantar recitando"—and are usually established as such either by the repetition of the same music for more than one strophe of text (while the "imitation of speech" obeys the madrigalistic principle that new words require new music) or by some explicit mention of the fact that the characters are indeed singing. There is, however, margin left for doubt.

[87] "Or non è maraviglia se i pastori d'Arcadia, massimamente nobili, abbellivano di vaghezze poetiche i loro ragionamenti, essendo essi, più di tutte l'altre nazioni, amicissimi delle muse. . . . Ma . . . veggasi quello che ne dice Polibio . . . : 'Che tutti gli arcadi eran poeti, che 'l principale studio, il principale esercizio loro era quel della musica, che l'apparavano da fanciulli, che le leggi a ciò fare li costringevano'"; *ibid.*, p. 253.

[88] *Ibid.*, p. 305. See also Vittorio Rossi, *Battista Guarini ed Il pastor fido* (Turin, 1886), pp. 123–131.

For instance, in Peri's *Euridice* the already mentioned "Funeste piagge" is clearly a song, but it is unclear whether Orpheus' following supplications in dialogue with Pluto and Proserpina are also songs, artfully improvised by the unusual singer, or passionate oratorical arguments.[89] Conversely, in the initial scene, the dialogue of shepherds and nymphs calling each other to share Euridice's happiness and to attend her nuptial preparations is already melodious from its beginning, but it gathers further momentum and culminates in open singing on its final line. The line is repeated three times, with different melodies, by three different characters, and a fourth time by the full chorus; of course, even in the bliss of Thessaly, no shepherd or nymph could ignore the fact that "Non vede un simil par d'amanti il sole" is a quotation from Petrarch [90] and needs to be put in some sort of quotation marks.

The lack of a clear-cut stylistic distinction was by no means restricted to the earliest operas. Even when the librettists began to separate recitative scenes more sharply from situations suitable for an aria, and began to exercise their ingenuity in providing more numerous occasions for the latter, the distinction was hardly made on the basis of musical style. Monteverdi always remained substantially faithful to the madrigalistic conception of a continuity and nuanced variety of musical expression. Cavalli's typical arias around and after the middle of the seventeenth century break into what we would consider recitative just at the point where they reach an emotional climax, as in Example 6; and vice versa, many of his recitatives suddenly take wing, even though for only the short flight of one single, more exalted line.[91]

[89] See the facsimile, pp. 32–37. The same applies to some extent to the songs of Orpheus in Monteverdi's score.

[90] It is line 9 of the sonnet "Due rose fresche e colte in paradiso"; for the music, see the facsimile, p. 4.

[91] Mention needs also to be made of certain recitative units, monologues as well as dialogues, which tend to organize themselves either in terms of an emotional crescendo, or, in more strictly musical terms, by adhering to a fundamental key in spite of dashing modulatory excur-

Example 6. Francesco Cavalli, *La Didone*, Act I, scene 4, first two stropes of an *ostinato* aria

Example 6 (cont.)

Domenico Mazzocchi's printed score of *La catena d'Adone* (Venice, 1626; it had been performed in Rome the same year) has two numbers which are labeled "arie recitative" in the index. The same term could be applied to the so-called unornamented version of "Possente spirto" in Act III of Monteverdi's *Orfeo*, as well as, in a somewhat different sense, to many an aria or lament on an *ostinato* bass.

The pastoral aura that made "recitar cantando" plausible was not the only legacy of pastorale to opera. Others, on which I cannot dwell, were the almost unbroken rule of the happy ending, the propensity for the depiction of tender passions, and the participation of comic characters, although on a lower social level than the main roles.[92] Still another deserves to be mentioned because it has some bearing on the use of set pieces. This is the striving of both genres toward a classic balance between, on one side, poetic freedom and emotional intensity and, on the other side, the effectiveness of an impressive formal composure.

It has been said that the pastorale was, after all, the fullest attainment of the Italian Renaissance in its attempt to recreate ancient tragedy. The goal could be reached only by repudiating the tenet that the subjects should be historical—too prosaic and depressing—and by avoiding the insidious shoals of the ethic catharsis—never too clearly understood, and anyway too dangerous in times of intensified control of the arts during the Counter Reformation. Instead, a more tangible catharsis was offered the audience not only by the pleasurable relief provided by the happy ending,[93] but also by the continuous balance of interest between the contents and the ingenuity of their artistic

---

sions and by exploiting the recurrence of significant phrases in both text and music. Cavalli was particularly fond of such effects.

[92] See my "*Commedia dell'Arte* and Opera," *Musical Quarterly*, XLI (1955), 305–324. The *commedia dell'arte* exerted a direct influence on opera at a slightly later time than the pastorale; yet pastorale, *commedia*, and opera are only different manifestations of the same general trend.

[93] A similar attitude is explicitly endorsed by Caccini in the passage quoted above, n. 78.

formulation. On the operatic side, I have deemed it possible, on occasion, to compare Peri's *Euridice* to a frieze of metopes, and Monteverdi's *Orfeo* to the triangular tympanum of a classic temple.[94] Such similes have limited significance, but they try to translate into words the sense of a classic balance, too vividly present in the scores to be viewed as a mere coincidence.[95] Although it was soon to give way to the Baroque conception of a play as a continuous building of tensions, to be released time and again by sudden changes of mood, the interest in a balanced pattern of organization can still be perceived in some of the Roman operas, for instance, in *La morte d'Orfeo* (1619) and *Sant' Alessio* (1631 and 1634), both by Stefano Landi.

The means available to the composer for achieving this sense of balance were mainly the distribution and interrelation of set pieces, either those belonging to the realistic type—musicians shown in the act of making music—or, even more often, those depending on formal theatrical conventions that had been established and accepted long before the beginning of opera. Such are the prologue and choruses which I have listed above along with the *arie* of *Euridice*. Were we to establish a similar list of set pieces for *Orfeo*, we should add the duets and tercets that are so prominent in its first two acts. Choruses no less than *arie* are

[94] In "Monteverdi e i problemi dell'opera," a lecture given in March, 1963, at the Fondazione G. Cini in Venice, to be published soon by the foundation.

[95] See Grout, *Short History of Opera*, p. 52, for a summary and diagram of the symmetries in *Orfeo*. It seems to me, however, that the overall symmetry has generally been overstressed, for to view Acts I and V as a balance of prelude versus postlude does not take into account that a daring tragic finale had been planned, which would probably have challenged Monteverdi more than the mellifluous apotheosis included in the score. I am more impressed by the symmetry in the first act, to be viewed in the general context of text and action rather than as a pure element of musical form. For a similar symmetry in the finale of *La morte d'Orfeo*, see Donald Grout, "The Chorus in Early Opera," in Anna Amalie Abert and Wilhelm Pfannkuch, eds., *Festschrift Friedrich Blume* (Kassel, 1963), pp. 160–161.

self-contained, set pieces; they share with many *arie* a strophic verse-pattern and need even more than *arie* to be reconciled with *vraisemblance*. Yet, despite much Renaissance talk about imitation of nature, and despite the realistic bent of Italian comedy and tragedy, the remarkably unlikely fact that a number of characters could find extempore not only a mutual agreement but also the way of vocalizing it in a harmonious ensemble never seems to have been questioned. In tragedy it was legitimized by classic precedent—indeed, it was one of the most obvious formal features of the model; in comedy it had a less official status, yet it became accepted, usually in the guise of a masquerade, as one possible form of *intermedio*.[96] In a similar way, although playwrights often preferred spoken prologues as the vehicles of their programmatic utterances,[97] sung prologues had also been an admissible choice at least from the beginning of the sixteenth century. The pattern of four-line verses sung by a single allegorical personage or mythological character, which we find applied with such uniform regularity in the early operas, appears to be the continuation of accepted practices in previous theatrical forms.[98]

Prologues and choruses, little more than convenient theatrical properties in the early Renaissance theatre, came to opera with

[96] *Intermedio* usually reminds us of the most spectacular examples, a category apart from the simpler forms which were most currently in use. To the masquerade type belong the *intermedi* of both Machiavelli's *Mandragola* and *Clizia*. Among the other types, I must particularly mention the instrumental interlude; well-known examples are the *sinfonie* of both Cavalieri's *Rappresentatione* and Monteverdi's *Orfeo*. The latter were needed, following the choruses that end each act, to accompany the change of scenery which took place before the eyes of the audience; each *sinfonia* is placed in the score at the end of an act, but actually partakes of the expressive mood of the following act.

[97] Particularly intriguing is the spoken "Proemio" of Cavalieri's *Rappresentatione*, a hybrid between the programmatic prologue and the spoken, humorous *frottole* (no relation, but for the name, with the musical form) of previous religious plays.

[98] The same pattern is also occasionally adopted by heavenly messengers in the course of the plot.

the more exalted status they had acquired in the pastorale with its emphasis on all kinds of artistic devices, and more particularly on those having musical implications. In the same spirit also duets and trios, if not used realistically as the concerted singing of two or three characters, acquired formal importance either as an extension of the Renaissance concept of chorus [99] or as the equivalent of another classic device, the stychomythia.[100] Thus the utopian optimism of the pastoral world, while yielding to the escapist tendencies of the time, nevertheless allowed, through the flexibility of its *vraisemblance*, ingenious formal effects which were the last residuum of the classic ideal.

V. "RECITAR CANTANDO" AND ARIA IN THE FIRST DECADES OF OPERATIC HISTORY

The history of the first half-century of operatic activity can hardly be described as a straight line. In spite of the initial strong impact of the pastorale, many other influences and occasional or local conditions made their mark on individual works, while, under the persisting habit of humanistic conceptualism, the real motivation was rapidly estranging itself from the essence of classicism. It is not my intention to give here any detailed account of that period, for which I can refer to the basic outline provided by Donald Grout's classic work on opera. I shall limit myself to examining some of the conventions that made *arie* and set pieces possible within the frame of *vraisemblance*, if not realism, which opera had inherited from the rules of the Renaissance theatre.

[99] Most usually, a normal operatic chorus was formed when two to six of the individual characters present on stage joined their voices to express a common feeling. See Grout, "The Chorus in Early Opera," pp. 151–153.

[100] Most duets may be included in the definition of a chorus as given in the preceding note; there are cases, however, in which two characters sing to express individual, even antithetic, feelings. Alternation and reassociation of the two voices are procedures similar to those of stychomythia; in addition, the duets often took advantage of the more typically musical technique of imitation.

I have singled out Peri's *Euridice* to mark the beginning of opera as a gentle, lovable, and viable (albeit frail) creature. Its viability as a work of art, however, was not necessarily sufficient to grant viability to its genre against adverse conditions and fierce competition. Opera had to compete against, on one side, the richer articulation of plot and dialogue of the spoken theatre and, on the other, a number of other genres in which music associated with less dramatic but more spectacular action. The competition was especially strong in Florence, where the two sides had long combined their forces in the exhibitionistic tradition of spoken comedies with lavish portentous *intermedi,* while normal court life favored a number of lesser, more easily staged musical entertainments.[101] As a result, a Florentine phase of the history of opera is practically nonexistent, beyond its inception in 1600, until about the middle of the seventeenth century.[102] The new genre might even not have survived had it not been transplanted and injected with new vigor first in Mantua, then in Rome, and finally in Venice.

In each of these places competition had to be met again and again, and acceptance won, through perseverance, ingenuity, and a certain amount of compromise. In Mantua, for instance, the two spectacular apotheoses which replaced the finales that had originally been planned for both *Orfeo* and *Arianna* clearly represented a compromise with the genre of the *intermedio.*[103] In

---

[101] A concise but comprehensive and up-to-date survey is given by Federico Ghisi in section 3 ("Le feste medicee, gli spettacoli teatrali, gli intermedi e la nascita dell'opera in musica") of the article "Firenze," *Enciclopedia dello spettacolo,* Vol. V (Florence, Rome, 1958), col. 376–381.

[102] There is no record of new operas performed in Florence between 1600 and 1628—Francesca Caccini's *Liberazione di Ruggiero* (1625) was a sung ballet introducing a tournament; then, with the exceptions of *Flora* (1628), *Le nozze degli dei* (1637), and *Celio* (1646), one has to wait until a habit of operatic performances was inaugurated by *Tancia* (music by Jacopo Melani) in December, 1656.

[103] In the case of *Arianna* it is recorded that a committee headed by the Dowager Duchess of Mantua found the plot "too dry" and suggested

the case of *Arianna,* opera's first conscious attempt to compete
with the spoken theatre, the compromise worked also in a different, though related, way. Rinuccini, who had already toyed with
the idea of tragedy at the time of *Euridice,* must have been glad
when the opportunity arose to produce a regular tragedy, or at
least a play with many features of a regular one, having no less a
musician than Monteverdi at his side. The experiment, however,
more daring than we realize, caused no little concern at the
Mantuan court, where the plot was felt to be too dry—too
human, that is; for it is a fact that, while the fishermen of Naxos,
replacing the shepherds and nymphs of Arcadia in the plot of
Arianna, can still praise the primeval simplicity of their life, the
pastoral aura and the blessed innocence of the Golden Age have
completely abandoned Theseus, Arianna, and their retainers.
They are but men and women, bound by custom, law and even
political considerations, from which arise their troubles, hardly
suitable to be put into song unless they reach a paroxysm of
despair. The compromise suggested by a committee and realized
in the Mantuan performance must have involved not only the
already mentioned spectacular and melodious apotheosis, but
also a considerable amount of vocal floridity brought about by
Venus and Love in the first episode.[104]

The two trends thus inaugurated in Mantua can be viewed as
separated in theory, but often intertwined in practice. We can
perceive the influence of the *intermedi* in such operas, usually

---

modifications (Angelo Solerti, *Gli albori del melodramma* [Milan,
1905], I, 92); it is easy to recognize these modifications in the added
dialogue between Venus and Love in the first episode, and the final
invervention of the gods, Venus rising from the sea, and Jupiter impart-
ing his blessing from the sky, both of which upset the classic "regularity" of the play. The original finale must have ended, after the arrival
on stage of Bacchus and Arianna, with the triumphal chorus "Spiega
ormai, giocondo nume." A similar intervention by those in power must
have averted the slaughter of Orpheus at the hands of the Bacchantes,
still present in the printed libretto of *Orfeo* but replaced by a different
finale in the printed score.

[104] See above, n. 103.

big courtly events, which incorporated danced choruses and gradiose stage effects. These were placed at the ends of acts, evidently to function as *intermedi*—in which category we can place the already mentioned *Catena d'Adone* (Rome, 1626), *La Flora* by Marco de Gagliano (Florence, 1628), and, as late as 1667–1668, Cesti's *Pomo d'oro* (Vienna). To a certain extent one can also recognize the influence of the *intermedi* in the evolution of the prologue, which was first expanded by adding a chorus and spectacular action to the original one-character strophic singing, and later transformed into an extensive dialogue, or dispute, between a number of gods or allegorical characters, requiring a set of its own and, more often than not, ingenious stage machinery.[105] This new type of prologue, however, quite often introduces into the ensuing plot a different level of motivation than that of human actions. This motivation can be expanded by other related scenes (not always placed at the proper place for an *intermedio*) into a counterplot of mythological or allegorical nature, which interferes with the principal plot (although the human characters may or may not be aware of its existence) and often determines the sudden twists of the peripeteia. Well-known instances of this two-level procedure are Cavalli's *Didone* (1640), as well as Monteverdi's *Ritorno d'Ulisse* (1640) and *Nozze d'Enea con Lavinia* (1641?).[106] They borrow

[105] The pattern of four-line strophes sung by a single character is still present in some of the earliest Venetian operas. In the *Armida* of Benedetto Ferrari (1639), the prologue is sung by Fortune alone, but the strophic pattern is broken; it is reestablished in *Il pastor regio* (1640).

[106] Previous instances are the pastoral counterplot of *Erminia sul Giordano* (Rome, 1633) and the assistance given by angels and by the personification of Religion to the protagonist of *Sant' Alessio* (Rome, 1631 and 1634) in his fight against the schemes of the Devil. In *Amore trionfante dello Sdegno* by Marazzoli, the personifications of Love and Indignation influence the actions of the human characters, thus also explaining their abrupt psychological changes; in other cases, rivalries among gods also affect the actions of the humans, and their pacification (or discomfiture in the case of an evil power) is a prerequisite for the denouement. Sudden transitions from indifference or hatred to love, and vice versa, are often the effect of Love's arrows.

it from their Virgilian or Homeric models. We also find this procedure applied without any similar justification, however, in most of the early Venetian operas, not to mention those plots which are still completely pastoral or mythological.[107]

One must conclude that, as had been the case for the audience of *Arianna* thirty years before, the Venetian public was not fully prepared for the novelty of "recitar cantando" as the normal means of expression for human beings; accordingly, it was only natural for the librettists to select themes that either still retain the mythological or pastoral aura, or could be developed on a double level, one of which at least would allow the composer a freer hand and compensate for the restraint to which he was obliged when handling human characters.[108] This assumption is confirmed by the fact that even on the lower level librettists and composers multiplied the occasions for "cantar recitando." In Benedetto Ferrari's *Andromeda* (1637), a group of nymphs concludes a successful boar hunt with singing and dancing; in his *Maga fulminata* (1638), two wandering knights sing a duet while traveling in a boat and are answered by no less than three sirens. The convivial singing of Penelope's suitors in *Il ritorno d'Ulisse* is paralleled by a concert offered in *La finta pazza* (1641) to a group of visitors. A festival gives the main characters of *Gli amori di Giasone, et di Issifile* (1642) the opportunity of singing in honor of Venus and Bellona; they are joined by two

[107] Mythological pastorales are Cavalli's *Nozze di Peleo, et di Teti* (Venice, 1639), the first opera to be called a "festa teatrale," and his *Amori di Apollo, e di Dafne* (Venice, 1640), as well as Manelli's *Delia* (Venice, 1639). Benedetto Ferrari's *Ninfa avara* (Venice, 1641) has no gods, but is entirely pastoral and is called "favola boschereccia."

[108] See, for instance, the floridity of the recitative of La Religione in *Sant' Alessio*, Act III, sc. 5, given by Hugo Goldschmidt, *Studien zur Geschichte der italienischen Oper im 17. Jahrhundert* (Leipzig, 1901), I, 237. Although Monteverdi did not wait for the pretext of the supernatural to justify his using whatever musical means best suited his intentions, yet in *Il ritorno d'Ulisse* Minerva's, Juno's, and Neptune's vocalizations are the most daring ones and Telemachus is never as melodious as when he travels with Minerva on a flying chariot.

comic characters, who sing for Bacchus and Priapus, and by three girls, who praise the three Graces. *La Venere gelosa* (1643) has a singing competition which reminds one of *Tannhäuser*. Finally, very few operatic heroines neglect to indicate in a song how free they are, initially, from all concerns of love; many of them are noted for their ability to accompany their singing on the harp or the zither; [109] and one, Aventina of *La finta savia* (1642), gives a full-dress recital when she describes the statues of a garden in a series of songs.

The luxuriant growth of the Venetian opera, after its initial phase of adjustment, richly exemplifies the many ways in which composers strove for public acceptance of "recitar cantando." Yet one has to realize that opera would have never become the kind of spectacle we know without a number of circumstances connected with its previous development in Rome. Strong objections had been raised there by the papal government against the professional *comici dell'arte*, whose performances represented elsewhere a welcome alternative to the more sophisticated, but expensive and infrequent, court spectacles. This gap, only partially filled by amateur performances, [110] gave opera the chance to be more than a tentative competitor of the spoken theatre.

The first operatic performances had been given in Rome by Florentines—as was the case of *Aretusa* by Filippo Vitali, performed in 1621 with the participation of Caccini's son Pompeo as a scenery painter and a singer—or had followed the Florentine pattern musically and dramatically, as for instance Stefano Landi's *Morte d'Orfeo* (1619). A different trend was inaugurated in 1623 with the advent of Maffeo Barberini as Pope Urban VIII and with the emergence of his three nephews as the arbiters of

[109] Dafne, in Cavalli's *Amori di Apollo, e di Dafne*, asks for her zither and sings; Archimene in *Il Bellerofonte* (Venice, 1643) plays the harp. Even later, in Cavalli's *Serse* (Venice, 1654), Xerxes falls in love with Romilda by hearing her singing.

[110] Plays, with or without music, were often performed by the students of various colleges; and, later, performances of comedies were organized by such artists as Lorenzo Bernini and Salvator Rosa.

Roman social life; an almost regular habit of operatic performances was soon established. The performances were held every
year during the Carnival season, or on the occasion of princely
visits, in one or the other of the various Barberini palaces, or in
the Palazzo della Cancelleria, the official residence of Cardinal
Pietro Barberini.[111] Opera thus became the main form of theatrical activity in Rome, and as such it expanded the scope of its
plots and the range of its subjects, including, along with the
traditional pastoral, mythological, and allegorical topics, plots
derived from the most famous poems of Italian epic literature
(*La catena d'Adone*, 1626; *Il ritorno di Angelica dalle Indie*,
1628; *Erminia sul Giordano*, 1633; *Il palazzo incantato
d'Atlante*, 1642), from hagiography (*Sant' Alessio*, 1631 and
1634; *Santa Teodora*, 1635; *San Bonifatio*, 1638), or even from
the *commedia dell'arte* (*Il falcone*, 1637, performed again in
1639 as *Chi soffre speri*).[112] One external indication of change

---

[111] Although performed in the house of a Baron Hohen Rechberg,
Diana schernita (1629), with the Barberini lily and golden bees appearing in its finale, can be considered the first Barberini opera. It derives
its inspiration from the favorite theme of an old follower of the
Barberinis, Francesco Bracciolini, author of *Lo scherno degli dei*
(1617); it also makes humorous references to the invention of the
telescope by another one-time protégé of Urban VIII, Galileo Galilei.
The performances of *Sant' Alessio* seem to have been given first in the
older palace in the Via dei Giubbonari, and then in the new one in the
region called Quattro Fontane. Concerning the theatre, see above, n. 3;
Professor Irving Lavin informs me that only in 1639 was some kind of
semipermanent theatrical installation created in the new palace.

[112] The trend of hagiographic plots had already been inaugurated in
1625 with a *Sant' Eustachio*, music by Sigismondo d'India (another
Sant' Eustachio, libretto by Rospigliosi and music by V. Mazzocchi,
was performed in 1643); it lasted at least until 1668, when *La comica del
cielo*, text by Rospigliosi (by now Pope Clement IX), music by A. M.
Abbatini, was performed. *La catena d'Adone* (1626) and *Il Ciclope*
(1630) combine mythology and Christian piety through far-fetched
moral allegories. The influence of the *commedia dell'arte*, already felt
in the comic parts of *Sant' Alessio* (including a dance of peasants in the
costumes of Punchinello, and the comic tricks played on the servants by
the Devil), is particularly strong in *Chi soffre speri*. With the expan-

was the gradual abandonment of such names as "favola" or "pastorale" in favor of "commedia per musica," or even simply "commedia." [113] Under the growing influence exerted on Italian theatrical activity by the Spanish theatre, the term had lost its connotation of a precisely defined comic genre; it meant rather any kind of theatrical action developed mainly through dialogue, and was as neutral as "opera," a term soon to prevail in the musical theatre.

In itself, the transition to plots derived from epic poems was not too great a departure. The warrior world of Ariosto's and Tasso's tales, the golden age of chivalry, was no less unreal and utopian than the pastoral Golden Age.[114] However, it offered no specific justification of "recitar cantando." It would seem then that less than two decades of opera had been sufficient to establish continuous singing, initially the privilege of shepherds and gods, as an accepted theatrical convention. Audiences and

---

sion of the operatic scope goes the shift from the classic number of five acts to the more practical division into three acts, reducing the number of required *intermedi* from four to two. It was easy, however, to rearrange the number of acts; for Monteverdi's *Ritorno d'Ulisse* we have a three-act score and various five-act libretti.

[113] For instance, in the *Argomento et allegoria della commedia musicale Chi soffre speri* (Rome, 1639); for the allegory, see Stuart Reiner, "Collaboration in *Chi soffre speri*," *Music Review*, XXII (1961), 265–282. The habit of referring to operas as comedies, an intriguing and often confusing feature of Roman chroniclers, occasionally spread outside Rome. See Henry Prunières, *L'opéra italien en France avant Lulli* (Paris, 1913), which contains many French and Italian letters that refer to operas as comedies.

[114] Charlemagne and his knights had become the heroes of popular mythology long before Ariosto's whimsical and ironical treatment of them in his epic. As for Tasso, his attempts to reconcile his romantic stories with history were a futile afterthought; his characters derive from Homeric, Virgilian, and Ariostesque models—a literary rather than a popular mythology—to which he merely added his note of pathos. In both Ariosto and Tasso, a host of fantastic or allegorical figures are introduced into the action and the art of magic is often present. However, no character in either Ariosto's or Tasso's works is noted for his musical gifts.

critics had become accustomed to the novelty and ceased to question its legitimacy; for it is a fact that the willingness of the audience to accept a mode of representation in the theatre, or any other artistic framework, matters more than the author's rationalizations. Once the acceptance is established, usually through mere repetition and habit, the illusion is created no matter how faithful to, or divergent from, reality the representation is.

The desire of the Barberini and their favorite librettist, Monsignor Rospigliosi, to eliminate the often scurrilous performances of the *commedia dell'arte* by equating opera with spoken theatre may have contributed to the rapid establishment of "recitar cantando" as the equivalent of speech on stage. In any case, it is a fact that the enlarged scope of the action, the increased number of characters, the introduction of secondary plots, of peripeteia, of disguise and recognition, created large sequences of action in which rapid delivery and communication of the text were more essential than musical setting. The only reason for hesitating to identify this procedure with the later "recitativo secco" is that the latter was chiefly characterized by a mode of accompaniment, not necessarily by a lack of musical interest.[115]

Of course, we are lucky to have in our possession a number of scores from this period. We must realize, however, that they put us only one step ahead of having only the libretti, and in a sense the latter are the most essential clue to works that were basically conceived as plays. As for the music, it was only one of the many elements contributing to the projection of that basic outline across the footlights; it was seldom more important than stage design, costumes, acting, the jokes of the comic characters, and, last but not least, what would now be called "special effects." The fact that music was only one of the many ingredients in the theatrical recipe explains the great difference of musical interest—one could say of musical dosage—in the various surviving scores. Impassioned recitative is still the center of attention, alter-

[115] See above, n. 69.

nating for the sake of variety with choruses and dances, in *La catena d'Adone* of 1626; but *Diana schernita* of 1629 (as far as we know, its most immediate successor) develops its satirical and even stripteaselike action mainly in a plain parlando style, relieved by only one extensive song of Endymion's (Act III) and by a choral finale in which, quite incongruously, Endymion's corpse is changed into the lily and golden bees of the Barberini arms. The parlando style is prominent in varying degrees in the Barberini operas that followed. In *San Bonifatio* (1638), not only is recitative seldom interrupted by arias, but further lack of musical variety is created by the fact—certainly due to the occasion and circumstances of the performance—that all characters, including the Devil and a Spanish braggart soldier, are sopranos.[116]

On the whole, the most prominent feature of the Roman opera, and its most typical legacy to the genre, far from being its emphasis on the chorus (often confined to the detachable and interchangeable *intermedi*), lies in its affinity to—actually meant as a refinement of—the mode of performance of comedy. This affinity led, on one hand, to the kind of compelling drive that characterizes the rhythm of comedy and, on the other, since the "comedy" is after all a musical one, to the creation of points of specific musical interest, functioning in most cases as either preparation or culmination of the "comic" action—or as a temporary diversion. This does not mean that the "comic" action was entirely devoid of musical interest; on the contrary, many of the procedures that lend remarkable musical interest to Cavalli's monologues and dialogues had already been attempted in the Roman opera.

[116] The Spanish soldier, Capitan Dragon y Vampa Sparaparapiglia, obviously derives from the *commedia dell'arte* and is paradoxically inserted in a classic plot. The "comedy" was probably performed by young students of a college; a manuscript libretto in the Biblioteca Casanatense in Rome (cod. 1293) includes the *intermedi*, in one of which the difficulties of an all-soprano cast are discussed and a reference is made to the diminutive stature of the performers.

The realistic procedure, the song as such, is by far the easiest way to introduce and justify passages of more specifically musical interest, as we have already seen while speaking of the pretexts for song invented by the librettists in Venice. In Venice, however, in the absence of the special conditions that had made Roman opera into a substitute for spoken theatre, the audience had to be gradually introduced to the novelty of operatic conventions. But realistic "cantar recitando" is by no means missing in Rome; we can take as an example scene 4 of Act II in *Chi soffre speri*, where the servants Zanni and Coviello—a Bergamasque and a Neapolitan, both familiar characters in the *commedia dell'arte*—entertain a young shepherd and finally succeed in cheating him of his food while singing a *bergamasca* and a warlike song. Act III of the same opera is opened by the same shepherd, who praises his carefree life in a song. This is an obvious reminder of the pastoral tradition; at the same time, however, it is related to the practice of showing a character in the act of singing to himself while performing some usual chore or sport. The selection and content of the song, and the activity in which he is involved, as well as additional recitative, are all intended to provide an insight into his personality. Shepherds, young girls picking flowers and adorning themselves, or minor gods stepping on stage to deliver some message, are most likely to be introduced in such a way. The procedure is even more straightforward with comic characters, whose monologue scenes often become a direct address to the audience with satirical or ribald remarks on contemporary life—an even more ludicrous situation when the character is a mythological figure expected to have classic composure.[117]

Serious characters lend themselves less easily to a straightforward singing situation. In their case the monologue takes the shape of a recitative with ups and down of emotional intensity and occasional changes of mood. Yet Stefano Landi did not hesitate to conclude the monologue introducing Sant' Alessio to

[117] Mercury or one of the Muses is most often cast in such a role.

the audience (Act I, sc. 2) with a two-strophe "arietta" summing up the saint's meditation on the vanity of life.[118] In *La catena d'Adone* (Act III, sc. 1) a philosopher's anguished reflections on Falsirena's rash actions periodically revert to a "mezz'aria" in which he states that "reason is the loser where sensual passion prevails." [119] In Monteverdi's *Ritorno d'Ulisse* (Act I, sc. 1), the description of things "returning" in nature assumes arialike features in Penelope's long self-introductory monologue (the short interruptions of Ericlea do not alter the basic situation); then the thought of Ulysses' continued absence brings the recitative back to a more impassioned (and, therefore, also musically relevant) conclusion.

Penelope's monologue and Alessio's meditation facilitate the transition to lament and prayer, the most impressive set-piece conventions of the early opera, for both of which Monteverdi's example was a decisive contribution. I name the lament first because it had been largely exploited even before the one sung by Arianna in 1608 moved the audience to tears and impressed itself in the mind of every music-loving Italian. After *Arianna* composers became so conscious of the effectiveness of the lament

---

[118] Modern edition in Goldschmidt, *Studien . . . italienischer Oper*, I, 208–209.

[119] See my "Falsirena e la più antica delle cavatine," *Collectanea Historiae Musicae*, II (1957), 355–356, including a partial transcription. We have coined the term "arioso" for this kind of transition from a declamatory pattern to a full, even though short-winded, melody. The seventeenth century used, if any, a number of different expressions. One is "mezz'arie," mentioned in the index of *La catena d'Adone* as present in the score, but not listed. Short, not formally organized, melodic passages are sometimes labeled "ariette" or even "arie" in the score of the anonymous *Pio Enea* and of Marazzoli's *Amore trionfante dello Sdegno* (both performed about 1641–1642). The inconsistency with which the two terms are used should not be surprising considering that even full-fledged arias were not always so labeled, either out of carelessness in the copying or because of the obviousness of their being arias. Finally, the word "cavata," which I indicated to be the antecedent of "cavatina," appears in some later scores, such as the Viennese copy of Sartorio's *Orfeo*.

that they abused it to the point of caricature. This is the case in *Aretusa*, which opens with Alfeo declaring to the audience his unrequited love for Aretusa, followed by Aretusa troubled by a menacing dream, by her father fretting over some obscure premonition, by her brother worrying lest something should happen to her while hunting, by a shepherd bringing on stage the sad news of her death and of Alfeo's despair, then by Alfeo himself and a dismal choral finale. A few cases of "cantar recitando" and choruses do not provide sufficient relief from this orgy of musical deploration.

The lament was initially conceived as a madrigalistic recitative, yet was already formalized to some degree in Peri's *Funeste piagge* and Monteverdi's *Lasciatemi morire*. During the 1620's it borrowed from the rising "cantada" the form of an *ostinato* aria, which I have already qualified as one sort of recitative set piece.[120] Even later, when the contrast between recitative and *ostinato* had lost its impressiveness through repetition, the lament became a plaintive aria, usually prepared by a recitative, and occasionally, but not necessarily, breaking into recitative at its climax.

Even more personal a contribution was the prayer of Act III of Monteverdi's *Orfeo*, where the double version in the score provides us the privilege of catching some glimpse of the growth of a poetic conception. There is no doubt in my mind that the unornamented version of this piece is not a schematic one, to be embellished at will by the performer, but a full realization of the prayer following the oratorical principles of the early "stile rappresentativo." [121] It is also a prayer in the familiar terms of human misery and of confident hope in a superhuman power. It

---

[120] See above, p. 86.

[121] The full artistic validity of both versions is strongly asserted by the direction at the head of the piece in the 1609 print (p. 52): "Orpheus sings only one [or "either one"] of the two parts to the accompaniment of the wooden organ and one *chitarrone*" ("Orfeo al suono del Organo di Legno, & un chitarrone, canta una sola de le due parti").

took a stroke of genius, after having quite effectively conceived the whole series of strophic recitative variations on a repeated bass line,[122] to give the same basic material—the same aria I would call it, and not in a merely formal sense—a completely new and more sophisticated twist, reworking it into an "orphic" rite, a highly stylized and hieratically formalized incantation, through which a superhuman singer soothes and subdues the forces of darkness crossing his path.

Both as a prayer and as an incantation Orpheus' song left its mark on history. No less than three prayers are included in *Sant' Alessio:* one is the "arietta" mentioned above, an invocation to death to come; a second one is a chorus (Act I, sc. 5) asking divine protection for Alessio "wherever he may be"; and the third is again a strophic aria (Act II, sc. 7), saluting the arrival of death, at last, announced by an angel to Alessio.[123] Another prayer is addressed to Juno by Psyche in *Amore e Psiche* (Venice, 1642; Act II, sc. 4), but its music is no longer extant. Aside from these examples, prayers are not too common in the world of opera. We need not to be surprised that the three included in *Sant' Alessio* all follow an arialike pattern, considering that more than a quarter of a century had lapsed since *Orfeo.* We have more reason for wonder when the magician Falsirena of *La catena d'Adone* evokes Pluto in an "[aria] recitativa per ottave." [124] But *La catena d'Adone* is probably the last among the Roman operas in which the ideals of the early "stile rappresentativo" are still applied in full vigor. Furthermore, Falsirena's evocation of Pluto is interpreted as a prohibited formula to be uttered in secrecy; the same penumbral concept also applies to Pluto when he reluctantly answers Falsirena's questions, again in a "recitativa per ottave."

[122] The text is a Dantesque *terza rima*, six three-line verses plus a concluding line. The rhythm of the bass pattern is freely organized, but substantially altered only in the fifth *terzina* and in the final line.

[123] Goldschmidt, *Studien . . . italienischer Oper*, pp. 217–223 and 230–231.

[124] Both Falsirena's and Pluto's "arie recitative" are set to a bass pattern repeated for the two halves of the *ottava.*

There must have been many other examples of the incantation aria, for magicians and enchantresses abound in seventeenth-century opera, as, for that matter, in most of the operatic history. Monteverdi's counterpart of Falsirena, the shadowy project of his *Armida*, is to us nothing more than a title; [125] but Armida returns in *Erminia sul Giordano* (Rome, 1633), where, with the help of theatrical machinery, she suddenly conjures up the walls of Jerusalem merely because she wants to know how the siege is progressing. She regains the title role in Benedetto Ferrari's *Armida* (Venice, 1639) and has a sister in his *La maga fulminata* (Venice, 1638). She is the leading female character in *L'Amore trionfante dello Sdegno* (Ferrara, 1641 and 1642), music by Marazzoli to a libretto by Ascanio Pio di Savoia. [126] But plots in which Armida appears are not the only ones to include magic. We need only recall Luigi Rossi's *Palazzo incantato d'Atlante* (Rome, 1642), in which the machinations of magicians form the central theme. Either the scores are lost or composers did not continue to utilize scenes of magic and incantation, for the only other example I can mention from this time is the well-known one of Medea in Cavalli's *Giasone* (Venice, 1649).

Monteverdi was also the originator, as far as we know, of the musical description of madness, another operatic feature which enjoyed some success with composers and audiences. Although related to the monologue—it is indeed a monologue even though other characters may be present—the dramatic sequence of musical folly is a comic one, committed not to a crescendo of

[125] The earliest mention of this project is in a letter of May 1, 1627, to Alessandro Striggio the Younger: "I have with me many *stanze* of Tasso which I have set. . . . Armida begins: *O tu che parti parte tu tuo' di me parte ne lassi*, followed by her whole lament and wrath, with Ruggiero's answers" (in Gian Francesco Malipiero, *Claudio Monteverdi* [Milan, 1929], p. 250). The following letters are mostly occupied with discussions of *La finta pazza Licori*; then two letters of September 18 and 25, also addressed to Striggio, speak of *Armida* (the first one, *ibid.*, p. 273, mistakenly reads *Aminta*) as a sizable composition which would require two months to be finished.

[126] Manuscript score without a title in the Vatican Library, Chigi, Q VIII 189.

emotional intensity, but to abrupt shifts from one idea to another, on which the mad character (or the simulator of madness) concentrates time after time with utmost intensity. In Monteverdi's words, "since the imitation of . . . madness must only consider the situation as it is present, not in its past or future; and since, consequently, the imitation must rest upon each individual concept, not upon the meaning of the whole sentence, then the mention of 'war' shall require imitation of war, 'peace' of peace, 'death' of death, and so forth. Also, since the transitions and imitations shall be enacted in quick succession, she who is entrusted with a role of such primary importance, which moves to laughter and sympathy, such a lady shall of necessity omit any imitation other than the momentary one suggested by the prescribed text." [127] The role described by Monteverdi is that of "Licori finta pazza inamorata d'Aminta," to which a larger number of his extant letters refer than to any other of his works. His enthusiasm for this comic pastorale, which he completed in 1627 in a few months of happy work, but which never reached the stage, is made more tantalizing by the fact that both libretto and score are lost.

Monteverdi, always faithful to the original comprehensive concept of "stile rappresentativo," and more extreme in its application than any other musician, must have displayed in the score, and more particularly in the description of Licori's simulated madness, the full riches of musical invention that are present in its tragic counterpart, *Il combattimento di Tancredi e Clorinda* (circa 1626).[128] As it was later revived on the Venetian operatic stage, the "imitation" of madness, real or simulated, must have relied more heavily on verbal expression, and consequently on a recitative relieved by short insertions of caricatural song. This

[127] Translated from a letter to Striggio in Malipiero, *Monteverdi*, p. 252; my translation does not agree with the one given by Leo Schrade, *Monteverdi: Creator of Modern Music* (New York, 1950), pp. 309–310.

[128] It is evident from Monteverdi's description that Licori's madness attracted him as an ideal situation for those extreme accents and abrupt shifts of mood that are typical of his "stile concitato."

much transpires, at least, from the only surviving score which contains scenes of folly, Cavalli's *Didone* (Venice, 1640). There, furthermore, the sequence of Jarba's madness, although essentially comic, also sounds, if only briefly, a note of his misery. The scores of *La ninfa avara* and *La finta pazza* (both Venice, 1641), in both of which madness is a central theme, are lost. To have the music of a similar scene one has to wait until Cesti's *Orontea* (Venice, 1649), and then the delirious character is a secondary one and the cause no longer folly but drunkenness.[129]

To express himself in song still seemed incongruous for a serious character,[130] but incongruity, if any was still felt, could only make a comic one more comical. To come on stage singing one or another type of song placed an immediate label on the ribald or the coward, the glutton, or the drunkard. In addition to that, comic characters also had a way of expressing their simple wisdom and coarse common sense in aphorisms and proverbs, which needed to be placed in quotation marks by the composer with a shift from parlando to an arialike rhythm and pitch. The Roman *Chi soffre speri* (1637 and 1639) with its multitude of *commedia dell'arte* types provides all kinds of examples of how comic characters can be musically handled. In Venetian operas, following a series of dramatic upsets, a comic character often remains alone to make derogatory comments, or easy generalizations embodying his practical or cynical wisdom, in an aria.

The tradition of giving comic characters simple tunes sounding like popular ones goes back to the last pastoral operas. Such are the songs of Pan in both *La Flora* (Florence, 1628) and *Diana schernita* (Rome, 1629); in the former there is also a

[129] I have given a partial transcription of it following "Le prime opere di Antonio Cesti" in Pietro Castiglia, ed., *L'orchestra* (Florence, 1954), pp. 176–177.

[130] See Francesco Sbarra: "I know that such ariette as those sung by Alexander and Aristotle will be held to be adverse to the dignity of persons of such stature," translated from the foreword to the printed libretto (1652) of *Alessandro vincitor di sè stesso* (see *ibid.*, p. 164).

suggestion of pastoral amoebean singing, for Pan's couplets expressing his unrequited love alternate with symmetrical, although differently tuned, rebukes of his beloved, also of a rather popular flavor. The popular sound is evident in the two-voice arietta of the pages Curtio and Martio in *Sant' Alessio* (Act I, sc. 3), with its thrice-repeated interlude (three times vocal imitation of instruments, the last time actually an instrumental ritornello);[131] this in turn compares with the *strambotti* sung by Zanni, Coviello, nymphs, and shepherds in the first *intermedio* of *Chi soffre speri*. The tradition was to be continued at least up to the time of Melani's *Tancia* (Florence, 1657); since Tancia is a peasant girl, she and her rustic lover are entitled to similar songs.[132] Even without these or similar references to popular singing, however, comic *arie* usually have simple and direct rhythms and an almost syllabic rendering of the text.

To be sure, comic characters could also sing, on occasion, virtuoso or pathetic arias. The first is possible when a character engages in extensive vocalization either because he has pretensions or delusions of grandeur and prowess or simply because he stutters. Concerning the second type, it is a well-known fact that misadventures and despair of an essentially comic character produce a ludicrous affect, which is enhanced the more exaggeratedly pathetic his laments. In both cases, however, the comic effect is doubled by the awareness of the fact that the lowly character is usurping expressive conventions that belong to another class or type.

This leads me to the last of my present considerations, that of situations in which the self-consciousness of operatic conventions lends itself to intentional caricature. This is obviously the case, for instance, in *Chi soffre speri* (Act II, sc. 11), when the main character decides on, and "laments," the sacrifice of his favorite falcon to the dinner table and is lamentably echoed by Zanni in his Bergamasque dialect idiom, or else in the monologue

[131] Goldschmidt, *Studien . . . italienischer Oper*, pp. 210–212.
[132] *Ibid.*, pp. 357–358.

of Iro in *Il ritorno d'Ulisse*, Act III, sc. 1.[133] More subtly, but on a larger scale, the parody of operatic conventions is a clue to *Il palazzo incantato d'Atlante* and *Orfeo* by Luigi Rossi (Rome, 1642 and 1647) and to a later *Orfeo* (Venice, 1672) by Antonio Sartorio.

❧❦

No elaborate conclusions can be drawn from my rambling survey of the conventions that lent a measure of *vraisemblance* both to opera as a whole and to its individual components. It would better suit the operatic traditions of the time to end with a short epitomizing choral line, in which case no other comment would be more fitting than the one which concludes the Chorus of Phantoms and Act I of *Il palazzo incantato d'Atlante:* "Oh, ch'è lieve ingannar chi tosto crede" ("How easily is beguiled he who wants to believe").

Another section, if not a conclusion, could be added to this article, which would revert to the question: What makes an aria? Such an investigation would not delineate the form and tonal plan of the available operatic arias; this would be a legitimate pursuit only if we realize that formal problems *per se* still were of secondary importance at the time under consideration. The continuity of both dramatic and musical action, the rhythm of "comedy" or "opera," were more urgent concerns of the composer, so that what lay outside the set pieces had no less interest than the pieces themselves. My endeavour, perhaps more ambitious, would examine, and possibly relate to a single principle, the many uses of the term "aria" for apparently different and even contradictory phenomena.

The realization of such a project must be left for another occasion. Here, only its projected title can be ironically quoted: "Exit on aria (though no exit aria)."

[133] In this category is also the parody of the incantation scene by Bruscolo in *Tancia*, Act III, *ibid.*, p. 371.

Giacinto Andrea Cicognini's and Antonio Cesti's *Orontea* (1649)

By WILLIAM C. HOLMES

The pioneering studies of Hermann Kretzschmar, Egon Wellesz, Henry Prunières, and Hellmuth Christian Wolff long ago focused attention on the important place occupied in music history by the composers and operas of seventeenth-century Venice. More recently, Wolfgang Osthoff, Simon Townley Worsthorne, and Nino Pirrotta have further enlarged our knowledge of the Venetian operatic stage, particularly during its early development between 1630 and 1655.[1] Pirrotta, especially, with his concept of a "pan-Italian" style of composition in mid-seventeenth-century Italy, has helped to clarify one of the more confused periods in the history of opera. In addition to these primarily musical studies, there is a great body of bibliographical material concerning the Venetian stage of this time. Allacci,

[1] Osthoff, "Antonio Cestis 'Alessandro vincitor di se stesso,'" *Studien zur Musikwissenschaft*, XXIV (1960), 13–43; Worsthorne, *Venetian Opera in the Seventeenth Century* (London, 1954); Pirrotta, "Tre capitoli su Cesti," Guido Chigi *et al.*, *La scuola romana* (Siena, 1953), pp. 27–79; Pirrotta, "Le prime opere di Antonio Cesti," Pietro Castiglia, ed., *L'orchestra* (Florence, 1954), pp. 153–181; and Pirrotta, "*Commedia dell'Arte* and Opera," *Musical Quarterly*, XLI (1955), 305–324. See also Pirrotta's entry on "Cesti" in *Enciclopedia dello spettacolo*, Vol. III (Rome, 1956), cols. 462–467. I wish here to express my gratitude to Professor Pirrotta, who very kindly made available films of his copies of the *Orontea* scores.

Ménestrier, Bonlini, Ivanovich, Crescimbeni, Quadrio, Ricco-boni, Arteaga, Galvani, and Molmenti have all faithfully, though not always accurately, enumerated the theatres of Venice and documented the works produced upon their stages.

In contrast to this documentation, the music of the operas, with a few notable exceptions, has not been made widely available in modern editions. Likewise, the librettos and their relationship to the spoken stage of the time have received scant attention from modern writers—perhaps because historians of both music and the theatre have hesitated until recently to venture into unfamiliar areas.[2]

Interestingly, what began as both a conscious and unconscious exchange between the lyric and the spoken stage later developed into fierce competition. As Ivanovich points out somewhat ruefully, the public's changing tastes all but ruined the companies of *comici*. He asserts that before the introduction of opera to Venice the *comici* had been much esteemed and very successful. Once opera had become a popular entertainment, however, the *comici* could no longer earn enough money to continue their performances. Ivanovich feels that the popular victory of opera over spoken comedy was generally detrimental not only to the art of the theatre, but to the whole state of culture in Venice. The *comici*, unable to earn a living on the stage, deserted the city, leaving it in the hands of the opera companies. Something had to be done to save the *comici* from oblivion.[3] The adoption

---

[2] Pirrotta is an exception. His article "*Commedia dell'Arte* and Opera" is devoted to an examination of the intimate connections between some of the early Venetian opera librettos and the *scenari* of the traveling companies of *comici*. A. A. Abert in her article "Schauspiele und Opernlibretti im Italienischen Barock," *Die Musikforschung*, II (1949), 133–141, and her *Claudio Monteverdi und das Musikalische Drama* (Lippstadt, 1954) also concerns herself with the connections between the opera libretto and the spoken stage in the first half of the seventeenth century.

[3] "*L'introduzione de' Drami in Musica hà levato il concorso alle Comedie ormai ridotte al niente. Prima che s'introducessero i Drami in Musica in Venezia, era molto gradita la Comedia. Le compagnie de'*

by the operatic stage of many of the accoutrements of the
popular prose theatre and its abandonment of the ideals of the
classical-Renaissance theatre provoked violent reactions from literary critics. The sharp attacks by Crescimbeni and his followers, from 1698 onwards, have left present-day students with a
prejudiced and often false view of mid-seventeenth-century operatic dramaturgy. To help clarify this situation is the principal
aim of this study: an examination of the libretto of Antonio
Cesti's first opera, *Orontea*, will demonstrate that this work, one
of the most widely performed in the seventeenth century, embodies an esthetic conception that regarded a certain balance of
ingredients necessary.

By 1649, the year of the first performance of Cesti's *Orontea*,
Monteverdi had been dead some six years and his pupil Cavalli,
often called the "founder" of the "Venetian School," had already written fourteen operas.[4] As we now know, however, the

Comici erano famosissimi . . . [here a list of *maschere*]. Ma questi
vedendo diminuirsi quì il concetto à loro virtuosi impieghi, da che hà
principiato la Poesia vestita di Musica, di caminare col fasto sù i
Teatri, schivano al più non posso l'esercizio in Venezia; dove in
mancanza del primiero nobile concorso, non rifiuta loro quel decoro, e
quell' utile, che li valeva d'allettamento allo studio, e all'applicazione
così dilettevole, e prosicua. Restano dunque à questa causa essi Comici
esposti più alle perdite, ch'à guadagni per le spese, che necessariamente
impiegano per mantenersi nel posto, e se i Teatri musicali non prender-
anno qualche alterazione del tempo, quelli delle Comedie anderanno
deteriorando la condizione con evidente pericolo, ò di svanire, ò di
prender qualche altro espediente, che pure sarà difficile à ritrovarsi in
competenza della Musica avanzata à segni incredibili della soddisfa-
zione universale, che si compra a vil prezzo, già introdotto come si dirà a
suo tempo da un privato fine di putrido interesse à pregiudizio della
Virtù"; Cristoforo Ivanovich, *Minerva al tavolino* (Venice, 1681), pp.
393–394.
[4] Osthoff (in "Antonio Cesti's 'Alessandro vincitor di se stesso,'" p.
13, n. 4) presents convincing arguments for placing the first performance of *Orontea* in 1650 rather than in 1649. This descrepancy results
from the so-called *mos venetus*, the official Venetian calendar in use
until the time of the fall of the Republic in 1797. Under this lunar
calendar, the year began on March 1 rather than January 1. Thus, any

term "Venetian School" is at best misleading and equivocal. Rather, at this time the fundamental characteristics of opera in Venice and in other Italian cities were determined by the traveling companies of performers and composer-performers, many of whom were trained in Rome.[5] Cesti, whose *Orontea* was written for the Venetian stage, can be connected with Rome, both biographically and stylistically. He was a close friend of Salvator Rosa, who was very active in Roman theatrical and musical circles, and he studied, first at Città di Castello and perhaps later in Rome, with the respected opera composer Antonio Maria Abbatini, who was for many years *maestro di cappella* at the Roman basilica of Santa Maria Maggiore.[6] Thus, in Cesti's music (aside from *Il pomo d'oro*, which is in every respect exceptional) we have a clear example of the mid-seventeenth-century

---

work dated between January 1 and March 1, Venetian style, would necessarily carry the date of the following year, Gregorian style. Cicognini's dedication in the first libretto of *Orontea* carries the date (Venetian style?) of January 20, 1649. Were January 1650 accepted as the date of the first Venetian performances, the presumed performances of *Orontea* in Lucca later the same year by the company of the *Febi armonici* (perhaps with Cesti himself singing) would make perfect sense, since the work had only recently been prepared for Venice.

[5] See Pirrotta, "*Commedia dell'Arte* and Opera," for the most recent discussion of this question. Perhaps the best-known description of the training of Roman singers is found in Giovanni Andrea Angelini Bontempi, *Historia musica* . . . (Perugia, 1695), pp. 170 ff. "Le scuole de Roma obligavano i Discepoli ad impiegare ogni giorno un' hora nel cantar così difficili e malagevoli per l'acquisto della esperienza; un'altra, nell'esercitio del Trillo; un'altra in quello de' Passaggi, un'altra negli studij delle Lettere; e un'altra negli ammaestramenti e eserciti del canto, e sotto l'udito del Maestro e davanti uno Specchio." This rigorous schedule of singing practice in front of a mirror took place in the morning; in the afternoon they studied counterpoint for half an hour, theory for half an hour, composition for one hour, and another hour of literature. What was left of the day was spent practicing singing, harpsichord, or composition.

[6] Abbatini's two best known operas, *Dal male il bene* (1653), written in collaboration with Marco Marazzoli, and *La comica del cielo* (1668) were composed in Rome and received many performances there.

"pan-Italian" style. That this style was prevalent can readily be observed when one confronts a scene from an opera by Cesti with, for example, a cantata by Luigi Rossi, who, though born and trained in Naples, is considered one of the leaders of the "Roman School" of composers. It is precisely because of such biographical and stylistic connections between composers in various parts of the peninsula that recent studies on seventeenth-century opera have abandoned such long-accepted terms as "Florentine opera, "Roman opera," "Venetian opera," and "Neapolitan opera." [7] Cesti's *Orontea*, as much as any other opera of the time, illustrates how meaningless these terms can be: it was written for the Venetian stage by a composer from Arezzo who studied with Roman teachers, and its libretto was by a Tuscan.

Before beginning our discussion of the work, however, it would be well to list all the librettos known to me of Cicognini's and Cesti's *Orontea*. Though it may not be complete—such lists seldom are—it is considerably more accurate than any other compilation from Allacci (1666; 2d ed., 1755) through Schlitzer (1953).[8] Each item contains the libretto's title, place and publisher, date of publication, any useful information from the preface, and also references to publications in which (if at all) it is mentioned and the libraries in which it is found.[9]

[7] Compare chapter headings in the first and second editions of Donald Grout's *Short History of Opera* (New York, 1947 and 1965) for a dramatic demonstration of this fact.

[8] Professor Claudio Sartori, director of the Ufficio per la Ricerca dei Fondi Musicali of the Biblioteca Nazionale Braidense in Milan, very graciously made available to me his office's extensive catalogue of opera librettos. I wish to thank him here for his many kindnesses.

[9] The references cited are: Leone Allacci, *Drammaturgia* (2d ed.; Venice, 1755); Alfred Loewenberg, *Annals of Opera* (2d ed.; Geneva, 1955); Ulderico Rolandi, *Il libretto per musica attraverso i tempi* (Rome, 1951), which discusses librettos in Rolandi's personal collection—more than 32,000 items—now the property of the Cini Foundation in Venice; Franco Schlitzer, "Fortuna dell'Orontea," Chigi *et al.*, *La scuola romana* (Siena, 1953), a bibliographical study of the librettos

Orontea, drama musicale del D. Hiacinto Andrea Cicognini . . . da rappresentarsi in Venetia nel Theatro di SS. Apostoli: Nell Anno 1649. Venice, Giacomo Batti, 1649. 84 pp. Elaborately figured frontispiece. Dedication by Cicognini to Giovanni Grimani Calergi, dated January 20, 1649. Cesti not mentioned. Allacci, p. 584; Schlitzer, p. 82; Wotquenne, p. 104. Bologna, Conservatorio; Brussels, Conservatoire; Los Angeles, University of California (not yet catalogued); Milan, Brera; Naples, Conservatorio; Padua, Museo Civico; Rome, Santa Cecilia, Nazionale; Rovigo, Marciana; Venice, Marciana. Allacci has the following to say about the first performance and the theatre: "La rappresentazione di questo Dramma si fece in una Casa privata nella Via detta de' Proverbj, nella contrada de' SS Apostoli, ove più non sussiste il Teatro, e fu la prima, che si udisse in tal sorta di luoghi." The Teatro Santi Apostoli was a small theatre in the Cà Bellegno. It was used primarily for spoken comedies, and operas were performed there only in the years 1649, 1650, 1651, 1652, and 1687. There was another Venetian theatre named Santi Apostoli, but it was not built until 1707.[10]

Orontea regina d'Egitto, drama musicale del sig. dottor Giacinto Andrea Cicognini. Venice, no printer or date. 72 pp. Dedication by Bartolomeo Lupardi, the Roman book seller, to Pompeo Eugenii. Cesti not mentioned. Allacci, p. 584; Schlitzer, p. 84 (places performance between 1656 and 1660 in Rome); Sonneck, p. 836; Wotquenne, p. 104. Bologna, Universitaria; Brussels, Conservatoire; Florence, Marucelliana; London, British Museum (1670?); Milan, Brera; Rome, Vaticana; Washington, Library of Congress. Lupardi,

---

of *Orontea* from only a few sources; O. G. T. Sonneck, *Catalogue of Opera Librettos Printed before 1800* (Washington, 1914); Alfred Wotquenne, *Catalogue de la Bibliothèque du Conservatoire Royal de Bruxelles* (4 vols.; Brussels, 1898–1912).

[10] Allacci (*Drammaturgia*, p. 585) also lists a Neapolitan performance in 1654, with music by the Neapolitan composer Francesco Cirilli. The libretto for this performance has not been found. However, there is a collection of most of the arias of *Orontea* at the Conservatory in Naples and it bears the name of Cirilli. For more on this Neapolitan version, see Pirrotta, "Tre capitoli su Cesti," p. 42, and Schlitzer, "Fortuna dell'Orontea," p. 84.

in his preface, refers to "la presente operetta dell'Orontea regina d'Egitto di nuovo vagante e peregrina per mezzo della stampa. . . ."

Orontea, dramma musicale del Sig. D. Hiacinto Andrea Cicognini Accademico Instancabile di nuovo ristampata in Innsprugg nel Teatro Sala l'anno 1656: appresso Michael Wagner. Cesti's name not mentioned. The text of this libretto is closest to that of the extant scores. Cesti was in Innsbruck from 1652 until 1657. Schlitzer, p. 85. Rome, Nazionale.

L'Orontea, dramma musicale del dott. Giacinto Andrea Cicognini rappresentato in Firenze nell'Accademia de' Sorgenti. . . . Florence, 1661, nella stamperia di S.A.S. Dedication by the Academicians to Archduke Ferdinand Leopold of Austria. Cesti not mentioned. Schlitzer, p. 85. Florence, Nazionale.

Orontea, regina d'Egitto, dramma musicale del dottor Jacinto Andrea Cicognini. Genoa, Giovanni Calenzani. 72 pp. Dedication by the printer to Violante Grimalda Selvaga, dated November 29, 1661. Cesti not mentioned. Allacci, p. 584; Lowenberg, 1662; Schlitzer, p. 86; Sonneck, p. 836; Wotquenne, p. 104. Rome, Santa Cecilia; Munich, Theatermuseum.

Orontea, regina d'Egitto, drama musicale del dottor Iacint' Andrea Cicognini. Milan, Stampatori Archiepiscopali. Dedication by Manuel Beltram de Mesquida to D. Falaminio Crivelli, dated July 22, 1662. Cesti not mentioned. Allacci, p. 585. Milan, Brera, Conservatorio.

Orontea, regina d'Egitto, dramma musicale del dottor Iacinto Andrea Cicognini: Fatto rappresentare dal Signor Gio. Battista Abbatoni in Torino. Turin, Bartolomeo Zavatta, 1662. 69 plus 3 pp. The three final pages contain additions to various scenes. Dedication by the impresario. Cesti not mentioned. Schlitzer, p. 86; Sonneck, p. 836. Washington, Library of Congress.

Orontea, drama del Sig. Giacinto Andrea Cicognini, posto in musica del Sig. Cavalier Cesti: Da rappresentarsi nel teatro del Signor Marchese degli Obizzi. Ferrara, Alfonso and Giovanni Battista Maresti, 1663. Dedication by the publishers to Camillo Carnesecchi, dated January 7, 1663. Cesti is mentioned for the first time in a printed libretto. Note that here Cesti is designated "Sig. Cavalier" rather than by his title as a religious. Venice, Cini Foundation.

L'Orontea, drama per musica da rappresentarsi nel Regio Ducal Palazzo di Milano. Milan, Giulio Cesare Malatesta. 76 pp. Dedication by the performers to Don Paolo Spinola Doria, duca del Sesto, etc., dated November 22, 1664. Cesti is mentioned. Bologna, Conservatorio.

L'Orontea, drama musicale del sig. dottor Giacinto Andrea Cicognini fiorentino: Rappresentato nel Teatro di Macerata l'anno 1665. Macerata, Grisci e Gioseppe Piccini, 1665. 82 pp. Dedication by the impresario Giovanni Battista Ruggieri, to Monsignor Franciotti, Archbishop of Trebisonda, dated June 22, 1665. Cesti not mentioned. The dedication speaks of the "famosa Orontea, che à dispetto del tempo, e di Morte vive ancora gloriosa al mondo" and states that it has been performed "su gli più nobile Teatri delle primarie Città d'Italia." The prologue and the *intermedi* after Acts I and II all deal with the adventures of Aeneas in Carthage. This is the first libretto of *Orontea* to contain printed *intermedi*. Schlitzer, p. 87. Bologna, Conservatorio; Florence, Marucelliana.

L'Orontea, regina d'Egitto, dramma musicale del signor dottor Giacinto Andrea Cicognini. Bologna, Giacomo Monti, 1665. Cesti not mentioned. Schlitzer, p. 87. Bologna, Conservatorio.

L'Orontea, drama per musica di D. Hiacinto Andrea Cicognini da rappresentarsi nel Theatro Grimano di SS. Giovanni e Paolo l'anno 1666. Venice, Steffano Curti, 1666. 72 pp. Dedication by Stefano Curti to Madama Maria Mancini Colonna, Principessa di Roma, duchessa di Tagliacozzo, etc., dated January 10, 1666. From the Preface: "Spettatore. Dopo essersi per il corso di nove mesi dispendiato profusamente per farti comparire con pompa in Iscena la Doriclea Drama composto dalla felice penna del Sig. Giovanni Faustini di buona memoria, et che fu rappresentata l'anno 1643 in questa città con gli applausi maggiori, si sono fraposte tante difficoltà, che si è convenuto per necessità risserbarla a tempo più benigno, & propitio; onde in sua vece in soli dieci giorni si è posta all'ordine l'Orontea compositione del nobilissimo ingegno del Sig. Hiacinto Andrea Cicognini. . . . Goderai della musica celeste del sig. Cavalier Antonio

Cesti. . . . Il Prologo è lo stesso della Doriclea, compositione del signor Faustini." There are nine scene changes listed in the libretto. Wotquenne, p. 105. Bologna, Conservatorio; Brussels, Conservatoire; Florence, Marucelliana; London, British Museum; Milan, Brera, Conservatorio; Padua, Museo Civico; Paris, Bibliothèque Nationale; Parma, Conservatorio; Rome, Casanatense, Santa Cecilia, Nazionale; Venice, Cini Foundation, Marciana.

Orontea. Brescia, Giacomo Perini, 1667. Parma, Conservatorio.

L'Orontea, drama musicale del signor D. Hiacinto Andrea Cicognini, Academico Instancabile: Di nuovo ristampata e rappresentata in Bergamo l'anno 1667. Milan, Lodivico Monza. 59 pp. Dedication by Dominico de Tobia Manganoni to Gasparo Giacinto Martinengo Marchese di Pianezza, dated April 9, 1667. Milan, Brera (badly damaged), Conservatorio.

Orontea, drama per musica del signor D. Giacinto Cicognini da rappresentarsi nel Teatro de' Borghi in Lucca l'anno 1668. Bologna, Giovanni Battista Ferroni, 1668. 70 pp. Schlitzer, p. 89. Florence, Marucelliana; Lucca, Archivio di Stato; Rome, Santa Cecilia.

L'Orontea, regina d'Egitto, drama musicale del signor dottor Giacinto Andrea Cicognini. Bologna, Ferroni, 1669. 74 pp. Allacci, p. 585; Schlitzer, p. 89. Bologna, Conservatorio; Modena, Estense; Venice, Cini Foundation.

Orontea, opera drammatica per musica rappresentata in Bologna l'anno 1669. Bologna, per l'Herede del Benacci. 81 pp. Contains texts for *intermezzi* after Acts I and II. Schlitzer, p. 89. Bologna, Conservatorio; Modena, Estense; Rome, Nazionale.

Orontea, dramma del sig. Giacinto Andrea Cicognini posta in musica dal sig. Cavalier Cesti da rappresentarsi nel Teatro del Co. Rinaldo Cato in Porto Maggiore. Ferrara, Alfonso e G. B. Maresti, 1670. 82 pp. Dedicated to the Abbot Ferrante Bentivoglio. Ferrara, Communale.

Orontea, regina d'Egitto. Naples, Carlo Porsile, 1674. Dedication by the Filomolpi to the Principessa d'Avellino, Donna Geronima Pignatelli. This libretto's text is considerably altered from the original. Schlitzer, p. 90. Naples, Conservatorio.

L'Orontea, dramma musicale del cavalier Cesti e poesia del Cicognini; rappresentata nel teatro di Reggio. Reggio, Prospero Vedrotti, 1674. 66 pp. Dedication by Leone Parisotti to Francesco II d'Este. Schlitzer, p. 89. Bologna, Conservatorio; Reggio, Municipale.

Orontea, regina d'Egitto, drama musicale del sig. Dottor Giacinto Andrea Cicognini. Rome, Giuseppe Corvo e Bartolomeo Lupardi, 1667. Dedication by F. Lupardi to Paolo Albertazzi. Cesti not mentioned. In this libretto many of the recitatives are shortened and many arias are added. Schlitzer, p. 90. Bologna, Universitaria; Florence, Marucelliana; Rome, Santa Cecilia.

L'Orontea, drama per musica da rappresentarsi nel Teatro Grimano di SS. Giovanni e Paolo l'anno 1683. Venice, Antonio Bosio. 59 pp. Dedication by Nicola Navarra to Prince Cesare Ignatio d'Este, General of the Venetian Republic, dated February 17, 1683. Contains *intermezzi* and *balli*. Allacci, p. 585; Schlitzer, p. 90.

L'Orontea, opera in musica rappresentata dalle dame di corte. Wolfenbüttel, August 1686. Dedicated to the Dukes of Saxony. Mentioned by Schlitzer, p. 91, with no references.

Giacinto Andrea Cicognini (1606–1651), the librettist of *Orontea*, was a Tuscan by birth, but spent some years in Venice. The popularity of his many comedies made him one of the most widely performed Italian playwrights of his day. Although most of his works were written for the spoken stage, toward the end of his life Cicognini prepared four opera librettos: *Celio* (Florence, 1646), *Giasone* (Venice, 1649), *Orontea* (Venice, 1649), and *Gl'amori di Alessandro magno* (Venice, posthumously, 1651). Great as Cicognini's reputation was to his contemporaries, he soon became an object of derision to later writers, anxious to reform what they considered to be the barbarous state of the Italian stage. Cicognini's fondness for the dramatic intrigues and linguistic extravagances of the Spanish stage and his use of these in his own plays especially irritated his critics. G. M. Crescimbeni, in his *Dell'istoria della volgar poesia*, first printed in

1698 and later reprinted and revised many times, was among the
first to criticize Cicognini's comedies and librettos so severely.
He claims that with *Giasone* (1649), in order to please the
generally low tastes of the public, the true arts of comedy and
tragedy were dealt a death blow and in their place arose a
hopeless *mélange* in which the classical rules of neither comedy
nor tragedy were respected. He also criticizes the introduction
of arias into the action and in general decries the rise of popular
opera.[11] Though there is some truth in these accusations, Cicognini perhaps has been singled out as a scapegoat rather unjustly.
Spanish comedy was in vogue throughout Italy at this time.

[11] "Fu poi l'Arte istrionica anch'essa seguitata, finchè Giacinto Andrea Cicognini intorno alla metà di quel secolo con più felice ardi-
mento introdusse i Drammi col suo Giasone, il quale per vero dire è il
primo, e il più perfetto Dramma, che si trovi; e con esso portò
l'esterminio dell'Istrionica, e per conseguenza della vera, e buona Comica, e della Tragica stessa; imperciocchè per maggiormente lusingare
colla novità lo svogliato gusto degli spettatori, nauseanti ugualmente la
viltà delle cose Comiche, e la gravità delle Tragiche, l'inventor
de'Drammi unì l'una e l'altra in essi, mettendo pratica con mostruosità
non più udita tra Re, ed Eroi, ed altri illustri Personaggi, e Buffoni, e
Servi, e vilissimi uomini. Questo guazzabuglio di personaggi fu cagione
del total guastamento delle regole Poetiche, le quali andarono di tal
maniera in disuso, che nè meno si reguardò più all locuzione; la quale,
costretta a servire alla musica, perdè la sua purità, e si riempiè
d'idiotismi"; G. M. Crescimbeni, *L'istoria della volgar poesia*, VI:
Della bellezza della volgar poesia (Venice, 1730). Dialogue VI, 106–107.

Later, Stefano Arteaga, to cite only one of the many other critics of
Cicognini, echoed Crescimbeni when he wrote: "Il mentovato Cicognini verso la metà del secolo trasferendo al melodramma i difetti soliti
allora a commettersi nelle altre poesie drammatiche, accoppiando in uno
avvenimenti, e personaggi seri coi ridicoli, interrompendo le scene in
prosa colle poetiche strofi, che arie s'appellano, e mischiando squarci di
prosa alle scene in verso, confuse tutti gli ordini della poesia, e il
melodramma Italiano miseramente contaminò. Fù nondimeno à suoi
tempi per ristorator del teatro: i suoi drammi furono ristampati non
poche volte come cose degne di tenersi in gran pregio: i letterati se'l
proponevano per modello d'imitazione, e le muse, anche elleno, le
vergini muse concorsero a gara per onorar con inni de laude chi più
d'ogni altro recava loro vergogna ed oltraggio"; *Le rivoluzioni del
teatro musicale italiano* (3 vols.; Bologna, 1783–1788), p. 256.

Many of the *scenari* and characters of the *commedia dell'arte* came from the Spanish stage, and most Italian playwrights, with the notable exception of those who frankly imitated the academic traditions of the Renaissance, adapted Spanish plots and consciously constructed their plays in Spanish style—in three rather than five acts, with a mixture of noble and common people constantly onstage, and a complete disregard for the classical unities. From the many examples of such borrowing one might cite two in particular: Cicognini's playwright father, Jacopo, in the introduction to his *Trionfo di David* (Florence, 1633), acknowledged his debt to Lope de Vega; later, Giulio Rospigliosi, who was to become Pope Clement IX, based his libretto for *Dal male il bene* (Rome, 1653) on a Spanish model. Maligned as Cicognini was by many later critics, however, at least one of them, Francesco Saverio Quadrio, spoke more gently and more accurately when he described Cicognini's work—again the opera *Giasone* is the example—as, on the whole, acceptable artistically. He noted that especially in opera it was Cicognini's followers who were led to gross excesses.[12]

Cicognini was perhaps the first librettist to document in print the changing esthetics of opera in his time. As early as 1646, in the preface to his *Celio*, he wrote categorically, "Io compongo per mero capriccio." In his preface to *Giasone* (music by Cav-

---

[12] "Avendo poi la Comica in prosa incominciato a confondersi colla Tragica, ed essendosi preso a tessere Commedie Eroiche, Politiche, Regie, e Morali, anche la Drama Musicale pasò di così fatte qualità a vestirsi. Ma siccome le cose non giungono al loro stato, che a poco a poco, così le Poesie Drammatiche Musicali non divennero Tragicomiche, chè coll'andar di qualche tempo. Giacinto Andrea Cicognini, Fiorentino, fu quegli, che l'ultimo mano loro diede. Perciocchè il suo *Giasone*, per vero dire ha tutte le circostanze de' Drammi, che poi furono seguitati, e che seguitano tuttavia. Ven è però da avvertire, che non andò egli mai tanto lontano dalla buona arte, quanto poscia ne andarono alcuni suoi successori, i quali volendo, strafare, vituperarono affatto la Drammatica Musicale, allorchè s'avvisarono d'ingrandirla"; Francesco Saverio Quadrio, *Storia e ragione d'ogni poesia* (5 vols.; Bologna and Milan, 1739–1752), pp. 433–434.

alli), written in the same year as *Orontea*, he not only repeated this statement, but amplified it.[13] It is obvious here that, by 1649, aristocratic opera, which by its very nature had limited public appeal, was a thing of the past. Instead, in Venice, with its numerous theatres and larger public, the principal purpose of both the librettist and the composer was to please the public. In 1651, Francesco Sbarra, the librettist of Cesti's second opera *Alessandro vincitor di sè stesso,* presented the new esthetic in its final and definitive form:

I know that some people will consider the *ariette* sung by Alexander and Aristotle unfit for the dignity of such great characters; but I know also that it is not natural to speak in music . . . and nevertheless it is not only permitted but even accepted with praise. For today this kind of poetry has only the aim of pleasure and therefore we need to adapt ourselves to the usage of our time. If the recitative style were not intermingled with such scherzi [read "arias"], it would give more annoyance than pleasure. Pardon me this license, which I have taken only in order to make it less tiresome for you.[14]

[13] "Io compongo per mero capriccio, il mio capriccio non hà altra fine, che dilettare: L'apportar diletto appresso di me, non è altro, che l'incontrare il genio, & il gusto di chi ascolta, ò legge; Se ciò mi sarà sortito con la lettura, ò recita del mio Giasone, haverò conseguito il mio intento" (from Cicognini's introductory remarks to *Giasone* [Venice, 1649]). This attitude is remarkably similar to that expressed in 1609 by Lope de Vega in his oration *The New Way of Writing Comedies,* translated with an introduction by Brander Matthews (New York, 1915).

[14] "So che l'ariette cantate da Alessandro, e Aristotile, si stimeranno contro il decoro di Personaggi sì grande; ma sò ancora ch'è improprio il recitarsi in Musica, non imitandosi in questa maniera il discorso naturale, e togliendosi l'anima al componimento Drammatico, che non deve esser altro, che un'imitazione dell'attioni humane, e pur questo difetto non solo è tolerato dal Secolo corrente, ma recevuto con applauso; questa specie di Poesia hoggi non hà altro fine che dilettare, onde conviene accomodarsi all'uso de i Tempi; se lo stile recitativo non venisse intermezzato con simili scherzi, potrebbe più fastidio che diletto; condonami però quell'errore, che solo hò commesso per meno tetiarti" (preface to *Alessandro vincitor di sè stesso* [Venice, 1651]). The English translation in the text is taken, for the most part, from

These statements by Cicognini and, especially, Sbarra, can only be interpreted as the esthetic manifesto of all Italian opera for at least a century afterwards. That Cesti chose these men as his librettists for his first and second operas is ample evidence of his forward-looking attitude toward the lyric stage.

~⚹~

The story of *Orontea*, though it incorporates the complications common to many opera librettos, is essentially centered around one dramatic idea—against her will, Orontea, queen of Egypt, falls in love with the young painter Alidoro, who returns her love. Orontea's ambivalent feelings towards her regal duties and Alidoro's rather frivolous attitude towards love—two other women are attracted to him and he is not unattentive to them—complicate the relationship, but finally all these contretemps are resolved to the benefit of the happy couple. It should be noted that, as was the rule in the seventeenth and eighteenth centuries, there are many versions of the opera and, though all the extant librettos agree in substance, there are often discrepancies as to the number of arias in each scene and the number of scenes in each act. The profusion of scenes does not necessarily indicate great length, as it was customary to label the entrance of each character as a new scene. Thus, whereas one scene with Orontea alone might cover ten pages of score at the beginning of Act II, the same number of pages at the end of Act III includes five scenes because of the rapid dénouement. The basis for my plot summary will be the Innsbruck libretto (1656), since it agrees most closely with the extant manuscript scores of the opera.

Pirrotta, "*Commedia dell'Arte* and Opera," p. 321. The statement "conviene accomodarsi all'uso de i Tempi" is noteworthy as an early example in print of the literary conflict between the traditionalists, who maintained that Aristotelean principles should be retained on the stage, and the newer breed of playwrights, who felt that contemporary fashion should determine the structure of stage pieces.

The Prologue of the Innsbruck libretto presents Filosofia and Amore arguing their respective merits. This is one of the many prologues to the opera and has no relevant connection with the plot.

Act I can be divided neatly into five groups of scenes. Orontea, after announcing her opinions on duty and love, meets the painter Alidoro, and they are attracted to one another (1–5). Gelone, the drunken servant, has a comic scene (6). The love affair of Corindo and Silandra, two members of the court, is presented (7–8). The relationship between Orontea and Alidoro becomes closer, but is complicated by Silandra's attentions to Alidoro, attentions which Alidoro does not try to hamper (9–11). Two comic drunken scenes involving the servant Gelone and the page Tibrino end the act. (12–13).

Act II introduces further psychological and emotional complications into the plot. Orontea, her sense of duty overcome, capitulates completely to her love for Alidoro. At this point her friend and former servant Giacinta (a transvestite role with Giacinta masquerading as the young man, Ismero) assumes a more important role in the story. Orontea's falling in love with a common painter has also alienated her court (1–5). There follow comic love scenes between Alidoro's old "nurse-mother" Aristea and the transvestite Giacinta, who is the unwilling object of Aristea's affections (6–7). Silandra continues to pursue Alidoro, to the misery of her former lover, Corindo (8–10). Orontea at first cannot contain her jealousy, but after Alidoro faints from fear at her raging, she relents and decides to forgive him and make him her husband. She leaves him a letter telling of this decision, and when he returns to consciousness, he is delighted, in his rather vapid way, by this turn of events (11–18).

Scenes rush by in Act III to bring the plot to its happy and somewhat forced conclusion. Silandra is desolate at having lost Alidoro to Orontea, but Orontea, meanwhile, has heeded the advice of her counsellors and decides to forsake Alidoro. Fickle Alidoro, when he hears of this, begins to woo Silandra once again. She this time rebuffs his advances (1–6). Gelone has another comic scene (7). Silandra writes a note to ask forgiveness from her old lover Corindo, who in turn wishes to take revenge on Alidoro (8–9). There follow more comic love scenes between the old nurse Aristea and Giacinta–Ismero. Giacinta, smitten by Alidoro, passes on to him a gift which she has received from the old nurse (9–13). By one of the oldest dramatic ploys, Alidoro is first accused of being a thief and then proved to be a noble prince kidnapped from home as a baby. Orontea can now marry Alidoro and, in an improbable act of *noblesse oblige,* she sends Silandra back to the arms of Corindo (14–20).

Table 1 graphically illustrates the relationships of the various characters in the opera.

Table 1. Relationships between characters in *Orontea*

Act and scene	Emotional relationships	Comic love scenes	Servants' comic scenes
I, 1–5	Orontea–Alidoro		
I, 6			Gelone
I, 7–8	Corindo–Silandra		
I, 9–11	Alidoro–Orontea– Silandra		
I, 12–13			Gelone–Tibrino
II, 1–5	Orontea–Alidoro		
II, 6–7		Aristea–Giacinta	
II, 8–10	Alidoro–Silandra– Corindo		
II, 11–18	Orontea–Alidoro		
III, 1–2	Silandra–Alidoro		
III, 3–4			Tibrino–Gelone
III, 5–6	Orontea–Alidoro– Silandra		
III, 7			Gelone
III, 8–9	Corindo–Silandra		
III, 10–13		Aristea–Giacinta– Alidoro	
III, 14–20 (dénoue- ment)	Alidoro–Orontea Corindo–Silandra		

The principal relationship, of course, is that between Orontea
(soprano) and Alidoro (tenor), though this becomes a triangle
when Silandra (soprano) enters the scene. Psychologically
Orontea is beautifully portrayed by both the librettist and the
composer. From the very opening of Act I we are presented
with a queen who will forsake love because of her sense of duty:

> Orontea: Superbo amore,
> Al mondo imperi,
> Ma nel mio core
> Regnar non speri.   (I, 1) [15]

This aria, which opens the opera without the customary preceding recitative—a noteworthy occurrence in itself—affords the
dramatic soprano of the queen the opportunity to display itself
in all its grandeur. By the fifth scene of Act I, however, Orontea's staunch opposition to love wavers—especially after she has
met the handsome Alidoro, who has been wounded in a street
fight:

> Orontea: Così dunque Orontea,
> Nemica inesorabile d'Amore,
> D'un oggetto straniero
> Farà schiavo il suo core? (I, 5)

By the end of scene 9, in the first lengthy conversation between
the queen and Alidoro, Orontea is obviously fighting her emotions:

> Orontea: Fa ciò che vuoi, purche da me non parta.
> Alidoro: Comanda qual mi vuoi seguace, or scorta.
> Orontea: Vieni, resta, no, sì, O Dio son morta.   (I, 9)

Her confused state of mind is here graphically represented by
sudden rests alternating with the music of the recitative.

At the opening of Act II, Orontea openly expresses her love
for the young painter:

---

[15] Music in Pirrotta, "Le prime opere di Antonio Cesti," p. 170.

S'io non vedo Alidoro
Par che manchin li spirti,
E lunghi dal suo bel quasi mi moro. (II, 1)

She then bursts into an aria:

Adorisi sempre,
Nè mai muti tempre.
Chi serve al suo bene
Fra ceppi e catene,
Le doglie l'asprezze.
Sian tutte dolcezze. (II, 1) [16]

In spite of the violent objections from her advisers, she intends at any cost to have Alidoro:

Sì, ch'io l'amo e l'adoro.
Odami il mondo tutto, amo Alidoro. (II, 5)

But as it becomes apparent that Alidoro is responding to the advances of Silandra, Orontea's jealous rage boils over:

E che vorresti?
E che si vuole?
Con si sfacciato ardire,
Con si sfacciata brama,
Ne i real gabinetti tratta
Un vil peregrino una mia dama?

. . .

Immodesta Silandra,
Temerario Alidoro,

. . .

O contumaci o rei,
Cadrete ambo cadrete
Vittime del mio sdegno, a piedi miei. (II, 13)

By the final scene of the act, however, Orontea relents and, over the unconscious body of Alidoro, sings her best-known aria:

[16] *Ibid.*, p. 178.

Intorno all' idol mio,
Spirate pur spirate
Aure soavi e grate,
E nelle guance elette
Baciatelo per me cortesi aurette. (II, 16) [17]

She leaves her sceptre and a letter offering him not only her love but also her kingdom.

All is not solved by so rash an act on the part of the queen. Creonte (bass), her counsellor, convinces her that she must give up Alidoro, who is after all a common painter:

Orontea: E che far deggio?
Creonte: Sbandirlo, allontanarlo
　　　　 Da gl'occhi, e più del core.
Orontea: Non più. . . . Al tuo consiglio
　　　　 Mi soscrivo, e m'appiglio.   (III, 4)

But her heart is not in her actions and, once the true identity of Alidoro is discovered, she ecstatically receives him as her consort. Though the final reconciliation seems forced, the fact that Orontea never really wanted to renounce her love for Alidoro strengthens the dénouement from a dramatic point of view.

Alidoro, who is uncomfortably cast in the role of hero, is a much less complicated personality than Orontea. His first words, as he enters wounded, are:

Ohimè, misero, ohimè.
Quanto, deh quanto indugia
L'alma a partir da me? (I, 4)

and throughout the opera his bloodless and fickle actions display a permeating undertone of self pity. For example, his immediate reaction to Orontea's ambivalent attitude towards him is to re-

---

[17] An incomplete version of this aria appears in Charles Burney, *A General History of Music from the Earliest Ages to the Present Period* (4 vols.; London, 1776–1789), IV, 66–67. Burney gives only the voice and continuo parts; the upper strings are missing.

peat her words—and music—and wonder if somehow her interest might cause unpleasantness for him:

> Troppo me fan' temere
> Questi contrarii, irresoluti accenti.
> Cielo! e quando havran fine
> I miei danni, il mio duolo, le mie rovine? (I, 10) [18]

He has little time to reflect further on this matter, for after he
has sung an arietta, Silandra, Orontea's lady-in-waiting, enters,
looks at him, and announces that she is in love. In their following
duet, Alidoro allows that

> Donzelletta vezzoletta
> D'ascoltarti non mi pento.
> Con gl'accenti tuoi pungenti
> Scherza pur, ch'io son contento. (I, 11)

We assume he does not yet know that Silandra is affianced to the
courtier Corindo (alto), though this has been made abundantly
clear to the audience by the love scenes between the two (I, 7
and 8).

In Act II, Silandra definitely decides to pursue Alidoro further
and, in her most important solo scene, sings first "Addio Corindo" in a lively fashion and, later, "Vieni Alidoro," set in the
manner of a lament over an ostinato bass composed of a descending tetrachord (II, 8). She then informs Corindo that "Io più
non t'amo" (II, 9).

As Alidoro paints Silandra's portrait, their love scene unfolds
in the standard *spagnoleggiante* language of the seventeenth-
century Italian theatre:

> Alidoro: Così ti ferma, io do principio all' opra.
> Silandra: Immobile mi vedi.
> Alidoro: Appena i'l credo.
> Silandra: Perchè!
> Alidoro: Perchè non suole
>   Star immobile il sole.

[18] Music in Pirrotta, "Le prime opere di Antonio Cesti," pp. 174–175.

> Silandra: Tu mi burli o mio core.
> Alidoro: Ah non burla chi more.   (II, 12)

It should be noted, however, that this sort of repartee plays a much smaller role in *Orontea* than one might assume from reading criticisms of Cicognini's style.

When Alidoro awakens at the end of Act II to find Orontea's sceptre and note, he accepts his sudden good fortune in his typical manner—asking no questions and marveling at his luck:

> Così mi basta, non aspiro a meglio.
> M'addormentai mendico e Ré mi sveglio. (II, 18)

This apparent solution is far from final. Once more, in Act III, Orontea accuses Alidoro of presumptuousness and infidelity and compares him to Icarus, who also set his sights too high (III, 5). Alidoro, undaunted by this reversal of his fortunes, approaches Silandra once again—only to be reviled by her as well (III, 6). In an aria he accepts his downfall as stoically as he had accepted his sudden good fortunes at the end of Act II.

> Il mondo così va;
> Dianzi grandito
> Hora schernito.
> Provo stratii e crudeltà,
> Il mondo così va. (III, 6)

To the reader, Alidoro's vapid personality and fickle nature can be exasperating, but there is also little doubt that a singing actor could interpret his not always innocent but often openly ingenuous response to serious crises so as to convey his attractiveness across the footlights to the audience.

The two principal comic characters, the drunken servant Gelone (bass) and the old nurse Aristea (alto), are of the types which had appeared before in opera and were to remain standard for another century and a half. They differ, however, from their forebears and contemporaries. This is especially true of Gelone, who, though his solo scenes really have little to do with the development of the plot line, also appears in many other scenes (I, 7, 8; II, 15, 16; III, 8, 9, 17, 18, 19) where he is completely integrated into the story.

Aristea is very amusing in the scenes in which she woos the transvestite Giacinta (II, 6, 7; III, 10), though, as might be expected, this sort of humor can weigh heavily in a very short time. Aristea sings pleasant little strophic arias in her big scenes, and it is precisely these arias which save her role from lapsing into vulgarity.

Gelone is a much more interesting person—his humor is not derived from physical defects, intellectual naïveté, or a speech dialect, as was the case with most comic servants, but from his habitual drunkenness. He not only constantly extols the virtues of wine, but seldom appears onstage without having had too much of it. His first appearance, a solo scene, finds him setting forth his basic philosophy:

> Chi no beve
> Vita breve
> Goderà.
> Il buon vino
> Che è divino
> Viver fa. (I, 6)

This serves as a prelude to his delightful—and lengthy—drunken scenes which close the first act. Here, in his state of drunkenness, he passes through all states of mind from:

> Suonisi il cembalo,
> Toccate gli organi,
> Io vuo ballar (I, 13)

through:

> In grembo ai fiori
> Lieto mi sto.
> Tra grati odori
> Io dormirò (I, 13)

to his conclusion, as he is led offstage by the page Tibrino:

Gelone and Tibrino: O che gusto, o che piacer;
a dormir, a gioir, a ber.   (I, 13) [19]

Gelone's appearances in Act II are limited and are integrated into the plot; it is not until Act III that he once again is given important solo scenes. The first of these is shared with the young page Tibrino, who, in his adolescent enthusiasm for the military life, has much in common with his descendant Cherubino. Gelone, of course, entertains no such romantic illusions about himself:

Tibrino: Soldato son io.
Gelone: Io son bevitor.
Tibrino: La spada è'l cor mio.
Gelone: Il vino il mio cor.
Tibrino: Picciol Marte io sono in terra.
Gelone: Bacco è'l nume mio divino.
Tibrino: Alla guerra!
Gelone: Al vino!   (III, 3)

Gelone's final solo scene is among the earliest in a long line of *basso buffo* scenes which characterized one facet of Italian opera until the late eighteenth century. The servant is alone onstage and, for a time at least, he rises above his menial position in real life. He becomes philosopher, adviser, and king. The world must now listen to his advice and, more importantly, heed it.

Gelone: Amanti udite me.
A pianger notte e dì,
Voi siete pazzi a fè.
Io non vuo far così.   (III, 7)

From this point until the end of the opera, Gelone is very much in evidence—carrying information, delivering notes, and commenting upon the increasingly confused situation. Only in the

[19] Music to parts of this scene appears in *ibid.*, pp. 176–177.

final scene does he stand aside, as an onlooker, while the two happy couples are finally brought together.

It is apparent, I think, that *Orontea* is much more than a *commedia* in the early seventeenth-century meaning of the word—there is considerably more to it than a series of farcical situations, unconnected with the central plot which eventually leads to a *lieto fin*.

Crescimbeni's description—though not his judgment—of Cicognini's work was just. Cicognini did indeed create a *dramma* which had little or nothing to do with the classical conceptions of comedy. For our purposes here, it is less important to trace the influences of the Spanish theatre and the *commedia dell' arte* in the development of the new type of libretto [20] than it is to realize that it was Cicognini who first concocted this new *dramma* from various and diverse ingredients. In *Orontea* we have an example of romantic comedy in which characters from all stations of life—queen, painter, courtier, servant—interact with one another, psychologically, in such a way as to create human situations that can elicit the gamut of emotional response from raucous laughter at Gelone's antics to, perhaps, misty-eyed comprehension when Orontea seems hopelessly lost in what appears to her an impossible love affair.

Of course Cesti's role in the success of *Orontea*, though it has only been touched upon here, is very great.[21] With his apparent concern with the libretto as it was being written, he assisted in the creation of a work which, more than any other opera before it, allowed ample space to arias at crucial points in the action. The balancing of the scales between recitative and aria was indeed an innovation which was to have important results in operatic composition for 150 years or more, especially as the

[20] Pirrotta has dealt with this question in "*Commedia dell'Arte* and Opera" and "Tre capitoli su Cesti."

[21] For more on this see Pirrotta, "Tre capitoli su Cesti" and "Le prime opere di Antonio Cesti." See also my "Comedy—Opera—Comic Opera," *Analecta Musicologica*, Vol. V (1968).

scales tipped more in the direction of the musical set piece. It is obvious that such a balance could not have been achieved by musical means alone: Cicognini, the literary Tuscan, had to supply the composer with the right sort of plot. That this was the case once again serves to remind us that the importance of the construction of the libretto cannot be overestimated in the history of opera.

Alessandro Scarlatti's
Il Mitridate Eupatore (1707)

By JACK ALLAN WESTRUP

Italians seem to adopt a rather casual attitude to the music of their countrymen. Even when they produce a complete edition of a single composer, as in the case of Monteverdi, the result cannot be accepted without reserve. In any other country a composer as celebrated as Alessandro Scarlatti would by now have been commemorated in a series of volumes incorporating at least all the surviving operas and oratorios. A start has been made with the oratorios, but the operas still remain virtually in limbo. They are referred to respectfully in histories of music, but only those who have the leisure to visit Italian libraries or to assume the labor necessary to obtain microfilms can speak with any authority about the music. In fact very little has been done since Edward Dent published his pioneer volume in 1905, when he was under thirty. If that book did not stir Italian scholars into activity, it did at least draw a tribute from Alessandro Longo, whose Dantesque poem *Symphonia* included a handsome tribute to the English musicologist:

Di dì in dì la nebbia si disserra
A te d'intorno, e ciò, per caso strano,
Alla nebbiosa devesi Inghilterra:
   Dove Eduardo Dent, un anglicano
Che sì conosce l'arte antica, ed ama,

Da non equivocar tra loglio e grano,
  Molto adoprossi a ravvivar tua fama;
Ed un suo libro d'abile scrittura
I musicisti a l'opera tua richiama.[1]

Dent recognized the superior quality of *Il Mitridate Eupatore*, first produced in Venice in 1707. Perhaps it was his enthusiasm that induced Giuseppe Piccioli to produce a vocal score of the work, which was published by Curci, Milan, in 1953. A performance of this version took place at the Piccola Scala in Milan in May 1956. Piccioli describes his score as a *ricostruzione scenica e strumentale*. This in itself is enough to rouse suspicions, particularly as no indication is given of what has been added to Scarlatti's original or omitted from it. The full score, available only on hire, does not help very much. The critical reader may suspect that a good deal of the orchestration is not the composer's, but there is no kind of editorial commentary and nothing to say where cuts have been made. With a knowledge of Scarlatti's original it is possible to restore the orchestration; and if one is willing to accept the very substantial cuts, Piccioli's version can then be used for performance, though naturally enough the result will hardly represent completely the composer's intentions.

As Dent points out, Count Girolamo Frigimelica Roberti's libretto is based on the story of Orestes. Eupator (corresponding to Orestes), exiled from his native Pontus, returns to avenge his murdered father by killing his mother Stratonica (Clytemnestra) and her lover, now husband, Farnace (Aegisthus). By a nice touch of dramatic irony he represents himself as an Egyptian envoy, bringing back his own head in an urn. His sister Laodice (Electra) at first does not recognize him, but having done so aids and abets him. In order to enlarge the cast, Eupator is provided with a wife, Issicratea, who spends most of the opera in male disguise under the name Antigono. Laodice has a rustic husband,

[1] Quoted from the second edition of Dent's *Alessandro Scarlatti*, ed. Frank Walker (London, 1960), p. vii.

Nicomede. Neither Antigono nor Nicomede contribute much to the action, but they play a larger part than they are allowed to by Piccioli, who removes all their arias. The only other character is Pelopidas, a two-faced individual who originally serves Farnace but has no hesitation in changing sides when the favorable moment arrives. The complete list is:

> Laodice, soprano
> Nicomede, soprano
> Eupator, soprano
> Antigono, alto
> Stratonica, soprano
> Farnace, tenor
> Pelopidas, alto

In Piccioli's version Nicomede, Eupator, and Pelopidas are tenors, and Farnace is a baritone. There is only one chorus in the original, in Act III (Act II in Piccioli), where the people give their assent to the pact with Egypt. Piccioli adds two further choruses—one (page 111) an adaptation of a march of priests in the opera *Il Ciro* (Dent, page 123), the other (page 160) a perversion rather than an adaptation of a ballet of furies from the same opera (Dent, page 121). He also introduces the chorus into an aria assigned to Pelopidas, though originally sung by Stratonica (page 40), the aria sung by Eupator at the solemnization of the pact (page 91), and the finale of the last act. The original orchestration specifies a solo oboe, two trumpets and timpani in the orchestra (and the same offstage), strings, and continuo. It is reasonable to suppose that two oboes played with the violins in *tutti* passages and that a bassoon doubled the bass. The examples in this essay are taken from a manuscript copy in the library of the Paris Conservatoire, no. 22410 (now in the Bibliothèque Nationale). It is a good clean copy, and where it has mistakes they are always obvious. From internal evidence I suspect that this was the source used by Piccioli. A peculiarity of it is that it was obviously used at some time in the late nineteenth century

for a projected, perhaps an actual, performance in France. Cuts
have been marked in the recitative, and a French translation
added to everything that was meant to be sung. No information
about this performance seems to be available; it is in any case
irrelevant, except that the translator seems to have had little
respect for the manuscript.

The opera is in five acts, which Piccioli reduced to three. Dent
observes: "The last act is most disappointing; Scarlatti makes
nothing of the fine dramatic situation where *Eupatore* presents
Stratonica with the head, not of her son, but of her lover." I
should disagree with the latter part of this statement. Though the
scene is in recitative accompanied only by continuo it is highly
effective in the theatre; in particular Laodice's icy refusal to help
her mother is given a sinister significance by a change of harmony (Example 1). But Dent is quite right in suggesting that the
act as a whole is disappointing. Once Farnace has been killed
there is no excuse for prolonged delay. On the other hand,

Example 1

Stratonica

Ahi - mè!   il pie-de   e la ma - no nie-ga-no d'ub-bi-dir-mi,   al lo-to uf-fi-cio gli sol-
le - ci - to in-va-no.   La - o - di - ce a te, le-va a quel te-schio il ve-lo.   D'or-ror tut - ta   m'in-
chio-da un fie - ro   ge - lo.   L'ub-bi - dir - ti m'è tol - to.

Piccioli has been too ruthless in cutting everything that intervenes between Eupator's song of vengeance, "Uccidete, distruggete" (page 148) and the scene where Stratonica is confronted with the urn. It is difficult to believe that Farnace's head could have been so rapidly detached from his body and placed in the urn; and in the theatre, as I know to my cost, the swift exit of the urn and its almost immediate return is likely to arouse the mirth of an irreverent audience. In general, the cuts which Piccioli makes in the recitative do serve to speed up the action, though they sometimes involve modifications of the text. But this does not alter the fact that anyone who wants to study the opera will expect to have everything that Scarlatti wrote. Recitative may look tedious on paper, but it is an essential means of communication on the stage and can be made vivid by good actors even when it appears musically unexciting. There is, however, one detail of the recitative which Piccioli has treated with understanding—partly, no doubt, because the original score makes it inevitable. This concerns the cadences. Scarlatti regularly writes the penultimate chord for the continuo under the singer's last note or pair of notes, and allows no space for any postponement of the cadence, for instance, in the first scene (Example 2). I

Example 2

in - van m'a - pel - lo   al tri - bu - nal   dei ven - ti.

have argued elsewhere [2] that this was the normal practice in Baroque opera, though editors in general seem to be reluctant to admit it.

Apart from the offstage trumpets (*trombe marine*) at the beginning of Act IV (quoted by Dent, page 109) Scarlatti's

[2] "The Cadence in Baroque Recitative," Bjørn Hjelmborg and Søren Sørensen, eds., *Natalicia Musicologica Knud Jeppesen septuagenario collegis oblata* (Copenhagen, 1962), pp. 243–252.

treatment of the orchestra does not show a great deal of variety. There are, however, several instances of solo instruments playing obbligato parts. In the overture there is a short section for oboe solo accompanied only by the first violins—an example of spare texture which can be paralleled elsewhere in the opera (Example 3). The oboe also has a long and elaborate obbligato in Stratonica's aria "Bella gloria d'un gran re" in Act I, which is assigned by Piccioli to Pelopidas (page 40) and completely misrepresented. Further oboe obbligatos occur in Eupator's aria "Non è l'ozio

Example 3

riposo beato" in a popular style (Act II) and Nicomede's "Vado, vado" (Act III), both of which are omitted in Piccioli's version. The opening of Nicomede's aria is a further example of the delicate two-part texture to which reference has already been made (Example 4). The most notable example of this texture occurs in Laodice's wonderful lament for her brother in Act IV, which is all the more striking because it follows a sonorous ritornello for the full body of strings (Example 5), quoted by Dent, page 111. Dent thought that Handel may have remembered Scarlatti's funeral march for trumpets and timpani when he came to write the "Dead March" in *Saul*. What is much more probable is that he remembered this aria of Laodice's when he wrote "Cara sposa" in *Rinaldo*. Here the voice steals into the texture in much the same way, and the accompaniment, without cellos and basses, is almost equally tenuous (Example 6). We know from Hawkins [3] that Handel valued this aria highly, and with good reason. Dent's supposition that Handel had either seen *Il Mitridate Eupatore* in Venice or was familiar with the score seems very likely.

The trumpet was the heroic instrument of the Baroque orchestra. Hence it is introduced in Act III into the chorus "Sì, dà laude, sì applaude." It is used also as an obbligato to the aria "All'armi, a battaglia" (not in Piccioli) in Act IV, in which

Example 4

Nicomede summons the forces of resistance after Laodice has recognized her brother. There are two imposing instrumental movements for two trumpets and strings. The first occurs at the opening of scene 6 of Act I, where the stage directions read: "Sala reale nella reggia di Sinope, ornata in Festa per La sollennità Annuale in cui si celebra L'essaltazione al Trono dei due Tiranni." For reasons best known to himself Piccioli has disfig-

[3] *A General History of the Science and Practice of Music* (London, 1853), p. 868 n.

ured this passage by dividing the trumpet parts between horns in the orchestra and trumpets on the stage. Quite apart from the

Example 5

[sempre senza basso]

fact that Scarlatti did not use horns as early as 1707, the editorial version introduces a factitious contrast for which there is no authority in the score. The second appearance of trumpets and strings is in an equally imposing scene, at the beginning of Act III (Act II in Piccioli), before the solemn pact is concluded. The stately introduction is followed by a quick movement in 3/8 time, with florid parts for trumpets which Piccioli, nervous perhaps of his players, transferred to oboes. But the most remarkable use of trumpets is one to which Dent drew particular attention— the entry of Eupator with the urn at the beginning of Act IV (Act III, sc. 2, in Piccioli). Here the scoring is for "due Trombe in Orchestra alla Sordina" with timpani, answered by two "Trombe Marine," also with timpani. As Dent sensibly observed (page 109), the word *marine* is to be taken in its literal sense: these trumpets are supposed to be on board ship—in other words either behind the scenes (in which case it is difficult to balance the ensemble) or at the back of the stage. This must be one of the most original pieces of scoring in any Baroque opera. It is worth noting that since the insertion of a mute raised the pitch a tone the players in the orchestra would have had to use C trumpets.

Example 6

There are several places where Scarlatti has been careful to mark "violino solo," but there is one particularly spectacular cadenza which suggests that the leader of the orchestra at the Teatro S. Giovanni Crisostomo was an unusually accomplished player. It occurs in the introduction to Stratonica's aria:

> Esci ormai chè più non v'hai loco,
> Materno amore da questo sen.
> In regio petto un più bel foco,
> Amor v'accese del comun ben.

Here, after the solemnization of the pact, she proclaims with insolent hypocrisy that the welfare of her people has triumphed over her love for her son. After a brief stormy opening the solo

violin is left on its own above a tonic pedal. The copyist of the
Paris score has clearly misunderstood the original here. His in-
troduction of the treble clef at the junction of tutti and solo
(Example 7) is pointless if it is to be taken literally; and the same

Example 7

is true of a further treble clef which appears at the end of the
cadenza. The original score must have had a treble clef on the
first line (sometimes known as the violin clef), so that the correct reading should be that shown in Example 8. The soloist is

Example 8

then able to explore exalted heights and play a series of double
stops without having to face a virtually impossible challenge to
his technique (Example 9). Piccioli (page 104) has a naïve

Example 9

footnote on this passage: "Questa 'estensione' insolita (il violino
generalmente non oltrepassava il 're') è un'altra prova delle arditezze strumentali di Alessandro Scarlatti." Unfortunately he has
not noticed the copyist's error and transcribes the whole passage
in F sharp minor (over a pedal A), which not only makes
nonsense of the harmony but also expects the soloist to play

something which is exceptionally difficult at the present day and would have been regarded as unplayable in the early eighteenth century. The *arditezze strumentali* are there, undoubtedly; but that is no reason for making them impossible.

One of the interesting details of early eighteenth-century orchestration is the emergence of the cello as a solo instrument, not only in concertos but also as an obbligato instrument in opera and oratorio. There are notable examples in Handel which call for subtlety of interpretation as well as an accomplished technique. Scarlatti has a cello obbligato in Antigono's aria "Aria dolce e fiera ha in volto" in Act II, the omission of which in Piccioli's version leaves an unexplained gap, since Stratonica has asked for a description of her son (page 60) and is left without an answer. An aria for Nicomede in Act I, "Sento allore chi mi dice" (not in Piccioli), has obbligato parts for two solo cellos, beginning as shown in Example 10. It must be admitted that this

Example 10

claims attention more as an example of instrumentation than as evidence of originality.

There is a curious detail in the writing for strings in the overture that calls for comment. The final section (Piccioli, page 5, figure 6) is marked "allegro arpeggiato." This clearly applies to the upper strings, which have a succession of half-note chords. One might be tempted to regard this as a kind of shorthand for open-work figuration, if it were not that *arpeggiato* chords occur also in a recitative for Farnace in Act III (Example 11),

Example 11

not in Piccioli. It is difficult to believe that figuration is intended for the upper strings here, in spite of the warning indication "tenete la corda" for the basses. It would make ensemble exceptionally difficult and would be contrary to the nature of recitative. The intention must be that the extension of the Roman Empire is to be suggested by a series of quadruple and triple stops of which the upper notes are sustained. This would be much easier—and quite effective—with the bows in use in Scarlatti's time; it seems probable that a similar effect, producing a series of vigorous *sforzandi*, is intended in the overture. It certainly makes sense in performance.

Among the defects of Piccioli's edition is the fact that he has omitted all the arias for the secondary characters and all the duets. Pelopidas, it is true, is given an aria in Act I (page 40), but this was originally sung by Stratonica. The aria which he sings in Act III in praise of his master is not included. The absence of any arias for Nicomede reduces him almost to a cipher. Two of his arias have already been mentioned. A third, a song of triumph when victory has been won, is so buoyant and infectious in rhythm that its omission is difficult to understand. I quote the opening ritornello in Example 12. The words are conventional enough:

Example 12

Del pien diletto
Che ha un forte petto
Doppo gran pene
Vien a goder.

But their translation into music is the perfect expression of joy in victory. It is small compensation that Piccioli transfers to Nicomede a piece of recitative—"Canta giuliva la tua vendetta" (page 159)—that was originally sung by Laodice. Even more serious is the omission of duets, for example, those for Eupator and Antigono in Act II, for Laodice and Nicomede in Act III, and for Laodice and Eupator in Act IV (after the moment of recognition). Piccioli's edition merely serves to confirm the erroneous opinion that baroque opera consisted of a series of *da capo* arias interspersed with recitative. The term "recitative" itself covers a wide variety of expression. It includes things as different as the thrust and parry between Farnace and the supposed envoys (Piccioli, pages 61–65) and the passionate utterance in which Laodice laments that all she can offer to the brother whom she once held in her arms is a kiss to the dead (Example 13).

Dent observes (page 194): "To us Scarlatti's music often seems conspicuously devoid of emotional qualities." This may have been true in 1905, when musicians were still under the spell of Romantic composers. Today we are more ready to appreciate

Example 13

the subtleties of Baroque art. It is significant that on the same page Dent quotes Scarlatti's own admission that when he was writing *Il gran Tamerlano* he was moved to tears. Certainly there is no lack of emotion in the passage just quoted, nor indeed in the whole of Laodice's lament. Piccioli, who whatever his sins as an editor is not lacking in appreciation, is moved to describe it in a footnote as "questo stupendo recitativo." And there are subtleties in plenty, though they are rarely understood by singers, who are apt to look on a Scarlatti aria as an agreeably neutral piece that will help to fill out an "old music group" at a recital. For this reason, no doubt, it is precisely the more neutral arias that are the best known. The aria which Laodice sings in Act I (not in Piccioli) when she is denying Stratonica (Example 14)

Example 14

might appear to come into this category—good, clean-limbed music, one might think, where everything appears to go according to plan. Yet, as so often with Handel, the plan is more in our imagination than in the music. The *all'unisono* accompaniment to the voice (the small notes indicate a blank in the manuscript) sounds as if it might well keep going for some considerable time; but suddenly the texture is lightened at the words "io morirò," until the bass returns at the end of Example 14. How unexpected, too, is the change of harmony at these words, and the harmonic sequence as well. One may compare the totally unforeseen cadence in the A major aria which Eupator sings in Act I (Piccioli, pages 24–28):

> Se il trono domando
> Al cielo, al mio brando,
> Con quella che adoro sol bramo regnar.

The jaunty rhythm of the words finds no echo in Scarlatti, who substitutes a boldly assertive triple time (Example 15). Nor do

Example 15

the words "con quella che adoro" call for any modification of the robust style until we come to the cadence, where the music suddenly softens into an ambiguous minor (Example 16).[4]

Example 16

[4] The coloratura passage which immediately precedes this is emasculated in Piccioli's version.

Il Mitridate Eupatore does not appear to have had much success. One reason for this may be the story, which is entirely free from the conventional love interest (and the consequent intrigue) that clutters up so many Baroque operas and makes it difficult for a modern audience to take them seriously. Roberti was obviously too conscientious to corrupt the story of Orestes by introducing irrelevancies. Eupator has a devoted wife, and Laodice has a devoted husband. Nothing occurs to mar their marital happiness; on the contrary each pair has a single aim—to wreak vengeance on the tyrants. As Eupator says at the beginning of Act II (Piccioli, page 53):

> Ora lo stesso amor vuol che l'ingegno,
> La mente, il cor, la man sol pensi al regno.

There is no place here for love scenes. The only love that is truly passionate is between Laodice and her brother—a love which is so memorably represented in her lament and in the joy of recognition. The drama of this recognition can be paralleled in Gluck's *Iphigénie en Tauride*, also founded on a classic story. Orestes has his Pylades, as Eupator has his Antigono (otherwise Issicratea). But in both cases the "domestic" relationship, if it may be called so, is as nothing to the bond that links brother and sister.

It may well be that the purely musical qualities of *Il Mitridate Eupatore* provoked a no less strong reaction from the public. In spite of his voluminous production Scarlatti can hardly be said to have been a popular composer. His epitaph [5] records his achievements in glowing terms, but his contemporaries appear to have been less enthusiastic. It is not difficult to see why. The sensuous qualities of Italian melody are modified in Scarlatti by a certain austerity, evident particularly in the spare texture of much of his writing. This is much more music for musicians than music for singers, though it is well written for the voice and can be rewarding for any performer who has intelligence as well. The very characteristics of his harmony which we find appealing may well have seemed to his contemporaries irrational, if not

---

[5] Quoted by Dent, *Scarlatti*, p. 193.

uncouth. Dent very shrewdly observes that there was much in common between Alessandro and Domenico, different as they may appear on the surface. It might be true to say of both of them that they were never commonplace. Of Alessandro it would be certainly true to say that he was capable of a nobility of utterance which was surpassed by none of his contemporaries and by few of his successors. It is this sublimity that is so finely represented in the aria in Act II of *Il Mitridate Eupatore* where the exile, having gained entrance to the palace, prays to the gods of his fathers to hear him:

> Patrii Numi, amici Dei,
> Fausti udite il mio dolor.

The music is marked "senza cembalo," and indeed the richness and variety of the string writing make a keyboard instrument unnecessary. Above the tracery of the violin parts the singer embarks on a broad cantabile, becomes more urgent in the middle section, and returns again to the mood of the opening—a complete justification, if one were needed, of the *da capo*. The quotation of the entire aria is one of many welcome additions to the new edition of Donald Grout's *Short History of Opera*.[6] To him this modest essay is offered in friendship and admiration.

[6] Pages 175–178.

Quirino Gasparini and Mozart

By LUIGI FERDINANDO TAGLIAVINI

While several connections, direct and indirect, between Quirino Gasparini and Wolfgang Amadeus Mozart are known to scholars, the closest connection has not yet been sufficiently studied. Gasparini's name has attracted some attention ever since 1922, when Hermann Spies established the fact that Gasparini was author of the motet "Adoramus te," previously attributed to Mozart.[1] Recently Wolfgang Plath has identified the manuscript copy that led to the false attribution as the hand of Mozart's father Leopold,[2] so that this connection becomes rather tenuous.

[1] The "Adoramus te" appeared in the complete edition of Mozart's works, *W. A. Mozarts sämtliche Werke* (Leipzig, 1876–1905), as no. 30, 3d ser., Vol. II, and in the Köchel catalogue (Ludwig Köchel, *Chronologisch-thematisches Verzeichnis sämtlicher Tonwerke Wolfgang Amade Mozarts* [Leipzig, 1862]) as K. 327. In Alfred Einstein's revision of Köchel (3d ed.; Leipzig, 1937), it was transferred to the *Anhang*, and in the sixth and latest edition, by Franz Giegling, Alexander Weinmann, and Gerd Sievers (Wiesbaden, 1964), it is designated Anh. A 10. Gasparini was identified as the composer by Spies, then Kapellmeister at the Salzburg Cathedral, in his article "Ist die Motette Adoramus te . . . von W. A. Mozart? Eine kritische Untersuchung," *Gregorius-Blatt*, XLVII (1922), 25–29. See also Félix Raugel, "Quirino Gasparini (d. 1778) maître de chapelle de la cour du Piémont et de la cathédrale de Turin, auteur de l'Adoramus te à 4 voix attribué à W. A. Mozart," *Revue de musicologie*, XII (1931), 9–12, and "Un mottetto di Mozart . . . che non è di Mozart," *Musica d'oggi*, XIII (1931), 215–216.

[2] Plath, "Studien zur Mozart-Autographie, I: Die Handschrift Leopold Mozarts," *Mozart-Jahrbuch, 1960–1961*, p. 109.

Far more important is the fact that the first opera composed for an Italian theatre by the fourteen-year-old boy from Salzburg was based on the same libretto that the Italian composer had already set—the *Mitridate re di Ponto* by Vittorio Amedeo Cigna-Santi. *Mitridate* with Gasparini's music was performed in January and February 1767 at the Teatro Regio in Turin; in December 1770 and January 1771 *Mitridate* was performed at the Teatro Ducale in Milan with music by Mozart. We shall see that this relationship is more than a coincidence.

Before dealing with my central issue, the relations between Mozart and Gasparini, I should like to dwell a bit on the latter. Details of this Italian musician's life and work have come down to us through two especially interesting sources: a manuscript biography compiled with affection and care by Giovanni Simone Mayr (who was able to make use of first-hand documents) [3] and an impressive number of letters written by Gasparini to Padre G. B. Martini during the years 1759–1777. [4]

It would seem appropriate to print here the complete biography written by Mayr, which is found in the Biblioteca Civica at Bergamo. [5] In presenting it, I shall make a running commentary, integrating the biography with information taken from the letters and other sources.

---

[3] "Biografie di musicisti" [Q. Gasparini, G. G. Gastoldi, P. Giovanelli, A. Gonzales, F. Grazioli, G. Legrenzi], Bergamo, Biblioteca Civica, Sala 32, D.8.29/4 (8). I wish to thank the director and the personnel of the library for their courtesy and help. [These biographies are not listed in Arrigo Gazzaniga, *Il fondo musicale Mayr* (Bergamo, 1963), which is limited to the music in the collection.—W. A.]

[4] Bologna, Biblioteca Musicale "G. B. Martini," Carteggio Martiniano, Vol. XXV (labeled I/21) and Vol. XXXIII (labeled I/28). Vol. XXV contains thirty-seven letters by Gasparini (nos. 41 to 79—no. 59 is missing and nos. 67 and 71 are two sheets of a single letter). Vol. XXXIII contains four letters by Gasparini (nos. 104–107).

[5] The biography of Gasparini is preceded in Mayr's manuscript by information about some of the well-known people from Gandino, a town in the province of Bergamo. The Italian text of Gasparini's biography as it is found in the manuscript, pp. 1ʳ–2ʳ, is given in the Appendix to this article.

The Abbot *Quirino Gasparini* was not elected *maestro di cappella* in his own city, and it was well for him that he was not, for he was afterwards chosen *maestro di cappella* of the cathedral in Turin. He was then honored by being raised to the position of *maestro di musica di camera* to the royal, splendid, and worthy sovereigns there, who esteemed him greatly and rewarded him honorably. At court he found a generous Maecenas in Cardinal delle Lancie, who in addition to other favors, often invited him to dine and took him in his coach to the Basilica of Santo Benigno.[6]

Quirino was born in the town of Gandino [7] [near Bergamo] in the year 1721, the son of . . . .[8]

Since he displayed great talents for both theological studies and music, he was taken by his parents to Bergamo where he became a student of the Santi Silari [?] [9] In a very short time he was able to perform extremely difficult accompaniments as well as pieces from tabulature, and indeed even surpassed his teachers. He played the organ well and wrote many excellent and tasteful pieces for that beautiful instrument. After having studied counterpoint, he was held by all to be a prodigy in musical composition. Though at the mere age of sixteen he could compete with the most renowned composers, and though he was much sought after for many functions, receiving

[6] Letter from Gasparini to Padre Martini, February 25, 1767.

[7] At this point in Mayr's manuscript a note is indicated, but the note is lacking.

[8] Mayr apparently intended to fill in the names of Gasparini's parents. We find the birthplace confirmed on a portrait of Gasparini, painted in September 1775 by Giuseppe Mazza, which Gasparini sent to Padre Martini; this portrait remained until the beginning of the last war in the Conservatorio "G. B. Martini" in Bologna. It bears the following inscription: SACERD. QUIRINUS GASPARINI A GANDINO BERGOMENSI/ACCADEMICUS PHILARM.[cus] BONONIAE IN ECCLESIIS/METROPOLITANA ET CORPORIS X̃TI AUGUSTAE TAURINORUM MUSICES PRAEFECTUS MDCCLXXV. The portrait has disappeared since the war. Gasparini's birth date is confirmed in the "Miscellanea musicale," Biblioteca Musicale "G. B. Martini," UU/12, Vol. II, p. 622: "Gasparini D. Quirino Bergamasco scolaro di Fioroni nacque nel 1721 e morì nel settembre 1788 di 57 anni non compiti." Gasparini's birthplace and birth date were first published in Angelo Geddo, *Bergamo e la musica* (Bergamo, 1958), pp. 162–163. Geddo based his findings on the Mayr manuscript, but gives no references.

[9] Aside from this reference, this name is unknown. See Geddo, *Bergamo*, p. 163.

the greatest praise, he did not allow himself to be led astray by all
this acclaim which is so often fatal to talented youth. Instead he
went first to study with the celebrated Fioroni, *maestro* at the
cathedral in Milan, and later with the illustrious Martini in Bologna,
under whose expert guidance he was able to perfect his talents. At
the age of twenty he was taken into the Academy at Bologna [10] and
Martini requested his portrait to place in his private gallery. At the
same time Martini presented Gasparini with a portrait of himself. I
have the pleasure of owning both these portraits.[11] At the age of
twenty-eight he produced an opera of his with great success at the
Royal Theatre in Milan.[12] Soon after Cardinal Rezzonico was elected
pope on July 6, 1758, Quirino went to Rome, and then to the
musical center of Naples, in the train of Co[nte] D'Aziano di
Vercelli, who was both his noble student of music and his protec-
tor.[13] It was through the count's influence in 1760 that Abbot Gasparini was chosen to take part in the service *a otto reali* which is held
every year on the Feast of Sant' Eusebio in the cathedral of Vercelli.
It was at this time that, not being satisfied with the manner in which

[10] At this time Gasparini was already a priest. On August 12, 1750,
Giovanni Andrea Fioroni, in a letter to Padre Martini supporting
Gasparini's application for admittance into the Accademia Filarmonica
at Bologna, calls him "Priest and Doctor in Theology" (Biblioteca
Musicale "G. B. Martini," Carteggio Martiniano, Vol. XIII [I/10],
letter 73). Gasparini was admitted to the Accademia Filarmonica in
January 1751, after having submitted, as a requirement, an antiphon for
five voices on a *cantus firmus*. Copies of this antiphon are in the
Archives of the Accademia and in the Biblioteca Comunale at Assisi.

[11] See above, n. 8. Padre Martini sent his own portrait to Gasparini in
April 1776 (letter from Gasparini, April 17, 1776). Mayr's remark, "I
have the pleasure of owning both these portraits," apparently means
that he also had another portrait of Gasparini. The one Gasparini sent
to Padre Martini, as we have seen, remained in Bologna and eventually
became part of the collection of the Conservatorio di Musica "G. B.
Martini." As for the portrait of Padre Martini, it is possible that this is
the one originally owned by Gasparini.

[12] This refers to *Artaserse* (libretto by Metastasio) produced at the
Regio Ducal Teatro in Milan during the carnival of 1757.

[13] Mayr's manuscript here has the following marginal notation: "This
nobleman had excellent statues placed in the garden of his estate at
Assiano, among them one of his teacher Querino."

the *maestro di cappella* at Santa Maria Maggiore in Bergamo was elected, he did not compete for the position.[14] He was then chosen to go to Turin.[15] At Turin he then composed an opera for the Royal Theatre [16] as well as a Stabat Mater for two sopranos in the manner of Pergolesi. This last was printed and dedicated to Maximilian,

[14] Manuscript note: "The Abbot Querino objected that, though indeed the distinguished gentlemen of the jury were to award the decision, the merits of the various entries must be voted on by leading musicians from throughout Italy, to whom the solutions of the examination problem should be sent for this purpose. The jury, however, declined to follow this procedure since it seemed to reflect unfavorably on its own qualifications, whence Querino withdrew from the competition."

It is apparent from letters he wrote to Padre Martini (August 22 and September 5, 1759, and March 12 and June 3, 1760) that Gasparini very much wanted the post of *maestro di cappella* at Santa Maria Maggiore in Bergamo. He occupied himself with this matter from August 1759 through May 1760. Actually, the only post vacant at this time was that of substitute, with the right to succeed eventually to the principal position when it was vacated by the aged and ailing *maestro*, Lodovico Ferronato. In his letter of August 22, 1759, Gasparini asked permission to study with Padre Martini so that he might improve his counterpoint and thereby be in a better position to compete for the post. At the end of the competition Gasparini's work was warmly praised in testimonial letters by Martini and eight other musicians, but in spite of these recommendations the favored candidate was Carlo Lenzi, even though in Gasparini's view he "did nothing more than play the cembalo and perform some of his *arie*, all very ornamented and not at all appropriate for church" (letter of March 12, 1760).

[15] Near the end of May 1760, Gasparini left his "barbarous home city" and traveled to Turin, where the position of *maestro di cappella* at the cathedral was vacant. The fact that he was a priest and also a member of the Accademia Filarmonica in Bologna spoke in his favor, and he was elected *maestro di cappella* by the chapter (Gasparini's letters of June 3 and September 3, 1760). His official activity began on November 1, 1760, according to the archives of the Turin cathedral, *Libri dell'economo della cappella de' cantori*, vol. 1754–1767, anno 1760, c. 165. This information was kindly sent to me by Mlle. Marie-Thérèse Bouquet, author of the unpublished dissertation "Documents pour servir à l'histoire de la musique en Savoie (1650–1775)," Paris Conservatoire, 1967.

[16] This, Gasparini's second opera, was *Mitridate re di Ponto*, libretto by Vittorio Amedeo Cigna-Santi; it was produced during carnival, January 31, 1767 (letters of January 14 and February 25).

Duke of Bavaria, who was greatly pleased by it and rewarded the composer with regal munificence. No prince passed through the renowned city of Turin without searching out Quirino in order to have one of his compositions. Constant work, and going for entire weeks without sleeping, totally exhausted Quirino, who tried to stay awake by imbibing liquors and great quantities of coffee. He composed many highly prized sacred and chamber works, among them various duets and trios for the violin, which even today are held in great esteem. The city of his birth, honoring its virtuoso and renowned son in Turin, invited Quirino, along with other Italian composers, to take part in an extraordinary celebration, lasting for several days in 1762, during which the relics of Saints Fermo, Rustico, and Procolo were transferred to a new marble altar surmounted by a bronze urn and a portable silver urn of exquisite workmanship done by our celebrated Filiberti. On this occasion Quirino outshone his colleagues. The city made it clear that the aforementioned privilege was merited by very few. I should go on too long were I to list all the events in which he was called to take part by both the nobility and commoners, as well as the admiration, honors, and gifts bestowed upon him after his return to Turin. There was universal unhappiness at the news of his grave illness and then his death on September 23, 1778.[17] He was an exemplary priest of irreproachable habits and his memory lives on today in Turin, in his birthplace, and elsewhere.

Gasparini's correspondence offers us interesting information

[17] On September 30, 1778, Gasparo Gasparini wrote Martini of the death of his brother Quirino "after a short, but acute illness." According to the catalogue of the Biblioteca Civica at Bergamo, Gasparini's death certificate should be in the library as MS 37 R 19 (30), but I could not succeed in finding it. The incorrect date of October 11, 1778, given by Federico Parisini (*Catalogo della collezione d'autografi lasciata alla R. Accademia Filarmonica di Bologna dall'Accademico Ab. Dott. Masseangeli* [Bologna, 1881], p. 134), is repeated in Carlo Schmidl, *Dizionario universale dei musicisti* (Milan, 1887–1889; 2d ed. 1926–1929), and Hugo Riemann, *Musik-Lexikon* (Leipzig, 1882; 12th ed., Mainz, 1959). The correct death date is given by Geddo, *Bergamo*, p. 163, and Claudio Sartori, ed., *Enciclopedia della musica* (Milan, 1964).

about his contacts with his colleagues in Turin and his encounters with eminent personalities of the musical world of the time. He was on friendly terms with Gaetano Pugnani, with the brothers Besozzi, renowned oboe players, with the violinist Marc'Aurelio Canavasso, with the singer Gaetano Ottani, and with the composer Bernardino Ottani, whom he took under his paternal wing [18] and who later succeeded him as *maestro di cappella* at the cathedral in Turin. There was, however, dissension between him and the *maestro di cappella* at the Court, Francesco Saverio Giay, whom Gasparini described as "a man jealous of me." [19]

In June 1768, the celebrated violinist Maddalena Lombardini Sirmen, pupil of Tartini, appeared in Turin. "With her playing, she gained the admiration of all Turin. . . . Saturday I wrote old Tartini at Padua telling him about it, which will certainly give him satisfaction and consolation, so much the more because this performer played perfectly some of his sonatas." [20]

In February 1770, Gasparini presented and warmly recommended Giuseppe Mysliveček to Padre Martini. In the spring of that year Mysliveček's *Nitteti* was to be presented in Bologna.[21]

In July 1770, Charles Burney was in Turin. Gasparini did not have the fortune to meet him because he was out of the city at the time. He does, however, refer to the visit of "an English man of letters" in a curious letter to Padre Martini. In this letter he expresses grave concern that the English scholar, in the work he is about to publish, plans to mention insignificant musicians, while his own name is not to appear. He begs Padre Martini, when he sees Burney in Bologna, to make certain that "my name

---

[18] Letter from Bernardino Ottani to Padre Martini, from Turin, November 17, 1776 (Biblioteca Musicale "G. B. Martini," Carteggio Martiniano, Vol. XVI [I/13], letter 85).

[19] Letter from Gasparini to Padre Martini, April 24, 1765.

[20] Letter from Gasparini to Padre Martini, June 22, 1768.

[21] Letters dated February 27 and March 3, 1770.

is not left out" of the book.[22] In fact, in his resumé of his visit to Turin, Burney does not fail to mention that "the Maestro di Capella is Don Quirico [*sic*] Gasparini." [23]

[22] "Essendo passato da Torino un letterato inglese in questi scorsi giorni raccomandato a codesti Sig.ʳⁱ Besozzi dal Sig. Giardini professore di Violino che stà in Londra, il quale oltre le notizie che hà, scorre l'Itaglia per prenderne di nuove rapporto a Compositori, Cantanti e Suonatori celebri dal antico sino a qui per formare come genealogica istoria per dare alle stampe, Per il poco tempo che qui si è trattenuto io non l'hò potuto conoscere per esser in questi scorsi giorni statto fuori ad una vigna di un signore ma ho saputo che li Sig.ʳⁱ Besozzi si sono fatti sentire a suonare ed il lor nome ha esso notato per registrarlo in ditta Istoria. Essi gli hanno fatto una lettera appresso il Sig. Farinelli, che in passando per Bologna procurasse di fargli conoscere la pregiatissima di Lei Persona siccome di principal merito, così essi pur m'anno asserito. Hò indi da altra parte saputo che questo è statto dal Sig. Gaetano Ottani tenor teatralijsta servito per Torino, ed il nome di questo pur sara, come è probabile, statto notato, e siccome il Sig. Ottani è amicissimo di un tal Abate Finoglio, uomo per altro savio e prudente, reputato da diversi per qualche oracolo di musica, che dà solo lezzioni, ma a dirci in secreta confidenza senza appagare il publico, ne con un componimento, ne con un scolaro formato; non hà letteratura, ne discende da nessuna scuola di musica, ma solo da lettura de libri, ed è quello che pochi anni sono voleva far stampare un libro di regole musicali intitolato il *perchè della musica* essendo statto portato ma in vano dal fù Sig. GiamBattista Somis per esser accettato dalla Corte, così m'è insorto un dubbio, che il Sig. Ottani perchè gli è statto maestro in fargli imparare la parte quando qui hà recitato più volte con incontro e per la forte voce, recitare, e comica, possa aver portato questo sogetto ad essere ascritto al sud.ᵗᵒ Catalogo, il che se seguito fosse, io non ne avrei onore, mentre qui ho datto col aiuto del Cielo tutte le reali prove di quel poco che sò, e del qualche talento che Iddio mi hà donato, e perciò sono a vivamente supplicare la Benignità grande di V[ostra] P[aternità] M[olto] R[everen]da degnarsi d'esplorare del D.ᵗᵒ Inglese che da qui è partito solo 4tro giorni sono, tal cosa, ed è in qual caso, operare che la mia persona non rimanghi esclusa se non peraltro, che per gli onori ricevuti da Bologna a tutti noti per graziosissimo di Lei mezzo, e ciò non essendo io non ardirei di supplicarla di tentare l'ascrizzione del mio nome perche in altri stati di Itaglia vi sono altri migliori nel stil di Chiesa valorosi sogetti" (letter dated July 17, 1770).
[23] Charles Burney, *The Present State of Music in France and Italy* (London, 1773), p. 64.

We know of only two printed works by Gasparini: *Sei trio academici a due violini, e un violoncello,* op. 1 (Paris, Le Clerc, n.d. [c. 1755]),[24] and *L'Inno Stabat Mater a due soprani, con violini, e basso* (n. pub., n.d. [The Hague, Stechway and Comp., c. 1770]), dedicated to Maximilian, elector of Bavaria.[25] Many more of his compositions are preserved in manuscript in various libraries, as follows: Concerto per cembalo o pure organo (Genoa, Istituto Paganini);[26] Sonatas for organ (Naples, Conservatorio, and Brussels, Conservatoire);[27] Antiphon "Exi cito in plateas," the test-piece for five voices written for admission to the Accademia Filarmonica in Bologna (Bologna, Archivio dell' Accademia, and Assisi, Biblioteca Comunale);[28] Magnificat for eight voices and strings, and Miserere for three voices (Assisi, Biblioteca Communale);[29] Compline for four voices and instruments, "Quoniam in me speravit" for two tenors and instruments, and another "Quoniam in me speravit," incomplete, for

[24] The only extant copy of this publication is in the University Library at Cambridge, England (see E. B. Schnapper, ed., *The British Union-Catalogue of Early Music Printed before the Year 1801* [London, 1957], I, 362). Manuscript copies of trios for two violins and cello, probably extracted from this op. 1, are listed in the printed catalogues of Bologna (Biblioteca Musicale "G. B. Martini"), Genoa (Biblioteca dell'Istituto "N. Paganini"), and Brussels (Bibliothèque du Conservatoire Royal de Musique).

[25] That this work was published by Stechway is the hypothesis of the *British Union-Catalogue.*

[26] Salvatore Pintacuda, *Genova—Biblioteca dell'Istituto Musicale "N. Paganini": Catalogo del fondo antico* (Milan, 1966), p. 219.

[27] Guido Gasperini *et al., Città di Napoli—Biblioteca del R. Conservatorio di Musica di S. Pietro a Majella* (Parma, 1933), p. 552.; Alfred Wotquenne, *Catalogue de la Bibliothèque du Conservatoire Royal de Bruxelles,* Vol. IV (Brussels, 1912), no. XY 15.138: "Libro di Suonate d'organo di diversi Autori: Ad uso di Giacomo Poffa, da Cremona, l'anno 1743."

[28] A. Bonora, *Città di Bologna—Archivio della R. Accademia Filarmonica* (Parma, 1910–1911), p. 31; Claudio Sartori, *Assisi—La Cappella della Basilica di S. Francesco,* I (*Catalogo del fondo musicale nella Biblioteca Comunale di Assisi*) (Milan, 1962), p. 232.

[29] Sartori, *Assisi—La Cappella della Basilica di S. Francesco,* I, 232.

two voices and instruments (Bergamo, Biblioteca Civica); [30] "Domine ad adjuvandum" for four voices and instruments, and "Laudate pueri" for three male voices with violins (Bologna, Biblioteca Martini); [31] Miserere for four voices (Genoa, Istituto Paganini); [32] Kyrie and Gloria for four voices and instruments (Modena, Biblioteca Estense); [33] Aria, "Ma no, non ho stupore" (Turin, Archivio dell' Accademia Filarmonica); [34] Dies Irae for three voices and instruments (Venice, Marciana); [35] "Cum sancto spiritu" for four voices and continuo (Berlin, Staatsbibliothek); [36] "Adoramus te" and "Plangam dolorem meum" (Salzburg, Cathedral Archives). [37] Finally, we mention the two operas, *Artaserse* (of which the printed libretto is known) [38] and *Mitridate re di Ponto* (scores of which are found at the Archivio dell'Accademia Filarmonica in Turin and the Bibliothèque Nationale in Paris). [39]

[30] Bergamo, Biblioteca Civica "A. Mai," Fondo Mayr, faldone 176.

[31] Gaetano Gaspari, *et al.*, *Catalogo della biblioteca del Liceo Musicale* (facsimile ed.; Bologna, 1961), II, 228.

[32] Pintacuda, *Genova—Biblioteca . . . "N. Paganini,"* p. 219.

[33] P. Lodi, *Città di Modena—R. Biblioteca Estense* (Parma, 1923), p. 33.

[34] Andrea Della Corte, *Accademia Filarmonica di Torino—Estratto del catalogo dell'Archivio di Musica* (Turin, 1926), p. 19.

[35] *Città di Venezia—R. Biblioteca di S. Marco* (Parma, 1941), p. 248.

[36] Robert Eitner, *Quellen-Lexikon der Musiker* (Leipzig, 1900–1904).

[37] Spies, "Ist die Motette Adoramus te . . . von W. A. Mozart?"

[38] *Artaserse: Dramma per musica da rappresentarsi nel Regio Ducal Teatro di Milano nel carnovale dell'anno 1757* (Milan, 1756), in Biblioteca Musicale "G. B. Martini" (2013). Page 5ᵛ bears the following indication: "Compositore della Musica il Sig. Abate Gasparini Accᵒ Fil. di Bologna." A manuscript score of this opera is mentioned in the microfilm catalogue of the Warsaw National Library: "Quirino Gasparini, Artaserses, opera di Milano. Tom. III, ms. sec. XVIII, pp. 322," *Biblioteka Narodowa, Katalog Mikrofilmów Nr. 12, Muzykalia III* (Warsaw, 1965), p. 26, no. 71.

[39] Della Corte, *Accademia Filarmonica di Torino*, p. 19. This score cannot be located now, according to the president of the Accademia, Lodovico Avogadro di Cerrione (letter of January 21, 1967). The copy now at the Bibliothèque Nationale (D 4342/4344) comes originally from the Bibliothèque du Conservatoire. It would be well to mention here that several musical manuscripts in various libraries bear simply

A few of Gasparini's compositions have appeared in modern editions. The misattributed "Adoramus te" was re-edited by Hermann Spies as a *Notenbeilage* of his article; then by D. Deis for G. Schirmer (New York, 1951); by R. Ewerhart for Bieler (Cologne, 1956); and by Schaller-Vené for Ricordi (New York, 1957). The "Plangam dolorem meum" was printed in Paris by the Bureau d'édition, according to Félix Raugel. Most interesting are two sonatas for violoncello and continuo that Carl Schröder edited, unfortunately without mentioning his sources, in the collection of *Classische Violoncell-Musik* published by Augener (London, 1896, plate numbers 5515 and 5516). One is a sonata in D minor—largo, spiritoso, grazioso—and the other a sonata in B flat major—largo, allegro, andante, allegro. Both these sonatas are of notable musical interest.

It is not my purpose in this short study to attempt any stylistic criticism of Gasparini's works. Suffice it to say that he composed in various genres: sacred music in both the old and the *concertante* styles, opera, and instrumental chamber music. A rather cursory examination of his music shows him to be a cultivated musician, with poetic gifts, if not a true inventive genius. Among his sacred compositions in old style, the best are the celebrated "Adoramus te" long thought to be by Mozart and the "Plangam dolorem meum," both of which were composed for his own chapel, where, in addition to *concertante* music, it was customary to perform a cappella works.[40] The "Adoramus te" has been called a minor masterpiece by Félix Raugel, who was particularly attracted by its "pure beauté." Apparently Gasparini himself was especially fond of the "Plangam," which in February 1765 he sent—in the hands of Gianfrancesco di Majo—to Padre Martini for his opinion of the work.[41] In one of his most care-

---

the name Gasparini, without mention of a Christian name, so that one cannot be certain of their attribution.

[40] Gasparini's letter to Padre Martini, October 28, 1761.

[41] "Ad esso [Gianfrancesco Di Majo] ho consegnato alcuni miei poveri componimenti, fra quali desiderarei che V[ostra] P[aternità] M[olto] R[everen]da mi onorasse di visitar un picciol motetto a 4 da

fully worked out compositions,[42] the "Stabat Mater," alongside
conventional and banal passages can be found sections, particularly at the beginning, filled with genuine originality and emotion. Although Gasparini, in a letter written to Padre Martini in
August 1765, held that this work was "alien in style to that of the
late Giambattista Pergolesi," one does recognize certain reminiscences of Pergolesi in it. Giovanni Simone Mayr found the
"Stabat Mater" a "priceless" composition.[43] Gasparini's sacred

morto *Plangam dolorem meum* fatto facile in stil madrigalesco ad uso
della mia capella" (letter of February 18, 1765).

[42] Gasparini had to expend a great deal of time and energy on the
"Stabat Mater." On August 14, 1765, he wrote to Padre Martini to ask his
opinion on a section of the *Stabat Mater,* in A-flat minor ("alafa terza
minore"), where instead of seven or eight flats in the key signature he
proposed the enharmonic equivalent, with four sharps, in order to
facilitate reading: "avendo poi di tutto mio genio fatto un componimento a 2 Soprani con Violini sopra la verbale espressione del Stabat
Mater in elafà colla possibil facilità studiata tutto alieno nei passi da
quello del fù Sig. GiamBattista Pergolesi, non posso a meno di secreta-
mente ricorrere alla Benignità grande di V[ostra] P[aternità] M[olto]
R[everen]da supplicandola sinceramente favorirmi di sua opinione
veneratissima se l'accluso pezzetto possa scusarsi rilasciandolo alli
rifflessi del publico. Questo è posto in alafà 3^{za} minore mà siccome sul
procedimento della modulazione sarebbe venuto oscurissimo per li tanti
bemolli, hò stimato alcuni tochetti porli in 4ro#. Veramente si dà
in questi qualche divisione di genere dove esposto siane dalla declinazi-
one de # siane dalla alterazione de b molli in confronto di queste 2
nature, mà in tal guisa viene il tutto più facilmente eseguibile, e forma
un effetto curioso di flebilità in confronto degli altri pezzi da' quali
tutti insieme si sentono le qualità direttamente e indirettamente di tutti
i Toni e generi. Se V.P.M. R.^{da} giudicasse potesse da mè scusarsi nella
prefazione come così voluto per facilitar l'essecuzione, indi per dimo-
strar ancora qualche curioso inganno musicale a chi l'effettuarà, è pregata
suggerirmelo, quandoche non potesse aver una taccia positiva che in
mio discredito ridondar potesse, vieppiù che forse dedicato ad alto
Personaggio il detto componimento potrebbe venir stampato." The
"Stabat Mater" was printed a few years later and was indeed dedicated to
an "alto personaggio"—Maximilian, elector of Bavaria. Apparently either on the advice given by Padre Martini or because he himself
thought better of it, Gasparini changed the passage discussed in the
letter, for it does not appear in the published version.

[43] Geddo, *Bergamo,* p. 163.

"Army Encampment"—sketch by Bernardino Galliari (1707–1794) for Gasparini's *Mitridate*, Act III, scene 5 (from the Pinacoteca Nazionale in Bologna, Gabinetto dei disegni e delle stampe, Tom. XII, Br. 57).

"Terrace—Garden"—sketch by Fabrizio Galliari (1709–1790) for Gasparini's *Mitridate*, Act III, scene 6 (from the Pinacoteca Nazionale in Bologna, Gabinetto dei disegni e delle stampe, Tom. XII, B1. 58).

"Interior of a Fortress"—sketch by Fabrizio Galliari (1709–1790) for Gasparini's *Mitridate*, Act III, scene 7 (from the Pinacoteca Nazionale in Bologna, Gabinetto dei disegni e delle stampe, Tom. XII, B1. 61).

Scene from a puppet performance of Haydn's *The Burning House*, presented at Cornell University, May 20–21, 1966, under the musical direction of Professor William C. Holmes and Professor Barbara Troxell and staged by Professor H. Peter Kahn and his assistants.

compositions in *stile concertato*—for example, the "Domine ad adjuvandum" and the "Laudate pueri"—seem to me even more sincere and moving than his works in old style. With regard to his instrumental pieces, I can speak only of the Trios in A major and F major which I have seen in Bologna. These modest two-movement pieces (a bipartite first movement followed by a minuet) display a certain melodic grace, as can be seen in the example (the first theme of the Trio in A major), where the curve of the melody may remind us of similar themes in Mozart.

We should now like to fix our attention on Gasparini's opera *Mitridate re di Ponto*, which, as we have noted before, is based on the same libretto as Mozart's opera of the same name.[44] With the goal of ascertaining the similarities between the two scores,

[44] The libretto is by Vittorio Amedeo Cigna, or Cigna-Santi (Turin, 1725–1785), a poet and man of letters who was a member of the Academy of the Trasformati in Turin and wrote a number of librettos. See Tommaso Vallauri, *Storia della poesia in Piemonte* (Turin, 1841) II, 348, and Ulderico Rolandi, "Cigna-Santi," *Enciclopedia dello Spettacolo*, Vol. III (Rome, 1956), col. 748. The libretto was printed for the performances during carnival, 1767 (*Mitridate re di Ponto, dramma per musica da rappresentarsi nel Regio Teatro di Torino nel carnovale 1767: Alla presenza di S.S.R.M.* (Turin, Derossi, 1767). There is a copy in the Library of Congress (O. G. T. Sonneck, *Catalogue of Opera Librettos Printed before 1800* [Washington, 1914], I, 766). The libretto, with slight changes, was printed again on the occasion of the performances of Mozart's *Mitridate* (*Mitridate re di Ponto, dramma per musica da rappresentarsi nel Regio-Ducal Treatro di Milano nel carnovale dell'anno 1771* [Milano: Montani, 1770]). The composer, but not the librettist, is mentioned.

we should perhaps at this point outline the history of Mozart's setting.[45]

Innumerable difficulties surrounded the conception and composition of Mozart's *Mitridate*. It was, after all, the adolescent Mozart's first experience with the Italian opera theatre, and therefore it should not be surprising that among singers and other theatre people there were many doubts as to the boy's ability to assume such an arduous task. Thus, for example, Leopold Mozart points out that certain people tried to persuade the *prima donna*, Antonia Bernasconi, to sing other arias in place of those composed by the young boy from Salzburg. Leopold wrote on November 10 that "wir haben sie alle gesehen . . . sie sind alle neuen Arien, weder sie noch wir wissen aber, wer sie componiert hat." [46] Later, writing to Padre Martini on January 2, 1771, Leopold is more specific, saying that the substitute arias were by Gasparini, "that is, the arias composed in Turin." [47] It was apparently the intention of "enemies and jealous people" to substitute not only the arias of the prima donna, but also the duet between the prima donna and the *primo uomo*, this also in Gasparini's version. Fortunately, all the difficulties disappeared when the young Mozart composed arias and a duet which were more than satisfactory to the singers. Composing to order for the "virtuosi" must have been a tiring and difficult task, as we can see

[45] I have discussed the events surrounding the composition of Mozart's *Mitridate* in the preface to my critical edition of the work, *W. A. Mozart: Neue Ausgabe sämtlicher Werke* (Kassel, 1966), 2d ser., sec. 5, Vol. V. This edition also includes some consideration of the connection between Mozart's opera and Gasparini's.

[46] Letter from Leopold Mozart, Milan, November 10, 1770 (*Mozart, Briefe und Aufzeichnungen*, ed. W. A. Bauer and O. E. Deutsch [Kassel, 1962–1963], Vol. I, no. 218).

[47] *Ibid.*, Vol. I, no. 226. Antonia Maria Girelli was the prima donna in the performances of Gasparini's *Mitridate* at the Teatro Regio in Turin during carnival, 1767 (see Gasparini's letter to Padre Martini, February 25, 1767).

from Mozart's numerous sketches and revisions for the opera.[48]
What interests us most here, however, more than the desires and
taste of the singers, is whether or not Mozart used Gasparini's
setting of the opera as a model. It is obvious that both Leopold
and the young Mozart had seen the arias and the duet by Gasparini—those pieces which were to have been substituted. It is also
quite probable that Mozart had studied those pieces, since he was
literally in a rather risky competition with them. Thus for us to
compare the two scores—Gasparini's and Mozart's—seems most
desirable.[49] A preliminary examination of the mere outlines of

[48] The sketches and early versions of parts of *Mitridate* were
published for the first time in my critical edition of the opera (in
Mozart: Neue Ausgabe).

[49] The score of Gasparini's opera at the Bibliothèque Nationale (D
4342/4344) has been the one consulted. The score consists of three
oblong volumes (27.7 cm. × 22.7 cm.) bound in half-leather. On the
spine of each volume is stamped a coat of arms (with a crown and three
lilies) and the inscription MITRIDATE/ATTO I [ATTO II, ATTO
III] GASPARINI. The three volumes, in addition to the flyleaves, have 243,
173, and 131 pages respectively (numbered in pencil); the pages are
grouped into signatures of varying sizes (from one to nine leaves), all
with their original numeration (from 1 to 17 in Vol. I, where signatures
no. 12 and no. 16 are lacking; from 1 to 17 in Vol. II; and from 1 to 13 in
Vol. III, where signature no. 4 is lacking). The leaves of the score
contain three different watermarks: (1) a shield containing a lily, (2) a
figure resembling a small hut, (3) a shield with the letters FR. The
flyleaves' laid lines are larger than their chain lines; they have a
watermark consisting of a complex of nine little circles and the word
DISNEMALIN. The pages with music are laid out in ten staves throughout.
In Vol. I, on the first lined leaf (p. 1), there is the following inscription: *Opera   Seconda   1767./ Overtura/ Del   Sig.   D.   Quirino
Gasparini/ Mitridate*. On the first page of every volume appear earlier
call numbers (1526, 1527, 1528 and 3823[A], 3823[B], and 3823[C], respectively). I wish to express my thanks to the music division of the
Bibliothèque Nationale, and particularly Mme Nanie Bridgman, for the
cooperation and many kindnesses extended to me during my work with
Gasparini's manuscript. There is no known autograph of Mozart's
Mitridate, except for the sketches and early versions of some of the
numbers. There are, however, many contemporary copies of the score.

numbers points up many differences in the organization of the two works. We shall list the more outstanding ones here: (1) The aria of Sifare (Act I, sc. 8) has different texts: in Gasparini, "Tuoni adirato il vento"; in Mozart, "Parto, nel gran cimento." (2) Act II, sc. 5 in Gasparini closes with an aria by Arbate, "D'un padre l'affetto"; this aria is lacking in Mozart.[50] (3) The aria of Aspasia (Act II, sc. 8) has different texts: in Gasparini, "Fra' dubbi affetti miei"; in Mozart, "Nel grave tormento." (4) Act II, sc. 14, closes in Gasparini with a march; there is no analogous piece in Mozart. (5) At the end of Act III, sc. 5, in Gasparini there is an aria by Aspasia, "Secondi il ciel pietoso"; although this aria is printed in the libretto for the first perform- ance of Mozart's opera, there is no trace of the music. (6) The chorus which closes the opera has different texts in the two versions: in Gasparini, "Gran Monarca, al tuo perdono"; in Mozart "Non si ceda al Campidoglio."[51]

The most interesting difference is without doubt the missing aria of the prima donna, "Secondi il ciel pietoso." The presence of the text in the libretto suggests that the aria was indeed performed,[52] but with the music of someone other than Mozart.

[50] The British Museum score of Mozart's opera (m. 16058), copied by the contrabassist Domenico Dragonetti, contains an aria on this text, but the number is probably apocryphal.

[51] In addition to these discrepancies, we should add that the Paris score of Gasparini's *Mitridate* lacks the following numbers: Mitridate's cavata (no. 8) "Se di lauri il crine adorno," Mitridate's recitative (Act I, final scene) "Respira alfin," Farnace's aria (no. 16) "Son reo, l'error confesso," and Mitridate's aria (no. 20) "Vado incontro al fato estre- mo." Mitridate's three missing numbers are not, as might be sus- pected, pieces that Gasparini failed to compose, but are definitely parts lost from the Paris score. The three missing signatures mentioned above correspond exactly in position to the missing numbers. However, there is no corresponding missing signature to Farnace's aria; hence this may not have been set by Gasparini.

[52] In the libretto of Mozart's *Mitridate* there are a number of pieces that were not set to music, but these are always set off by quotation marks in the left margin. The text of the aria "Secondi il ciel pietoso" is

Evidently Mozart was not successful in forcing *all* his arias on
Bernasconi and her entourage. One is inclined to hypothesize
that the aria sung was the one composed by Gasparini, but this
seems a dubious hypothesis, since Gasparini's aria is in E flat
major and the preceding recitative in Mozart's score closes in F
major.

Not only the differences but also the similarities between the
two scores are worth consideration. In my opinion, these cannot
merely be ascribed to the fact that the same libretto was used by
both composers; they demonstrate, I believe, that Mozart had
Gasparini's opera in mind when he composed many of the
pieces, though he never resorted to exact imitation or to plagia-
rism. These similarities are nowhere more apparent than in the
structure of the accompanied recitative and cavatina, "Ah ben ne
fui presaga!—Pallid'ombre che scorgete," sung by Aspasia in
Act III. In both versions the two composers set it with the
unusual linking of recitative-cavatina-recitative. Another striking similarity can be found in the duet in Mozart's first version,
which follows that of Gasparini exactly—A-B-A'-B' (in Gasparini: moderato-allegro-moderato-allegro; in Mozart: adagio-
allegro-adagio-allegro). At the phrase "Barbare stelle ingrate,"
characterized by strong dynamic contrasts and tremolos in the
violins, Mozart was apparently inspired by Gasparini's setting.
Mozart's final version of this duet shuns the formal and musical
similarities to Gasparini found in the earlier version.[53] According
to Leopold Mozart, the final version filled the two singers Antonia Bernasconi and Piero Benedetti with enthusiasm.[54]

One can surmise that Mozart had seen the complete score of

not set off in such a manner; this seems to indicate that it was indeed
performed.

[53] It is noteworthy also that both Gasparini's and Mozart's first set-
tings of the duet lack the words "Ah che tu sol tu sei che mi dividi il
cor," which appear in Mozart's final version.

[54] Letter from Leopold Mozart from Milan, December 15, 1770 (*Mozart, Briefe*, Vol. I, no. 223).

Gasparini's version, not merely the arias of Aspasia and the duet. Even though Mozart's arias generally follow a structure different from those of Gasparini (Mozart shortened his *da capo* by eliminating its first section, while Gasparini cut its middle section), there are also numbers in each version which show certain structural affinities that cannot be explained away because the same libretto was set by the two composers. Particularly striking are the arias of Mitridate, "Tu che fedel di sei" (Act II, sc. 4) and "Già di pietà mi spoglio" (Act II, sc. 14). Other echoes of Gasparini's score seem to be present in the accompanied recitative of Aspasia, "Grazie ai numi partì" (Act II, sc. 8). Finally at the beginning of Act I, scene 10, where the libretto calls for "a joyous *sinfonia*," both composers write a march in D major.[55]

Even though the similarities mentioned here [56] are principally in the formal structure of the works and have only a little to do with their true musical and dramatic substance (such a comparison would certainly favor the setting of the young Mozart), they seem far from negligible. Scholars have often cited Italian composers, and composers in the Italian manner, from Piccini to Jommelli, Padre Martini, Anfossi, and Johann Christian Bach,

[55] This march is found in only one of the sources—the recently discovered manuscript score of *Mitridate* in the Ajuda Library (Lisbon). The march is identical to a piece known until now only by its incipit (K. 62); it had been composed earlier (probably in Salzburg during the summer of 1769), in all probability as the first movement of the Cassation in D Major, K. 100 (62ª). Wolfgang Plath, codirector of the *Neue Ausgabe*, made the identification, and the piece was published for the first time in my critical edition of *Mitridate*.

[56] There is another connection between the two operas: the sets for both were done by "i Signori Galliari fratelli piemontesi," the celebrated Bernardino (1707–1794), Fabrizio (1709–1790), and Giovanni Antonio (1714–1783) Galliari (see M. Viale Ferrero, *La scenografia del '700 e i fratelli Galliari* [Turin, 1963]). The Pinacoteca Nazionale in Bologna possesses a volume (Bk. XII, inventory no. 4382) containing sketches by Fabrizio and Bernardino Galliari, eight of which (pp. 54–61) are for sets in Gasparini's *Mitridate*. Another sketch by Fabrizio Galliari in the same library (NS 12 N 79) seems to be for Act III, sc. 10, of the same opera.

who were influential in the stylistic development of the young Mozart, especially during his trips to Italy. Too often Gasparini and his opera *Mitridate* have been overlooked in these discussions. Certainly *Mitridate*, appearing as it did on the eve of the young Salzburg composer's baptism in the Milanese theatres, stands not only as a symbol of a rivalry to be overcome but as an object worthy of scholarly study.

That Gasparini was an indirect and unwilling accomplice to the "enemies and jealous people" in Milan was not held against him by either Leopold or Wolfgang Mozart. In the latter part of January 1771, after the performances of *Mitridate* in Milan, the Mozarts went to Turin and met Gasparini, with whom they continued to maintain friendly contact.[57] In February 1778, Wolfgang wrote from Mannheim to his father asking him to send some arias for Aloysia Weber, and Leopold sent him, among others, "5 grosse Arien," one of which was by Gasparini.[58] Thus the Mozart family persisted not only in cordial respect but also in professional esteem for the *maestro di cappella* of the cathedral in Turin.

APPENDIX

The text of Mayr's biography of Gasparini as reproduced here is found in "Biografie di Musicisti," Bergamo, Biblioteca Civica, Sala 32, D. 8. 29/4 (8), pp. 1ʳ–2ʳ.

L'Ab. *Quirino Gasparini* non venne eletto a Maestro di Capella in sua patria, e fu bene per il medesimo perchè fu scielto a quella della

[57] Gasparini's name appears in Leopold Mozart's travel notes for January 31, 1771. On May 28, 1778, Leopold Mozart, writing to his son, says that he has sent "auch Complim. an Abbate Gasparini" via the oboist Carlo Besozzi, who was leaving for Turin (*Mozart, Briefe,* Vol. II, no. 450).

[58] Letters from W. A. Mozart dated February 4, 7, 14, 19, 22, and 28, 1778; letter from Leopold Mozart dated February 25–26, 1778 (*ibid.,* nos. 416, 419, 423, 426, 428, 430, and 431).

Cattedrale e della città di Torino, con onore d'esser innalzato a Maestro di Musica di Camera di que' Reggi, splendidi ed adorabili Sovrani che lo ebbero in pregio e lo premiarono onorevolmente; ivi trovò nel gran Cardinal delle Lancie un generoso Mecenate, che oltre i molti altri favori si compiaceva averlo spesso alla sua mensa, e conducendolo seco in carozza nella Basilica di S. Benigno.

Nacque Quirino nel Borgo di Gandino l'anno 1721 da [59]

Dimostrando somma inclinazione a' studi sacri, e alla Musica da suoi genitori fu condotto a Bergamo ove ebbe a Maestri i S. Silari [?]. In breve tempo riuscì capace d'eseguire i piu difficili pezzi d'intavolatura e di accompagnamento, e di superar gli stessi Maestri. Era dilettante in suonare l'organo pel quale scrisse infinite suonate tutte di buon gusto, e adattate a si bell'istromento. Studiato il contrappunto fu da tutti tenuto nella composizione un prodigio, giacchè di soli 16 anni emulava già i più rinomati Maestri e benche fosse ricercato per diverse funzioni, e piacesse la sua musica non si lasciò guidare dagli applausi, che per il piu sono fatali a' giovani, ma si diresse al celebre Fioroni Maestro del duomo di Milano, indi all'insigne Martini di Bologna, colle quali validissime scorte ebbe campo di perfezionare i suoi talenti. D'anni 20 fu agregato all'accademia di Bologna ed il Martini volle il suo ritratto per collocarlo nella propria galleria, ed al medesimo regalò il suo, ed io ho il piacere di possederli. Con particolare incontro d'anni 28 produsse nel regio Teatro di Milano una sua opera. Poco dopo la promozione al Pontificato del Cardinal Rezzonico, che successe li 6 luglio 1758 Quirino si portò a Roma poscia alla sede della Musica di Napoli in compagnia del Co[nte] d'Aziano di Vercelli suo scolaro Cav. dilettante della Musica e per tutti i titoli riguardevole Mecenate,[60] per il qual mezzo l'ab. Gasparini veniva scelto per la fonzione a otto reali che ogni anno si celebra nel giorno di S. Eusebio nella Cattedrale di Vercelli, nel 1760. fu l'epoca per cui non essendo soddisfatto del modo col quale si voleva eleggere il maestro della Cappella di S. Maria Maggiore di Bergamo non volle fare il concorso,[61] indi venne

---

[59] See notes 7 and 8.

[60] Marginal note: "Questo Signore nel suo feudo d'Assiano fece porre nel giardino eccellenti statue, fra le quali il suo Maestro Querino."

[61] Marginal note: "L'ab. Querino aveva infirmato che l'esame pel concorso fosse bensì approvato da que' Nob. Sig. Presidenti, ma sul voto de'

scelto per Torino. Ivi scrisse un opera per quel R. Teatro, poi ad imitazione del Pergolesi un Stabat a 2 Soprani, che fece stampare dedicandolo all' A. S. E. di Massimiliano duca di Baviera che fu aggradito, e premiato con regal munificenza. Non passava Principe per quella regia Città che non cercasse di Querino, per aver qualche sua composizione per il che oltremodo era affaticato stando al studio settimane intiere senza porsi a letto provando di star svegliato con liquori, e quantità di caffè. Produsse moltissimi pezzi da chiesa, e da camera assai pregiati, fra quali varj duetti, e Trii pel Violino, che sono assai stimati anche in oggi. Memore la Patria di aver in Torino un così virtuoso e rinomato Maestro in occasione che nell'anno 1762 si fece per più giorni una straordinaria e solenne festa per la traslazione de' SS. Fermo, Rustico, e Procolo ad un nuovo altare di Marmo con urna di bronzo, ed altra portatile d'argento, di squisito lavoro de' nostri celebri Filiberti fu Querino a tal funzione invitato con altri Maestri d'Italia, e Querino ne portò la palma. Fece conoscer la Patria, che l'esclusiva anzi detta non fu causata se non da alcuni pocchi. Ritornato a Torino troppo mi difonderei se volessi di notare le funzioni a cui era chiamato il concorso della prima nobiltà e popolo, gli applausi, gli onori, e doni ch'ebbe, e perciò il dispiacere universalmente provato nel sentirne la grave malattia indi la morte sopragiuntali il 23 settembre 1778. Fu esemplare Sacerdote, e di illibati costumi e la sua memoria vive ancor oggi in Torino nella Patria ed altrove.

---

primari Maestri d'Italia a' quali si dovesser spedire le produzioni estemporanee dei concorrenti; sembrando all Presidenza con tal metodo di pregiudicarsi non volle ciò accordare e Querino rinunciò al concorso."

Haydn's Italian Opera Repertory at Eszterháza Palace

By DÉNES BARTHA

This essay is designed to provide a fresh report on continuing research [1] in Joseph Haydn's opera-conducting activities at Eszterháza, with some additional remarks on current problems of operatic "repertoire history"—that special aspect of operatic history whose essential lines are traced by Donald J. Grout in his *Short History of Opera.*

[1] Four books and two long articles have been collated here; to facilitate the reader's either skimming or carefully checking all relevant discussions, abbreviations are used as follows:

Hárich 59—János Hárich, *Esterházy-Musikgeschichte im Spiegel der zeitgenössischen Textbücher* (Eisenstadt, 1959).

Hárich 62—János Hárich, "Das Repertoire des Opernkapellmeisters Joseph Haydn in Eszterháza (1780–1790)," *Haydn Yearbook,* I (1962), 9–110.

HMO—H. C. Robbins Landon, "Haydn's Marionette Operas and the Repertoire of the Marionette Theatre at Esterház Castle," *Haydn Yearbook,* I (1962), 111–199.

HOK—Dénes Bartha and László Somfai, *Haydn als Opernkapellmeister* (Budapest, 1960).

Horányi—Mátyás Horányi, *The Magnificence of Eszterháza* (London, 1962).

Pohl—Carl Ferdinand Pohl, *Joseph Haydn* (Leipzig, 1875–1882), completed by Hugo Botstiber (1927).

❧ ❀ ☙

Joseph Haydn spent the thirty years from 1761 to 1790 in the service of the princes Esterházy: [2] Paul Anton (1714–1762), who lived mainly at Eisenstadt, and his more famous successor, Prince Nicholas, who lived from 1762 to 1768 at Eisenstadt, and then from 1768 to 1790 at Eszterháza Palace, which he built on the model of Versailles,[3] mainly in the years 1764–1768. Prince Nicholas "the Magnificent," as he was called by his contemporaries, was a fervent patron not only of architecture but also of theatre and music. Besides supporting the Italian operas whose repertory we shall deal with in detail, and some German marionette operettas, which we shall note more briefly, Prince Nicholas hired the very best German theatre companies he could get from the nearby cities of Vienna and Pressburg. Until the completion of the new theatre building at Eszterháza Palace in 1768, the repertory of those traveling theatre companies consisted mostly of the so-called *Hanswurstiaden*, Austrian variants of the Italian *commedia dell'arte*. But, after 1769, Prince Nicholas succeeded in getting better companies, with a repertory of nonimprovised, "regular" dramas of high literary value. Such were the companies of Hellmann and Koberwein in 1769, with performances of works by such playwrights as Molière (*Le malade imaginaire*), Voltaire, and Lessing (*Miss Sara Sampson, Minna von Barnhelm*). During 1770 and 1771, a similar repertory was performed at Eszterháza by the company of Franz Passer, whose performances are notable in German theatrical history as having contributed much to the transition from buffooneries to regular drama.

[2] In foreign literature there has been some confusion as to the orthography of those names. The family name of the princes should be spelled "Esterházy" whereas the locality of Haydn's conducting was spelled "Eszterháza." In documents and letters using German or Italian spelling, the latter often was distorted into "Esterhaz" or "Estoras."

[3] Eszterháza palace is the most impressive late-Baroque building in Hungary.

The golden age of spoken drama at Eszterháza came in the years 1772–1777, when the company of Carl Wahr played alternately at Pressburg and Eszterháza. The company performed nothing but "regular" plays of high literary value, many of them being first performances in the German language. There were tragedies by Shakespeare (*Hamlet* and *Macbeth*, beginning in 1773, *Othello* and *King Lear*, in the original versions, in 1774, *Richard III* and *Romeo and Juliet* in 1776); by Goethe (*Clavigo*); by Regnard (*Le distrait*); and others. In the year 1777, Wahr's company left Eszterháza for Budapest, Pressburg, and Prague. From then on, Italian *opera buffa*, under the direction of Joseph Haydn, absorbed most of Prince Nicholas' interest in the theatrical arts.

During the golden age of Wahr and before the triumph of Italian opera playing under Haydn in the 1780's, another genre won a short-lived success at Eszterháza: the marionette operetta, much favored by Haydn himself. The apparatus of the marionette theatre was bought by Prince Nicholas from the director, Pauersbach, in July 1773. During the next six years this theatre produced a quite remarkable series of musical performances in the German "Singspiel" style, including pieces by Haydn himself and by his contemporaries Ordonnez and Pleyel. In September 1778, the "spiritus rector" of the marionettes, director Pauersbach (who may have written most of the libretti), left Eszterháza. After that year, only sporadic performances were given in the marionette theatre at Eszterháza: in 1782, two operas taken over from the "regular" opera repertory and, in 1783, one spectacular showpiece (*L'assedio di Gibilterra*) by an unidentified composer.[4]

Haydn's operatic activities in the first fifteen years of his service with the princes Esterházy (1761–1775) thus seem to have been limited to rather sporadic performances of his own operas, written for special festival occasions at Eisenstadt (1761–1768)

[4] See HMO.

or Eszterháza (1768–1775). The following list indicates all first performances now known. (Dates of composition are at most a year earlier.)

La comedia marchese (the title on the MS), or *La marchesa nespola* (the title given in Haydn's *Entwurfskatalog*). First performance, May-June 1762, Eisenstadt. (See Pohl, I, 231; HOK, p. 379; Horányi, p. 29.) The names that follow in Haydn's catalogue—La Vedova, Il Dottore, Il Scanarello—were believed (by Pohl and by Hárich 59) to designate other Italian comedies, though no music for them is preserved; more likely they are subtitles or simply the cast of characters in the same comedy—all are standard characters of the *commedia dell'arte*.

Acide. Festa teatrale. Libretto by Migliavacca. First performance, January 11, 1763, Eisenstadt (Pohl, I, 237; HOK, p. 381).

An unidentified opera, 1764; only mentioned, with no source given, by Hárich 62, p. 92.

La canterina. Intermezzo in musica. First performance (identified by Horányi), February 16, 1767, Pressburg; other, perhaps even earlier, performances may have been given at Eisenstadt. Modern edition edited by Dénes Bartha in Haydn, *Werke, herausgegeben vom Joseph-Haydn-Institut, Köln, unter der Leitung von Jens Peter Larsen* (Munich, 1959) (Pohl, II, 37, 349; Horányi, pp. 41–42).

Lo speziale. Dramma giocoso. Libretto by Goldoni. First performance, autumn 1768, for the inauguration of the new opera house at Eszterháza. Modern edition by Helmut Wirth in *Werke*, (Munich, 1959) (Pohl, II, 39, 349). Another performance took place in Vienna, at the house of Count Sumerau, March 22, 1770 (Pohl, II, 45).

La contadina in corte. Music by Sacchini(?), Piccini(?). This performance is mentioned, but no source is specified, by Hárich 62, pp. 37–38. Neither score nor libretto for a performance in 1769 is preserved.

Le pescatrici. Dramma giocoso. Libretto by Goldoni(?). First performance, September 16, 1770, Eszterháza (Pohl, II, 46, 350; HOK, p. 387).

L'infedeltà delusa. Burletta per musica. Libretto by Coltellini. First performance, July 26, 1773, Eszterháza; repeated for the Empress Maria Theresa on September 1, 1773. Modern editions by H. Robbins Landon (Vienna: Universal, 1961) and Dénes Bartha (*Werke,* [Munich, 1964]) (see Pohl, II, 60; HOK, pp. 388–390).

L'incontro improvviso. Dramma giocoso. Libretto by Karl Friberth(?). First performance, August 29, 1775, Eszterháza. Modern editions by Helmut Schultz (Leipzig, 1939) and Helmut Wirth (*Werke,* [Munich, 1962–1963]) (Pohl, II, 74, 350).[5]

Obviously, this list of eight known works in fifteen years constitutes no "repertoire" in the true sense. Up to 1775, Haydn was conforming to the typical practice of seventeenth- and eighteenth-century court residences, including Vienna, Prague, and Munich, that operas were required of the local chapelmaster for performance at special festive occasions. The accumulation of a regular "repertoire," comparable to Neapolitan or Venetian practice, was not started at Eszterháza until 1776, when Haydn first performed some operas by his friend Dittersdorf. Then there followed a long series of Italian opera performances under his direction, until the death of Prince Nicholas in September 1790. Accordingly, the year 1776 marks an important turning point in Haydn's activities at Eszterháza. From that year on, a large part of his energy was absorbed in selecting, preparing, coaching, and performing an Italian opera repertory that ranked, as we now know, second only to those of the great centers of Italian operatic life—Venice and Naples—and equaled or surpassed the important Viennese repertoire. Among the eighty-seven opera premières[6] prepared and performed under Haydn at Eszterháza during those fifteen years, only six works of his own

[5] For the additional marionette performances in the years 1773–1776, see HMO, *passim.*

[6] This is but a minimum figure; if Dr. Hárich comes forward with some additional evidence from the so far undisclosed Esterházy archive material, the figure may safely rise by two to four more first performances.

were presented—*Il mondo della luna* (1777), *La vera costanza* (1779; composed in 1776 for performance in Vienna, but then withdrawn), *L'isola disabitata* (1779), *La fedeltà premiata* (1781), *Orlando paladino* (1782), and *Armida* (1784)—while the remaining eighty-one first performances, plus at least six additional opera scores prepared by Haydn for performance in 1790–1791 but then left unperformed, were all works of his contemporaries: thirteen by Cimarosa, eleven by Anfossi, nine by Paisiello, seven by Sarti, five by Guglielmi, four by Dittersdorf, three each by Bianchi, Gazzaniga, Piccini, and Righini, two by Sacchini, Salieri, Traëtta, and Zingarelli, and one by Bertoni, Bologna, Caruso, Fabrizi, Felici, Grétry, Gassmann, Martin, Naumann, Prati, Stabingher, and perhaps Gluck.[7] These are impressive and significant numbers: Haydn and Prince Nicholas must have had very accurate and extensive information about the outstanding composers of Italian opera and their most important works.

Some readers may wonder why Mozart is missing from this list. But the standard practices of eighteenth-century opera scheduling give sufficient reason for the omission. The Eszterháza repertory was almost entirely confined to the genre of *opera buffa*. That means that *Idomeneo* and *Die Entführung aus dem Serail* were automatically excluded. To perform Mozart's *La finta giardiniera* was impossible because of Anfossi's opera of the same name (performed at Eszterháza in 1780); *Don Giovanni* (1787) was barred because of Righini's *Il convitato di pietra* (1781); and Mozart did not compose *Così fan tutte* until the year Prince Nicholas died. Thus, *Figaro* offered the only possibility for Haydn to pay tribute to the operatic genius of Mozart. Haydn's hesitating to start work on it until 1789 may be

---

[7] The divergence of the figures above from those given in Hárich 62 originates from the fact that Hárich's essay covered only the last decade (1780–1790) of Haydn's activity, while here we have added to his figures the roughly fifteen performances previously conducted by Haydn from 1776 to 1779 and then dropped from the repertory.

attributable to the limited number of its Viennese performances in 1786—nine performances in the months May to November. And we know from his correspondence that Haydn found it nearly impossible to get leave of absence from Eszterháza during this same period. In all probability, he had no opportunity to attend a Vienna performance of *Figaro* until the revival in August 1789. Then Haydn immediately started work on the opera, but his preparations were canceled by the death of Prince Nicholas.

Before proceeding to list the Eszterháza opera repertory for the decisive years 1776–1790, we must first consider the nature of our sources and the special difficulties of their evaluation, as shown in the divergences among the pertinent publications (Pohl, Hárich 59, HOK, Hárich 62, Horányi). When Haydn, after many years of resounding successes in symphonic and chamber music, started performing in 1776 some operas by Dittersdorf,[8] Sacchini, and Piccini, there was only a modest company of able singers available at Eszterháza and no operatic organization at all. There was not even a regular schedule or calendar of opera performances. What we know about the repertory of the years 1776–1779 has had to be reconstructed from libretto prints, printers' bills, costume tailors' or hairdressers' bills, and other archive documents only loosely related to music. It was not until 1778 that Prince Nicholas issued an "instruction" ordering his librarian, Ph. Georg Bader, to take charge of the organizational and administrative affairs of the Eszterháza opera. As a result of this instruction, we fortunately possess a fairly precise calendar of all the theatrical and operatic performances of the significant year 1778 (published by Pohl, II, 367–371, but with some composers' names falsely and arbitrarily added).[9]

---

[8] Shortly before, Dittersdorf had sold a stock of his manuscript opera scores to Prince Esterházy (see HOK, pp. 67–68).

[9] The operas *Il finto pazzo*, *Il barone di Rocca Antica*, and *Arcifanfano* were all operas by Dittersdorf and not by Piccini, Salieri, or Gassmann. This error by Pohl has given birth to a long sequence of

Unfortunately, this valuable document is unique in its genre. No similar calendar has turned up for either the earlier or later years in the vast Esterházy archives; the calendar for 1779 may have been destroyed, together with many other valuable materials, in the Eszterháza theatre fire in November 1779. Accordingly, the reconstruction of the Eszterháza repertory up to 1779 is an extremely difficult task, subject to many hazards and possible misinterpretations. More solid ground is reached only with 1780; from that year on we have a fairly continuous series of *Stabenen* reports—regular reports on fees for supernumeraries, with precise performance dates and opera titles. Thus, from 1780 on, nearly all the first performances and repetitions can be ascertained, whereas for the three years from 1776 to 1779 the available data are very incomplete and often hard to locate within the enormous material of the Esterházy archives. (There is no detailed index at all for the archive material in Budapest and none at Eisenstadt that has been available to me.)

In most of the Haydn literature up to 1959, there was little mention of Haydn's feverish activity as an opera conductor at Eszterháza. Along with the scarcity of the documents, Haydn's own statements may have been partly responsible for the strange neglect of this long period of his life as a musician. In the early 1800s when he spoke about his life to his biographers Griesinger and Dies,[10] Haydn was remarkably reticent about his opera-conducting activities at Eszterháza; in retrospect, the tremendous work of selecting, revising, coaching, and performing other composers' operas may have assumed the character of an oppressing, cumbersome duty. To Griesinger, Haydn spoke of "mechanische Arbeiten," leaving open the question whether he referred

erroneous assignments, especially concerning the alleged composition of *Arcifanfano* by Gassmann. In reality, there is no evidence whatever for Gassmann's having composed *Arcifanfano*. The opera performed in 1778 was by Dittersdorf.

[10] Their biographies are now made available in an excellent English translation with pertinent commentary by Vernon D. Gotwals (*J. Haydn, Eighteenth-Century Gentleman and Genius* [Madison, Wis., 1963]).

to the many baryton trios he composed for Prince Nicholas or perhaps rather to his work as opera conductor. Accordingly, there is no wonder if C. F. Pohl, the author of the first scholarly monograph on Haydn (2 vols.; Leipzig, 1875, 1882), dismissed Haydn's opera conducting with a few sketchy and meaningless words (Pohl, II, 8–9). There Pohl, relying evidently on the libretto collection then in the Esterházy archives, mentioned merely thirty-seven opera titles, that is, less than half the number we know today to have been performed in Haydn's time. Moreover, Pohl did not mention at all the fact that most of the performing scores and parts used by Haydn and his opera troupe were preserved in the Esterházy archives.

It took a long time and many years of archive work to get substantially beyond Pohl's incomplete listing. The pioneering work in this field must be credited to the archivist-historian of Prince Paul Esterházy, Dr. János Hárich, who in 1941 started compiling a precise catalogue of the Esterházy libretto collection, with complete title pages of the librettos. A typewritten copy of this catalogue is available in the Music Division of the National Library at Budapest. During the siege of Budapest in 1945, the whole Esterházy libretto collection was destroyed by fire; the title copies made by Hárich proved to be of outstanding value, since most of the librettos destroyed turned out to have been unique copies. Hárich's typewritten catalogue has supplied the basic material for the libretto listings in two subsequent publications: a short survey by Hárich himself, *Esterházy-Musikgeschichte im Spiegel der zeitgenössischen Textbücher*, and a monograph on the Esterházy theatre, *The Magnificence of Eszterháza*, by the literary historian Mátyás Horányi. Parallel to their work was the collecting of source materials in Budapest, carried out mainly by Dr. Arisztid Valkó, who had been commissioned to prepare a complete edition of Haydn documents preserved in Budapest.[11] A somewhat mechanical way of meeting

[11] Published in Vols. VI and VIII of *Zenetudományi Tanulmányok* (1957 and 1960).

his difficult task made Valkó's work less useful and complete than it was expected to be—the main criterion used for including or dismissing a document was whether or not it displayed Haydn's autograph signature. It took a certain time to recognize that many important operatic documents had not been countersigned by Haydn at all. Nevertheless, the libretto listings of Hárich and Horányi, plus the document copies of Valkó, seemed to provide a fairly solid basis for starting a monograph on Haydn's opera-conducting activities in Eszterháza, a task undertaken by László Somfai and myself in 1957. Results were published in our volume *Haydn als Opernkapellmeister*. For the chronological statistics of opera performances, we had to rely mainly on the preliminary work done by Hárich, Horányi, and Valkó, supplementing it with our own research in the Budapest section of the Esterházy archives, since political reasons at that time made impossible our use of the important Eisenstadt section of the archives. This limitation in source material showed up soon, when publication of the Eisenstadt material was finally begun by Hárich in the *Haydn Yearbook* for 1962. Today the nearly complete statistics of Haydn's opera performances can be combined from the two publications. The principal contribution of *Haydn als Opernkapellmeister* was that in 1960 it represented the first, if necessarily incomplete, endeavor to establish a precise chronology of operatic performances under Haydn, and that—going far beyond a mere listing of libretto titles, as published in Hárich 59 and Horányi—it was the first attempt to evaluate the music material itself (scores and parts) used by Haydn and his company for the Eszterháza performances. This *catalogue raisonné* of the operatic collection within the Esterházy archives (HOK pp. 179–451), with a complete list of Haydn's insertion arias, a critical listing of his copyists, and the watermarks in the scores and parts, constituted the most important section of our work. To our knowledge no substantial supplement or correction to it has been published so far. It seems that the supplements and corrections now published or planned concern chiefly the statistics of repetitions. To give readers here a quick orientation, the most efficient procedure is a simple list of the first performances conducted by Haydn, plus some pertinent remarks on the sources themselves.

We have already mentioned that the most important sources for the chronology of opera performances at Eszterháza—the *Stabenen* reports—unfortunately start only in 1780. For the four previous years we must rely mainly on the testimony of the librettos themselves, which provide no exact dates but only seasons—spring, summer, autumn. For this reason, even our present chronology for 1776–1779 may be subject to a certain revision, if Dr. Hárich should succeed in producing new data from the Eisenstadt archives.

1776

Il finto pazzo per amore. Operetta a 4 voci (opera buffa). Dittersdorf-Mariani(?). First performance at Eszterháza, April 1776. Libretto in National Library, Budapest; title page and cast (Hárich 59, no. 93; HOK, p. 66). MS score (contemporary copy, partly by Esterházy copyists) and orchestra parts preserved in National Library, Budapest; vocal parts lost. Slight changes and cuts by Haydn. (Description of sources, HOK, pp. 179–180).

L'isola d'amore. Operetta giocosa (opera buffa). Sacchini–A. Gori. First performance at Eszterháza, summer 1776 (continued performances in 1777). Libretto lost in 1945; title page (Hárich 59, no. 94; HOK, p. 66; Horányi, p. 200). Complete orchestra parts and one single vocal part (Nardo), Viennese professional copyist's work. Slight cuts in the parts, probably by Haydn (HOK, p. 180).

La buona figliuola. Dramma giocoso. Piccini-Goldoni. First performance at Eszterháza, autumn 1776. Libretto lost in 1945; title page and cast (Hárich 59, no. 96; HOK, p. 66; Horányi, p. 200). No Eszterháza performing material extant (probably lost in the Eszterháza fire, 1779).

Lo sposo burlato. Intermezzo (opera buffa) a 4 voci. Dittersdorf-(?). First performance at Eszterháza, autumn 1776. Libretto lost in 1945; cast unknown; title page (Hárich 59, no. 95; HOK, p. 66; Horányi, p. 200). Music: MS score (contemporary copy, made in and for Eszterháza) and nearly complete orchestra parts preserved in National Library, Budapest; vocal parts lost (HOK, p. 181). Dittersdorf's autograph score (Johannisberg, 1775) seems to be lost.

Il barone di Rocca Antica. Intermezzo a 4 voci (libretto); *operetta giocosa* (score). Dittersdorf-Petrosellini(?). First performance at Eszterháza, autumn 1776. Libretto lost in 1945; title page and cast (Hárich 59, no. 98; HOK, p. 67; Horányi, p. 200). Music: autograph score (probably originating from Johannisberg) and complete orchestra parts preserved in National Library, Budapest; vocal parts lost. Slight changes in orchestration and cuts by Haydn (HOK, p. 181).

(?) *Orfeo ed Euridice. Opera seria.* Gluck-Calzabigi. Unknown to Hárich 59, Horányi, and HOK. Only recently mentioned in Hárich 62, p. 13, which adds that a libretto was printed for that occasion; no source mentioned. So far neither libretto nor performing material has been located in Budapest, and no trace whatsoever of a performance of a Gluck opera at Eszterháza. Another opera, *Orfeo ed Euridice* by Bertoni, was included in the Eszterháza repertory in 1788 (see below, page 202).

Complementing these few performances, there is evidence for a whole series of marionette-operetta productions at Eszterháza in 1776. Listings and detailed descriptions are given by Landon in "Haydn's Marionette-Operas and the Repertoire of the Marionette Theatre at Eszterház," HMO, pp. 111–199; here we give only short notes.

Alceste. Opera parody. Ordonnez. Repeated from 1775 (HMO, p. 189). Libretto printed in October 1775; score in National Library, Budapest.

Didone abbandonata. Haydn-Bader. First performance at Eszterháza, March 1776. Music and libretto lost. Performances continued until 1778, when a new edition of the libretto was printed (preserved in Stadtbibliothek, Vienna). For title, outline, and further information, see HMO, pp. 175 ff.

Demophon. Composer and librettist unknown. First performance at Eszterháza, March 1776. Music and libretto lost (HMO, p. 190).

Genovefens I, II, III Theil. Music by Haydn(?). First performances at Eszterháza, spring summer, autumn 1776. Music and libretto lost (HMO, p. 191).

Die Fee Urgèle. Pleyel. First performance at Eszterháza, December 1776. Autograph score in National Library, Vienna; libretto at Eisenstadt (HMO, p. 191).

Das abgebrannte Haus (Die Feuersbrunst). Haydn(?). Libretto lost. Score (contemporary copy) Music Library, Yale University, New Haven. Modern edition by Landon (London, 1961). For description, see HMO, pp. 178 ff.

1777

L'Amore artigiano. Dramma giocoso. Gassmann-Goldoni. First performance at Eszterháza, spring 1777. Libretto in National Library, Budapest; title page and cast (Hárich 59, no. 99; HOK, p. 70; Horányi, p. 200). Revivals took place at Eszterháza in 1780 and 1790 (HOK, pp. 86, 161). Music: incomplete score (Act III is missing) of Viennese origin, full orchestra parts, and some incomplete vocal parts copied by Eszterháza copyists preserved in National Library, Budapest. The same performing material was used for the revivals in 1780 and 1790. For the last revival in 1790, Haydn composed three new insertion arias (see his letter to Marianne v. Genzinger of February 25, 1790). One of them, "Da che penso a maritarmi," was identified long ago by Pohl. A second one, with text missing, was identified in HOK, p. 398. The third one, "La mia pace oh Dio," was only recently found by Paul Kast in an Italian library and identified by Christa Landon as belonging to this opera.

Il mondo della luna. Dramma giocoso. Haydn-Goldoni. First performance at Eszterháza, August 3, 1777. Libretto in National Library, Budapest; title page and cast (Pohl, II, 80; HOK, p. 71; Horányi, p. 202). No performing material for Eszterháza preserved (probably destroyed in the fire of 1779). Fragments of Haydn's autograph score, representing different stages of Haydn's planning and divergent in many details, preserved in Budapest, Paris, Berlin, and Vienna. For a detailed description of the sources, see HOK, pp. 188–197, and the modern edition by Landon (Kassel, 1958).

La Frascatana. Dramma giocoso. Paisiello-Livigni. First performance at Eszterháza, summer 1777 (possibly preceding that of *Il mondo della luna*); other performances in 1778 and 1779. No libretto preserved in Budapest; title page (Hárich 59, no. 100; HOK, p. 71; Horányi, p. 202). No performing material for Eszterháza preserved (probably destroyed in the fire of 1779). Haydn inserted one aria of his own, "D'una sposa meschinella," in the opera (HOK, p. 402).

Arcifanfano. Dramma giocoso. Dittersdorf-Goldoni. First performance at Eszterháza, autumn 1777; performances continued until 1778. Libretto lost in 1945; title page and cast (Hárich 59, no. 102; HOK, p. 71; Horányi, p. 202). The 1778 performances were erroneously listed by Pohl, II, 368–369, as Gassmann's work; this error has been perpetuated in the Gassmann articles in Umberto Manferrari, *Dizionario universale delle opere melodrammatiche* (Florence, 1954–1955), and in *Musik in Geschichte und Gegenwart*. Dittersdorf's autograph score (originating in Johannisberg) and the orchestra parts (prepared by Eszterháza copyists) preserved in National Library, Budapest; vocal parts lost. Some slight changes in orchestration were made by Haydn (HOK, pp. 198–199).

Il marchese villano. Dramma giocoso. Paisiello(?)–P. Chiari. First performance in Eszterháza, 1777(?). So far no printed libretto for this performance has been found. Not listed in Hárich 59, HOK, or Horányi. First mentioned in Hárich 62, p. 82, which gives as the source the "Baucassa-Rechnungen" for 1777, the Eszterháza copyist Schellinger having billed some work for an opera of this title. To date this seems to be the only evidence for this performance in 1777. Hárich points to the fact that this title is merely a variant of Paisiello's *La contadina di spirito*, which was performed at Eszterháza in 1788–1789 with moderate success. Hárich contends that the two operas were identical. Since all the Eszterháza sources for *Il marchese villano* must have been destroyed in the fire of 1779, there is no possibility whatsoever of forming an opinion as to whether the two operas really were identical. In all probability, in the source used by Hárich (the bill from Schellinger) the composer's name is not given at all; in that case, the bill could have referred just as well to another opera, *Il marchese villano* by Galuppi, which was performed in nearby Vienna and at Schönbrunn in 1767 (see Pohl, II, 375, and Anton Bauer, *Opern und Operetten in Wien:* [Graz, 1955], n. 2795).

1778 [12]

La sposa fedele. Dramma serio-giocoso. Guglielmi–P. Chiari. First performance at Eszterháza, May 3, 1778; eleven repetitions during 1778. Libretto preserved in National Library, Budapest; title page and cast (Hárich 59, no. 103 [which erroneously lists it as Sarti's work]; HOK, p. 75; Horányi p. 202). No performing material is preserved at all (probably lost in the fire).

L'astratto. Dramma giocoso. Piccini-Petrosellini. First performance at Eszterháza, July 12, 1778; four repetitions. No libretto has been traced so far, if it was printed at all. Not listed in Hárich 59 or Horányi. See HOK, p. 76. Music: only the score (of Viennese origin) and a single viola part (copied at Eszterháza) are preserved. For a description of Haydn's changes in the score, see HOK, pp. 200–202.

Il geloso in cimento. Dramma giocoso. Anfossi-Bertati. First performance at Eszterháza, September 10, 1778; three repetitions in 1778, continued into 1779. Libretto lost in 1945; cast unknown; title page (Hárich 59, no. 104; HOK, p. 76; Horányi, p. 202). Music: only Act I of the score (of Viennese origin) is preserved, with some traces of having been exposed to the fire in November 1779; orchestra and vocal parts in the archives were copied for the revival in 1785 (HOK, pp. 102, 297).

La Locanda. Dramma giocoso. Gazzaniga-Bertati. First performance at Eszterháza, November 22, 1778; two repetitions in 1778. Libretto (printed in Vienna) lost in 1945; title page (Hárich 59, no. 105; HOK, p. 76; Horányi, p. 202). Music: complete score (of Viennese

[12] For that single year, we fortunately possess a theatrical calendar for Eszterháza, prepared by the theatrical secretary, Bader, and republished in the Appendix to Pohl, II, 367 (the composer's names are arbitrarily and erroneously added by Pohl); Horányi, p. 230.

origin) and orchestra parts (copied in Eszterháza), and some of the vocal parts are preserved. For a description of Haydn's changes, see HOK, pp. 202–203.

This adds up to a total of four premières in 1778, all of the *opera buffa* type. All further opera performances listed for 1778 in Pohl, II, 367, were merely repetitions from the repertoire of 1776 and 1777: *Il finto pazzo* (Dittersdorf, not by Piccini, as listed in Pohl; three repetitions); *Il barone di Rocca Antica* (Dittersdorf, not Salieri; two repetitions); *La buona figliuola* (Piccini, six repetitions); *Arcifanfano* (Dittersdorf, not Gassmann; seven repetitions); *La Frascatana* (Paisiello, eight repetitions). Regarding the marionette performances, see HMO, *passim*.

1779

For this year no theatrical calendar is preserved; if it existed, it must have been destroyed in the fire of 1779. Accordingly, no precise first performance dates can be given here.

Le due contesse. Intermezzo per musica. Paisiello-Petrosellini. First performance at Eszterháza, March 1779. Libretto lost in 1945; title page (Hárich 59, no. 106; HOK, p. 78; Horányi, p. 204). Music: the full score (of Italian origin), full orchestra parts, and one vocal part (Livietta) are preserved. For a description of Haydn's changes, see HOK, p. 204.

I visionarij. Dramma giocoso. Guglielmi(?) or Astaritta(?)–Bertati. First performance at Eszterháza, March 1779 (the evidence is an estimate for costume costs). No printed libretto and no music extant. A libretto printed for Vienna, 1774, naming Astaritta as composer, was extant in the Esterházy libretto collection, whereas Hárich 59, p. 42, gives Guglielmi as composer (perhaps evidence may be available at Eisenstadt). No performing material is preserved (probably destroyed in November 1779).

La vera costanza. Dramma giocoso. Haydn-Puttini. First performance at Eszterháza, April 1779. Originally, the opera was commissioned for Vienna, about 1776, but intrigue prevented its performance. Libretto lost in 1945; title page and cast (Pohl, II, 87; Hárich 59, no. 108; HOK, p. 79; Horányi, p. 204). Revivals took place in 1785 and 1786 (Hárich 62, pp. 69, 93; HMO, p. 131). Modern edition of score by Landon (Henschel-Universal). No performing material has been preserved. Haydn's autograph turned up in Paris (Pohl, II, 88).

La Metilde ritrovata or *L'incognita perseguitata. Dramma giocoso.* Anfossi-Petrosellini. First performance at Eszterháza, July 1779. Libretto preserved in National Library, Budapest; title page and cast (Hárich 59, no. 109; HOK, p. 79; Horányi, p. 204). Music: complete score and orchestra parts (both of Viennese origin) preserved; vocal parts lost. See HOK, pp. 205–209, for a detailed description of Haydn's numerous changes in the score, including a complete insertion aria, "Quando la rosa," (HOK, p. 394).

L'isola d'Alcina. Dramma giocoso. Gazzaniga-Bertati (based on Ariosto's poem). First performance at Eszterháza, summer 1779. A revival took place in 1786 (Hárich 62, pp. 70, 93). Libretto lost in 1945; title page (Hárich 59, no. 110; HOK, p. 80; Horányi, p. 204). Music: the 1779 performance material completely lost; some music for the revival in 1786 preserved; score and vocal parts lost; orchestra parts (made by Esterházy copyists) preserved. For a description of Haydn's changes, see HOK, p. 306.

Le gelosie villane. Dramma giocoso. Sarti-Grandi (based on Goldoni). First performance at Eszterháza, summer 1779. Continued 1780–1781 and revived 1784 (HOK, p. 117; Hárich 62, pp. 32, 93). Libretto lost in 1945; title page and cast (Hárich 59, no. 111; HOK, p. 80; Horányi, p. 204). All music for the 1779 performance is lost. The material for the 1780 and 1784 revivals is preserved: complete score (of Italian origin), complete orchestra and vocal parts (Esterházy copyists). For a description of Haydn's changes, see HOK, pp. 234–237.

La villanella incostante, or *Le nozze disturbate.* Naumann-Bertati. First performance at Eszterháza, autumn 1779. No music extant, and no libretto (if it was printed at all). Not listed in Hárich 59 or Horányi; in HOK, p. 85, only performances for 1780 are listed. Evidence for the 1779 performance first produced by Hárich 62, p.

32 (the source is an estimate for costumes in the "Baucassa-Rechnungen" of September 1779). The performing parts must have been lost in the fire. Only the score (probably of Dresden origin) is preserved. For Haydn's numerous changes in the score, see HOK, pp. 217–219.

L'Amore soldato. Dramma giocoso. Felici–N. Tassi. First performance at Eszterháza, October 1779. The libretto (preserved in National Library, Budapest) erroneously names Sacchini as composer, while the music material of Eszterháza gives the right composer's name: Felici. For title page and cast, see Hárich 59, no. 112; HOK, p. 82; Horányi, p. 202. Complete score and parts (both of Italian origin) are extant. For Haydn's numerous changes, see HOK, pp. 209–213.

L'isola disabitata. Azione teatrale. Haydn-Metastasio. First performance at Eszterháza, December 6, 1779. Because of the fire that destroyed the theatre on November 18, the performance had to be transferred to the marionette theatre. Libretto lost in 1945; title page and cast (Pohl, II, 99; Hárich 59, no. 122; HOK, p. 83; Horányi, p. 204). No performing material for Eszterháza is preserved; even Haydn's autograph score may have been lost in the fire.

This adds up to a total of nine premières (among them eight of the *dramma giocoso–opera buffa* type) for 1779. No information has been made available for the repetitions performed in 1779.

1780

This year begins a new period in the operatic life of Eszterháza. The change did not affect the spirit established by Haydn and Prince Nicholas, but it meant a more efficient organization of theatrical life. This results in a much more complete preservation of theatrical and statistical documents: among others, a nearly complete series of *Stabenen* reports (reports for supernumeraries, with precise dates of performances and repetitions) and dated estimates for costume tailoring, helping us to reconstruct the cast if the libretto was lost. It was precisely a methodical evalution of these archive sources for 1780–1790 that helped the Esterházy archivist, Dr. Hárich, in 1962 to get rather far beyond the performance statistics given in 1960 in HOK. Accordingly, for that important period 1780–1790 we have to combine the statistical data in Hárich 62 with the pertinent information on musical sources available in HOK. The short listing of the most important data below will provide a useful survey. For each opera, the date of the first performance at Eszterháza is shown; then later performances, with page references to Hárich. At the end of each entry are guides to the fullest extant libretti and music.

La forza delle donne. Dramma giocoso. Anfossi-Bertati. February 17, 1780. Thirty repetitions (!) until November 1780 (Hárich 62, pp. 26, 94). Libretto lost in 1945; title page and cast preserved in an estimate for costume tailoring from February 16, 1780 (Hárich 59, no. 123; HOK, pp. 84–85; Horányi, p. 207). Orchestra parts (of Italian origin): transpositions, reorchestration, small insertions by Haydn (HOK, pp. 214 ff.).

La vendemmia. Dramma giocoso. Gazzaniga-Bertati. April 27, 1780. Eight repetitions in 1780 and one more in 1781 (Hárich 62, pp. 27, 94). Libretto lost in 1945; title page and cast preserved in a costume estimate (Hárich 59, no. 124; HOK, pp. 85 ff.; Horányi, p. 207). Complete score and orchestra parts (both of Italian, presumably Florentine, origin) with Haydn's changes (HOK, pp. 219 ff.).

La scuola dei gelosi. Dramma giocoso. Salieri-Mazzola. July 21, 1780. Twelve repetitions in 1780, ten more in 1781 (Hárich 62, pp. 28, 94). Libretto lost in 1945; title page and cast preserved in a costume estimate (Hárich 59, no. 125; HOK, p. 86; Horányi, p. 207). Complete score and orchestra parts, Italian; Haydn's fairly numerous changes include two important inserted arias, "Dice benissimo" and another with its text missing (HOK, pp. 223, 394).

La finta giardiniera. Dramma giocoso. Anfossi-(?). October 29, 1780. Four repetitions by November 1780 (Hárich 62, pp. 29, 94). Libretto preserved in National Library, Budapest (Hárich 59, no. 126; HOK, p. 87; Horányi, p. 207). Score and orchestra parts,

Italian, with Haydn's fairly numerous changes, including some reorchestrations and transpositions, mostly for L. Polzelli (HOK, pp. 229 ff.).

Thus there were altogether four first performances (all of the *dramma giocoso–opera buffa* type) in 1780, with respectively thirty-one, nine, thirteen, and five performances. As for the statistics of the operas kept in the repertory from the previous years, Hárich 62, p. 30, provides the following figures: *L'Amor soldato*, three performances; *L'isola disabitata*, one; *L'Amor artigiano*, fifteen; *Le gelosie villane*, sixteen. (*Le nozze disturbate*, or *La villanella incostante*, seems to have been rehearsed but not performed in 1780.) The total number of performances during the 1780 season is therefore ninety-three.

1781

La fedeltà premiata. Dramma giocoso. Haydn–A. B. Lorenzi. February 25, 1781; the different date given by Pohl and accepted in most of the literature is an error. Seventeen repetitions in 1781, nine in 1782, nine in 1783, and one in 1784 (Hárich 62, pp. 33, 94). Libretto lost in 1945; title page and cast (Pohl, II, 167; Hárich 59, no. 127; HOK, pp. 87, 101; Horányi, p. 204). Only one fragment of the autograph score preserved, with many self-corrections and changes by Haydn (HOK, pp. 262 ff.).

Isabella e Rodrigo. Dramma giocoso. Anfossi-Bertati. April 1781. Four repetions, all in the same month; by May 1781 the piece had been dropped (Hárich 62, pp. 34, 94). Libretto preserved at Eisenstadt (Hárich 59, no. 128; HOK, p. 91; Horányi, p. 207). Complete score and orchestra parts, Italian; vocal parts mostly lost; changes by Haydn, mostly to enrich the poor orchestration by Anfossi (HOK, pp. 237 ff.).

L'avaro deluso. Dramma giocoso. Paisiello–Abbate F. B. A. F. May 1781. Fifteen repetitions in 1781, three more in 1782 (Hárich 62, pp. 35, 94). Libretto preserved in the National Library, Vienna; Budapest copy lost in 1945 (Hárich 59, no. 129; HOK, p. 92; Horányi, p. 207). Only Act I of the score and some vocal parts preserved, hence exact amount of Haydn's changes uncertain.

Il francese bizzarro. Dramma giocoso. Astaritta-(?). July 1781. Four repetitions within the next month (Hárich 62, pp. 36, 95). Libretto not preserved, but printer's bill from June 1781 testifies to its printing (HOK, p. 93). Only a fragment from Act I of the score, Italian; many changes by Haydn (HOK, pp. 240 ff.).

Il convitato di pietra. Dramma tragicomico per musica. Righini–N. Porta. July 1781. Four repetitions up to September 1781 (Hárich 62, pp. 36, 95). Libretto in National Library, Vienna (Hárich 59, no. 130; HOK, p. 93; Horányi, p. 207). Complete score and orchestra parts, fragmentary vocal parts, all of Viennese origin; numerous changes by Haydn, including an inserted aria for L. Polzelli, "Mora l'infido—Mi sento nel seno" (HOK, pp. 241 ff.).

La schiava riconosciuta, or *Gli stravaganti. Dramma giocoso (farzetta).* Piccini-(?). August 1781. Two more performances in July 1782 (Hárich 62, pp. 36, 95). Libretto not preserved, but listed in a printer's bill, August 20, 1781 (HOK, p. 94). Complete orchestra parts and score; many changes, including insertions for L. Polzelli and added dynamic markings (HOK, pp. 246 ff.).

Thus 1781 saw six first performances, five of the *dramma giocoso* type and one *dramma tragicomico,* with seventeen, five, sixteen, five, five, and one performance respectively. For the operas kept in the repertory from previous years Hárich provides the following figures: *La Vendemmia,* one; *Le gelosie villane,* two; *La scuola dei gelosi,* ten; *La contadina in corte,* seven; adding up to a total of sixty-nine performances during the 1781 season.

1782

Zemira ed Azor. Translated from a French Comédie ballet. Grétry-Marmontel. February 1782. Five repetitions (Hárich 62, pp. 40, 95). No libretto traced; cast known only from a costume estimate (Hárich 59, no. 132; HOK, p. 99). Full score, probably of Viennese origin, full orchestra parts, and fragmentary vocal parts; moderate changes by Haydn (HOK, pp. 252 ff.).

La fiera di Venezia. Comedia per musica. Salieri-Boccherini. February 1782. Nine repetitions ending in July 1782 (Hárich 62, pp. 40, 95). Libretto, with cast, preserved at Eisenstadt (Hárich 59, no. 131; HOK, p. 99). Full score, of unknown origin, perhaps Viennese, and orchestra parts; changes by Haydn include cuts and tempo changes, e.g. from *andante maestoso* to *allegro vivace* (HOK, pp. 250 ff.).

Il cavaliere errante. Dramma eroicomico. Traëtta-Bertati. March 1782. Seven repetitions ending in July 1782 (Hárich 62, pp. 41, 95). Libretto lost in 1945; title page and cast preserved in an estimate for costume tailoring (Hárich 59, no. 133; HOK, p. 100; Horányi, p. 208). Only a fragment from Act I of the score, of Viennese origin, and some orchestra parts; numerous and important changes by Haydn, including some insertions (HOK, pp. 254 ff.).

L'innocente fortunata. Dramma giocoso. Paisiello-Livigni. April 1782. One performance only (Hárich 62, pp. 42, 95). No Eszterháza libretto preserved, but printer's bill shows it was printed (HOK, p. 100; Horányi, p. 208). Complete score and orchestra parts, of Italian origin; Haydn's changes mostly limited to cuts (HOK, pp. 259 ff.).

Lo sposo disperato. Dramma giocoso. Anfossi-Bertati. August 1782. Thirteen repetitions ending in November (Hárich 62, pp. 42, 95). No libretto preserved, but again printer's bill (HOK, p. 101; Horányi, p. 208). Orchestra parts and most vocal parts; unimportant changes (HOK, pp. 260 ff.).

Il curioso indiscreto. Dramma giocoso. Anfossi-(?). September 1782. Ten repetitions in 1782, five more in 1783 (Hárich 62, pp. 43, 95). No libretto traced (HOK, p. 103). Complete score, Italian, complete orchestra parts, and some vocal parts; changes by Haydn include enriching of Anfossi's poor orchestration, transpositions, cuts (HOK, p. 266).

I filosofi immaginarii. Dramma giocoso. Paisiello-Bertati. October 1782. Eight repetitions in 1782, nineteen in 1783, and five in 1784 (Hárich 62, pp. 43, 95). No libretto traced; cast unknown (HOK, p. 103). Complete score and orchestra parts, both Viennese; limited changes by Haydn (HOK, pp. 268 ff.).

Orlando Paladino. Dramma eroicomico. Haydn–N. Porta (based on the poem by Ariosto). December 6, 1782. Three repetitions in 1782, nineteen (!) in 1783, and seven in 1784 (Hárich 62, pp. 45, 96). Libretto preserved in National Library, Budapest (Pohl, II, 194; Hárich 59, no. 135; HOK, p. 101; Horányi, p. 208). Haydn's autograph score partly in London, partly in Marburg; only some vocal parts for 1782 preserved in Budapest; MS copy of full score made for Mannheim in 1792, with German text, includes some autograph corrections by Haydn (HOK, pp. 265 ff.).

This list indicates a total of eight first performances (five of the *dramma giocoso* type, one translation from the French, plus two pieces called *dramma eroicomico*) in 1782, with respectively six, ten, eight, one, fourteen, eleven, nine, and four performances for the operas listed above. As for the operas kept on from the previous years, Hárich 62, p. 47, provides the following figures: *L'avaro deluso,* three; *La contadina in corte,* thirteen; *La schiava riconosciuta,* two; and *La fedeltà premiata,* nine; adding up to a total of ninety performances during the 1782 season.

1783

Il ratto della sposa. Dramma giocoso. Guglielmi-Martinelli. March 1783. Only one repetition (Hárich 62, pp. 48, 96). No libretto traced; Haydn's MS draft for the cast preserved at Eisenstadt (Hárich 59, p. 35; HOK, p. 106; Hárich 62, p. 48). Full score, complete orchestra parts, and one single vocal part—Polidoro; limited, routine changes by Haydn (HOK, pp. 269 ff.).

La vedova scaltra. Commedia per musica. Righini-(?). March 1783. Fourteen repetitions (Hárich 62, pp. 49, 96). No libretto traced; Haydn's MS draft for the cast preserved at Eisenstadt (Hárich 59, p. 35; HOK, p. 107). Complete score (Viennese), orchestra parts, and some vocal parts, copied in and for Eszterháza; numerous changes by Haydn including reorchestrations, inserted pieces (HOK, pp. 271 ff.).

L'italiana in Londra. Intermezzo per musica. Cimarosa-Petrosellini. May 4, 1783. Four repetitions in 1783, three in 1787, seven in 1788

(Hárich 62, pp. 49, 96). No Eszterháza libretto preserved; cast known from estimate for costume tailoring (HOK, p. 108). Complete score, orchestra parts, of Italian origin, and some vocal parts; routine changes by Haydn (HOK, pp. 274 ff.).

Giulio Sabino. Dramma per musica. Sarti-Giovannini. May 21, 1783. Seventeen repetitions in 1783, seven in 1784, nine in 1786, two in 1787 (Hárich 62, pp. 49, 96). Libretto preserved in National Library, Budapest (Hárich 59, no. 139; HOK, p. 109; Horányi, p. 214). Orchestra and vocal parts, copied in and for Eszterháza; Haydn's changes in this important *opera seria* limited to a few cuts (HOK, pp. 276 ff.).

Fra i due litiganti il terzo gode. Dramma giocoso. Sarti-(?) (based on a Goldoni play). August 10, 1783. Nine repetitions in 1783, eight in 1784 (Hárich 62, pp. 50, 96). No Eszterháza libretto preserved, but printer's bill shows it was printed; cast known from a costume estimate (HOK, p. 111). Complete score, of Viennese origin; full orchestra and fragmentary vocal parts, both copied in Eszterháza; routine changes by Haydn, mostly cuts (HOK, pp. 278 ff.).

Il falegname. Commedia per musica. Cimarosa-Palomba. November 1783. Two repetitions in 1783, one more in 1784 (Hárich 62, pp. 50, 96). Libretto lost in 1945; cast known from an estimate for costume tailoring (Hárich 59, no. 140; HOK, p. 111). Complete score, Viennese; complete orchestra and fragmentary vocal parts, copied in Eszterháza; Haydn's dynamic markings, insertions, cuts (HOK, pp. 279 ff.).

These six first performances (with respectively two, fifteen, five, eighteen, ten, and three performances of the works in 1783) included five *giocoso*-type works and one tragedy (*Giulio Sabino*, with its eighteen performances making it the most performed première opera of the season). As for the operas in the repertory from previous years, Hárich 62, p. 52, provides the following figures: *I filosofi immaginarii,* nineteen (!); *Orlando Paladino,* nineteen; *La fedeltà premiata,* nine; and *Il curioso indiscreto,* five; adding up to a total of 105 performances (premières plus repetitions) in 1783.

1784

Armida. Dramma eroico. Haydn-Durandi (based on the poem by Tasso). February 26, 1784. Twenty (!) repetitions in 1784, seventeen in 1785, seven in 1786, five in 1787, and four in 1788 (Hárich 62, pp. 53, 97). Libretto lost in 1945; title page and cast (Pohl, II, 200; Hárich 59, no. 142; HOK, p. 114; Horányi, p. 214). Haydn's autograph score preserved in the library of the Royal College of Music, London; modern edition by Wilhelm Pfannkuch in *Werke* (Munich, 1965).

I viaggiatori felici. Dramma giocoso. Anfossi-Livigni. March 21, 1784. Seventeen repetitions in 1784, fourteen in 1787, three in 1788 (Hárich 62, pp. 54, 97). Libretto lost in 1945; title page and cast reconstructed from an estimate for costume tailoring (Hárich 59, no. 144; HOK, p. 115; Horányi, p. 214). Complete score, Viennese; nearly complete orchestra parts and very fragmentary vocal parts, copied at Eszterháza (HOK, pp. 282 ff.).

L'amor costante. Dramma giocoso. Cimarosa–N. Porta (based on a Bertati play). April 27, 1784. Nine repetitions in 1784 (Hárich 62, pp. 54, 97). Libretto lost in 1945; title page and cast from a costume estimate (Hárich 59, no. 143; HOK, p. 116; Horányi, p. 214). Complete score, Italian; complete orchestra parts and fragmentary vocal parts, copied at Eszterháza (HOK, pp. 283 ff.).

La Didone abbandonata. Dramma per musica. Sarti-Metastasio. July 26, 1784. Eight repetitions in 1784, six in 1785 (Hárich 62, pp. 55, 97). Libretto preserved in National Library, Budapest (Hárich 59, no. 145; HOK, p. 118; Horányi, p. 214). Complete score, Viennese; complete orchestra parts and some vocal parts, copied at Eszterháza; Haydn seems to have respected Sarti's masterwork in the *opera seria* genre, keeping his changes within moderate limits (HOK, pp. 286 ff.).

La villanella rapita. Dramma giocoso. Bianchi-Bertati (based on Favart's play). August 29, 1784. Nine repetitions in 1784, seven in 1785, eleven in 1786, eleven in 1787 (Hárich 62, pp. 56, 97). Libretto lost in 1945; title page and cast from an estimate for costume tailoring (Hárich 59, no. 146; HOK, p. 119; Horányi, p. 214). Complete score, of Venetian origin; complete orchestra parts and fragmentary vocal parts, copied at Eszterháza (HOK, pp. 288 ff.).

L'isola di Calipso abbandonata. Componimento drammatico. Bologna–Cigna-Santi. November 11, 1784. One repetition in 1784, eleven in 1785, nine in 1786, ten in 1787, four in 1788, four in 1789, and one in 1790 (Hárich 62, pp. 56, 98). No libretto preserved; cast from an estimate for costume tailoring (HOK, p. 120). All performing material for Eszterháza lost.

Within this total of six premières (with respectively twenty-one, eighteen, ten, nine, ten, and two performances in 1784), there were three *giocoso*-type works, two tragedies (Haydn's *Armida* with its twenty-one performances having been the most performed première opera of the season), and one *componimento drammatico*. A strong preference for serious subjects is clearly evident. As for the operas kept in the repertory from the previous years, Hárich 62, p. 59, provides the following figures: *Fra i due litiganti*, eight; *Il falegname*, one; *I filosofi immaginarii*, five; *Orlando Paladino*, seven; *Giulio Sabino*, seven; *La fedeltà premiata*, one; *Le gelosie villane*, five; adding up to a total of 104 performances in the season.

1785

I contrattempi. Dramma giocoso. Sarti–N. Porta. April 1785. Two repetitions (Hárich 62, pp. 60, 98). No libretto for Eszterháza preserved, but printer's bill shows it was printed; cast preserved in estimate for costume tailoring (HOK, p. 117). Complete score, of Dresden or Viennese origin; complete orchestra parts, copied at Eszterháza; changes by Haydn include transpositions and reorchestrations for L. Polzelli (HOK, p. 284).

Montezuma. Dramma per musica. Zingarelli–Cigna-Santi. June 5, 1785. Five repetitions (Hárich 62, pp. 61, 98). Libretto lost in 1945; title page and cast from a costume estimate (Hárich 59, no. 148; HOK, p. 125; Horányi, p. 215). Complete score, Italian; orchestra parts copied for Eszterháza; many cuts and changes by Haydn (HOK, pp. 290 ff.).

Il matrimonio per inganno. Dramma giocoso. Anfossi-Bertati. July 3, 1785. Six repetitions (Hárich 62, pp. 61, 98). Libretto preserved in National Library, Budapest (Hárich 59, no. 149; HOK, p. 126; Horányi, p. 215). Complete score, of Italian origin, probably Florentine; orchestra parts copied at Eszterháza; changes by Haydn including transpositions, cuts, and the inserted aria "Signor voi sapete" (HOK, pp. 294 ff., 395).

Le astuzie di Bettina. Dramma giocoso. Stabingher-(?). October 1785. Three repetitions in 1785, nine in 1786 (Hárich 62, pp. 61, 98). Libretto preserved in National Library, Budapest (Hárich 59, no. 150; HOK, p. 126; Horányi, p. 215). Only Act I of the score (Italian), and some fragmentary orchestra and vocal parts, copied at Eszterháza (HOK, pp. 296 ff.).

Thus only a modest total of four premières (three of the *dramma giocoso* type and only one tragedy) was presented in 1785, with respectively three, six, seven, and four performances. As for the operas kept on the program from previous years, Hárich 62, p. 64, provides the following figures: *La vera costanza*, seventeen; *L'isola di Calipso*, eleven; *Armida*, seventeen; *Didone abbandonata*, six; *Il geloso in cimento*, eleven (enriched with a new inserted aria by Haydn, "Dica pure"; see HOK, p. 395); and *La villanella rapita*, seven; adding up to a total of eighty-nine performances in the 1785 season.

1786

Most of our information on the casts of this year is derived from a plan called "Piano dimostrativo per la distribuzione di dieci opere . . ." compiled by stage director N. Porta.

Alsinda. Dramma per musica. Zingarelli-Moretti. March 1, 1786. Twelve repetitions (Hárich 62, pp. 65, 99). A copy of the Eszterháza libretto preserved at the National Library, Vienna (HOK, p. 131). Complete score, Italian, probably Milanese; fragmentary orchestra and vocal parts, copied at Eszterháza; numerous changes by Haydn, including drastic cuts (HOK, pp. 300 ff.).

La ballerina amante. Melodramma giocoso. Cimarosa-Casini(?). April 2, 1786. Five repetitions (Hárich 62, pp. 65, 99). Libretto preserved at the National Library, Vienna (Horányi, p. 215; HOK, p. 131). Complete score, Italian; complete orchestra parts and fragmentary vocal parts, both copied at Eszterháza; drastic cuts by Haydn (HOK, pp. 302 ff.).

Chi dell'altrui si veste, presto si spoglia. Dramma giocoso. Cimarosa-Palomba. May 2, 1786. Two repetitions (Hárich 62, pp. 65, 99). Libretto lost in 1945; title page and cast (Hárich 59, no. 153; HOK, p. 131; Horányi, p. 215). Complete score, Italian; orchestra parts copied at Eszterháza; drastic cuts by Haydn (HOK, pp. 304 ff.).

Ifigenia in Tauride. Dramma per musica. Traëtta-Coltellini. July 4, 1786. Four repetitions (Hárich 62, pp. 65, 99). Libretto lost in 1945; title page and cast (Hárich 59, no. 154; HOK, p. 132; Horányi, p. 215). Complete score, Viennese; changes by Haydn include drastic cuts and an inserted aria, "Ah tu non senti amico" (HOK, pp. 307 ff.).

L'albergatrice vivace. Dramma giocoso. Caruso-(?). August 6, 1786. Seven repetitions (Hárich 62, pp. 65, 99). No Eszterháza libretto preserved, but printer's bill from July 1786 shows it was printed (HOK, p. 132). Fragments of the score (Italian), and some of the orchestra and vocal parts copied at Eszterháza; moderate changes by Haydn (HOK, pp. 310 ff.).

L'incontro inaspettato. Commedia per musica. Righini–da Ponte. October 1, 1786. Two repetitions (Hárich 62, pp. 65, 99). One copy of the Eszterháza libretto preserved in the Library of the Gesellschaft der Musikfreunde, Vienna (HOK, p. 133; Horányi, p. 215). Complete score (Viennese), and some orchestra parts; mostly simple cuts by Haydn (HOK, pp. 311 ff.).

Idalide. Dramma per musica. Sarti-Moretti. October 24, 1786. Five repetitions in 1786, four in 1787 (Hárich 62, pp. 68, 99). Libretto lost in 1945; title page and cast (Hárich 59, no. 155; HOK, p. 134; Horányi, p. 216). Complete score, Italian; fragmentary orchestra parts and some vocal parts, copied for Eszterháza (HOK, pp. 314 ff.).

I due baroni di Rocca Azzurra. Dramma giocoso. Cimarosa-Palomba. December 6, 1786. Two repetitions in 1786, two more in 1787 (Hárich 62, pp. 68, 99). No libretto for Eszterháza preserved (HOK, p. 135). Complete score, Italian; fragmentary orchestra and vocal parts, copied for Eszterháza (HOK, pp. 315 ff.).

These eight première operas (three tragedies and five of the *dramma giocoso* type—a rather happy balance of genres) had respectively thirteen, six, three, five, eight, three, six, and three performances. Kept in the repertory from previous years (Hárich 62, p. 71) were: *Le astuzie di Bettina,* nine; *La villanella rapita,* eleven; *La vera costanza,* four; *Il geloso in cimento,* ten; *L'isola di Calipso,* nine; *Armida,* seven; *Giulio Sabino,* nine; *Il matrimonio per inganno,* seventeen; and *L'isola d'Alcina,* two; adding up to a total of 125 performances.

1787

Il sordo e l'avaro. Dramma giocoso. Anfossi-Bertati. February 1787. Four repetitions (Hárich 62, pp. 72, 99). Libretto lost in 1945; title page and cast from an estimate for costume tailoring (Hárich 59, no. 156; HOK, p. 138; Horányi, p. 216). All performing material for Eszterháza lost.

Il disertore. Dramma per musica. Bianchi-Benincasa. April 1787. Five repetitions in 1787, nine in 1788, seven in 1789 (Hárich 62, pp. 73, 99). Eszterháza libretto preserved in National Library, Budapest (Hárich 59, no. 159; HOK, p. 138; Horányi, p. 216). Complete score, of Venetian origin; fragmentary orchestra and vocal parts, copied at Eszterháza; changes include a complete inserted aria, "Un cor si tenero" (see HOK, p. 396), and numerous dynamic and tempo markings, indicating that Haydn was remarkably impressed by Bianchi's music for this important dramatic piece (HOK, pp. 318 ff.).

La Quakera spiritosa. Dramma giocoso. Guglielmi-Palomba. June 3, 1787. Ten repetitions in 1787, four in 1788 (Hárich 62, pp. 73, 99). Eszterháza libretto lost in 1945; title page and cast (Hárich 59, no. 157; HOK, pp. 139, 321; Horányi, p. 216). Complete score, Italian; complete orchestra parts and fragmentary vocal parts, copied at

Eszterháza; numerous changes by Haydn including a complete inserted aria, "Vada adagio signorina" (HOK, pp. 396, 320 ff.).

Alessandro nell'Indie. Dramma per musica. Bianchi-Metastasio. July 26, 1787. Two repetitions in 1787, eight in 1788 (Hárich 62, pp. 74, 100). Eszterháza libretto lost in 1945; cast reconstructed from the score (HOK, p. 324; Hárich 59, no. 158; HOK, p. 140; Horányi, p. 216). Complete score, of Venetian origin; fragmentary orchestra and vocal parts, copied at Eszterháza; Haydn's inserted aria, "Chi vive amante" (HOK, pp. 324 ff., 396).

Le gare generose. Dramma giocoso. Paisiello-Palomba. September 18, 1787. Four repetitions in 1787, fourteen in 1788, six in 1789, one in 1790 (Hárich 62, pp. 74, 100). No Eszterháza libretto preserved, but a Viennese printer's bill, August 20, 1787, proves at least the printing of a new title page for Eszterháza (HOK, p. 140). Fragmentary score, Viennese; complete orchestra parts and fragmentary vocal parts, both copied at Eszterháza; many dynamic and tempo markings by Haydn, indicating that he was rather impressed by Paisiello's masterpiece (HOK, pp. 327 ff.).

Thus there was a total of five premières (among them two of the *opera seria* type) with respectively five, six, eleven, three, and five performances. Kept in the repertory from previous years (Hárich 62, p. 77) were: *I due baroni di Rocca Azzurra,* two; *L'isola di Calipso,* ten; *Idalide,* four; *Il geloso in cimento,* seventeen; *Armida,* five; *I viaggiatori felici,* fourteen; *La villanella rapita,* eleven; *Giulio Sabino,* two; and *L'italiana in Londra,* three; adding up to a total of ninety-eight performances.

1788

Giunio Bruto. Dramma tragico. Cimarosa-Acanzio. February 2, 1788. Two repetitions (Hárich 62, pp. 78, 100). Eszterháza libretto preserved in National Library, Budapest (Hárich 59, no. 160; HOK, p. 144). Complete score, of Italian origin, possibly Genovese; complete orchestra parts and fragmentary vocal parts, copied at Eszterháza; Cimarosa's original affected less than usual by Haydn's cuts (HOK, pp. 329 ff.).

I finti eredi. Dramma giocoso. Sarti-Bertati. March 9, 1788. Fifteen repetitions in 1788, three in 1789, one in 1790 (Hárich 62, pp. 78, 100). No Eszterháza libretto preserved, but a bill from the Viennese printer Facci proves existence of at least a new title page; cast reconstructed from notes in the score (HOK, p. 145). Complete score, Viennese; complete orchestra parts and some vocal parts, copied at Eszterháza; Haydn's numerous changes include the in-serted aria, "Se tu mi sprezzi ingrata," and another aria with text missing (HOK, pp. 331 ff., 396).

I due castellani burlati. Dramma giocoso. Fabrizi-Livigni. July 6, 1788. Seven repetitions in 1788, five in 1789 (Hárich 62, pp. 79, 100). No Eszterháza libretto preserved (HOK, p. 146). Performing mate-rial completely lost.

La vendetta di Nino. Melodramma tragico per musica. Prati-Moretti. August 1, 1788. Eleven repetitions in 1788, thirteen in 1789 (Hárich 62, pp. 79, 100). Libretto lost in 1945; title page (Hárich 59, no. 161; HOK, p. 146; Horányi, p. 218). All performing parts lost; only a substantial fragment of the score preserved, with title page and first section missing; some changes by Haydn (HOK, pp. 336, 373).

Orfeo ed Euridice. Azione teatrale. Bertoni-Calzabigi. September 1788. One repetition in 1788, two in 1789 (Hárich 62, pp. 80, 100). Eszterháza libretto preserved in National Library, Budapest (Hárich 59, no. 162; HOK, p. 147; Horányi, p. 218). All performing material lost.

Il marito disperato. Dramma giocoso. Cimarosa-Lorenzi. October 1788. Three repetitions (Hárich 62, pp. 80, 101). Eszterháza libretto lost in 1945; title page and cast reconstructed from MS notes in the score and an estimate for costumes (Hárich 59, no. 163; HOK, p. 148; Horányi, p. 216). Complete score, of Italian origin; complete orchestra parts and fragmentary vocal parts, copied at Eszterháza (HOK, pp. 336 ff.). Only slight cuts by Haydn.

Il tamburo notturno. Dramma giocoso. Paisiello–G. B. Lorenzi (based on Bertati's play). December 1788. One repetition in 1788, five in 1789, one in 1790 (Hárich 62, pp. 80, 101). No Eszterháza libretto preserved (HOK, p. 152). All performing material lost.

Total: seven premières (four of the *dramma giocoso* type, contrasted with three tragedies) with respectively three, sixteen, eight, twelve, two, four, and two performances. Repetitions from previous years (Hárich 62, p. 83) were: *Il disertore*, nine; *Le gare generose*, fourteen; *L'italiana in Londra*, seven; *I viaggiatori felici*, three; *Alessandro nell'Indie*, eight; *La Quakera spiritosa*, four; *Armida*, four; *La contadina di spirito*, four; *L'isola di Calipso*, four; *Il matrimonio per inganno*, four; adding up to a total of 108 performances.

1789

I due supposti conti. Dramma giocoso. Cimarosa-Anelli. February 1789. Six repetitions (Hárich 62, pp. 85, 101). No Eszterháza libretto traced; cast unknown (HOK, p. 153). Complete score and fragmentary vocal parts, Milanese; complete orchestra parts, copied at Eszterháza; Haydn's changes include complete inserted aria, "Infelice sventurata," and some other significant changes in Cimarosa's score (HOK, pp. 338 ff., 396).

Le gelosie fortunate. Dramma giocoso. Anfossi-Livigni. May 1789. Six repetitions (Hárich 62, pp. 85, 101). Eszterháza libretto lost; title page (Hárich 59, no. 164; HOK, p. 153; Horányi, p. 218). Complete score, Viennese; orchestra parts, copied at Eszterháza; Haydn's changes mostly drastic cuts—he eliminated even Mozart's aria, "Un bacio di mano," inserted for the 1788 Vienna performance (HOK, pp. 341 ff.).

Il pittore parigino. Dramma per musica (properly, *dramma giocoso*). Cimarosa-Petrosellini. June 1789. Nine repetitions in 1789, seven in 1790 (Hárich 62, pp. 85, 101). Eszterháza libretto lost in 1945; title page (Hárich 59, no. 166; HOK, p. 154; Horányi, p. 218). Complete score, Viennese; complete orchestra parts and fragmentary vocal parts, copied at Eszterháza; routine changes, mostly cuts (HOK, pp. 343 ff.).

La Circe, ossia L'isola incantata. Dramma per musica (properly, *dramma giocoso*). This is an Eszterháza *pasticcio* made up of the following: *La maga Circe* by Anfossi, providing most of the score;

L'ipocondriaco by Naumann; and finally some important additions by Haydn himself. There is no connection whatever with the *dramma per musica*, *Circe*, by Cimarosa. July 1789. Eleven repetitions in 1789, four in 1790 (Hárich 62, pp. 86, 101). Eszterháza libretto lost in 1945; title page (Hárich 59, no. 165; HOK, p. 154; Horányi, p. 218). Score and performing parts, put together from the above-mentioned three sources (HOK, pp. 345–353).

Le vicende d'amore. Dramma per musica (properly, *dramma giocoso*). Guglielmi-(?). October 1789. Four repetitions in 1789, nine in 1790 (Hárich 62, pp. 86, 101). Eszterháza libretto lost in 1945; title page (Hárich 59, no. 167; HOK, p. 154; Horányi, p. 218). Score, Viennese; only a few changes by Haydn (HOK, pp. 353 ff.).

L'arbore di Diana. Dramma giocoso. Martin–da Ponte. November 1789. Four repetitions in 1789, six in 1790 (Hárich 62, pp. 86, 101). Eszterháza libretto lost in 1945; merely a title-page version of a Viennese libretto printed in 1787 (Hárich 59, no. 168; HOK, p. 155; Horányi, p. 216). Complete score and vocal parts, purchased from Vienna; orchestra parts, copied at Eszterháza, with important notes on the cast; very limited changes—Haydn must have been impressed by this fine score by Martin (HOK, pp. 354 ff.).

The total for 1789 was six premières (all of the *dramma giocoso* type, notwithstanding the misleading subtitles in some of the libretti) with respectively seven, seven, ten, twelve, five, and five performances. Repetitions from previous years (Hárich 62, p. 87): *La vendetta di Nino*, thirteen; *Il tamburo notturno*, five; *Il disertore*, seven; *Le gare generose*, six; *L'isola di Calipso*, four; *Orfeo ed Euridice*, two; *I due castellani*, five; *La contadina di spirito*, one; and *I finti eredi*, three; for a total of ninety-two performances.

1790

Il barbiere di Siviglia. Dramma giocoso. Paisiello-Petrosellini (based on Beaumarchais's play). May 9, 1790. Eight repetitions (Hárich 62, pp. 88, 102). Eszterháza libretto, lost in 1945, was only a title-page version of a libretto printed for Vienna, 1783 (Hárich 59, no. 170;

HOK, p. 161; Horányi, p. 222). Fragmentary score, Viennese; fragmentary orchestra and vocal parts, copied at Eszterháza, mixed up with other performing materials with German text, used in a later performance; Haydn apparently fascinated by Paisiello's masterwork—usual changes limited to a few additions of expressive dynamic and tempo markings, and only a few cuts (HOK, pp. 355 ff.).

L'impresario in angustie and *Il credulo*. Both *Farse in un atto*. Cimarosa-Diodati. June 6, 1790; only one performance (Hárich 62, pp. 88, 102). Eszterháza libretto lost in 1945; title pages (Hárich 59, nos. 172, 173; HOK, p. 161; Horányi, p. 222). Scores, Italian; parts, copied at Eszterháza; Haydn's changes more numerous and obvious in the *Impresario*, including an inserted aria, "Il meglio mio carattere" (HOK, pp. 357 ff.).

L'amor contrastato. Commedia per musica. Paisiello-Palomba. July 13, 1790. Three repetitions (Hárich 62, pp. 88, 102). Eszterháza libretto lost in 1945; title page (Hárich 59, no. 174; HOK, p. 161; Horányi, p. 218). All performing material lost.

The death of Prince Nicholas on September 28, 1790, put a sudden end to the operatic performances at Eszterháza Palace. Thus the 1790 season was an unusually short one—February to September. In this time there were four premières (all belonging to the *giocoso* genre) including two one-act pieces performed on the same night, with respectively nine, one, one, and four performances. Repetitions from previous years (Hárich 62, p. 91): *L'arbore di Diana*, six; *I finti eredi*, one; *Il pittore parigino*, seven; *La Circe*, four; *Le gare generose*, one; *Il tamburo notturno*, one; *Le vicende d'amore*, nine; *L'amor artigiano* (in a remarkably reworked version with new arias by Haydn), eight; and *L'isola di Calipso*, one; adding up to a total of fifty-three unmistakably identified opera performances during that eight months' season. (Eight more performances are mentioned in Hárich 62, pp. 91–92, without a precise identification of the operas performed.)

Five more operas can be supposed to have been prepared for

1790; whether they were really performed, in August–September 1790, cannot be proved. These are:

Giannina e Bernardone. Dramma giocoso. Cimarosa-Livigni. No Eszterháza libretto traced. Score (Viennese) and orchestra parts, copied at Eszterháza, were ready for performance by August 1790; inserted aria by Haydn, "La moglie quando è buona" (HOK, pp. 363 ff.).

Le nozze di Figaro. Commedia per musica. Mozart-da Ponte. No Eszterháza libretto traced, but performing parts were copied and costumes designed; for detailed description of the music preserved, see HOK, pp. 366 ff. No changes by Haydn found.

Il rè Teodoro in Venezia. Dramma eroicomico. Paisiello–G. B. Casti. No Eszterháza libretto traced. Score and vocal parts purchased from Vienna; copying of orchestra parts just started at Eszterháza, then left unfinished in September 1790; a few changes by Haydn (HOK, p. 366).

Axur rè d'Ormus. Dramma tragicomico. Salieri–da Ponte. No Eszterháza libretto traced. Score purchased from Vienna; orchestra and vocal parts copied at Eszterháza; preparatory work by Haydn—some cuts—just started and then left unfinished (HOK, pp. 368 ff.).

Riccardo (an Italian version of *Richard Cœur de Lion*). Grétry-Sedaine. Score purchased from Italy; copying of vocal parts started in September 1790—one single sheet of a vocal part in an Eszterháza copyist's handwriting preserved; orchestra parts not even started; no trace of Haydn's usual changes.

SYSTEMATIC SURVEY OF HAYDN'S OPERA REPERTORY, 1776–1790.[13]

1776. 4 premières of the *giocoso* type (3 by Dittersdorf, 1 by Piccini), plus 1 serious drama by Gluck(?).

---

[13] In this survey we have to sum up all works of *opera buffa* character under the common denominator *giocoso* (including *dramma giocoso, operetta giocosa,* and *intermezzo*). It may be worth mentioning that the traditional term *opera buffa* was no longer used in the 1780's; for that very reason we have dismissed its use. *Opera buffa* was a perfectly adequate term for the lower-class farce up to 1750; the middle-class

1777. 5 premières, all of the *giocoso* type (Paisiello, 2; Dittersdorf, Gassmann, Haydn, 1 each). Number of "reprises" (continued performances) unknown.

1778. 4 premières, all of the *giocoso* type (Anfossi, Gazzaniga, Guglielmi, Piccini). 5 reprises (Dittersdorf, 3; Piccini, Paisiello, 1 each).

1779. 9 premières, 8 of the *giocoso* type, plus 1 *azione teatrale* (a neutral genre) (Haydn, 2; Anfossi, Gazzaniga, Guglielmi, Felici, Naumann, Paisiello, Sarti, 1 each). Number of reprises unknown.

1780. A somewhat disturbed season, immediately following the fire in November 1779. 4 premières, all of the *giocoso* type (Anfossi, 2; Gazzaniga, Salieri, 1 each). 5 reprises (Felici, Haydn, Gassmann, Naumann, Sarti).

1781. 6 premières (by Anfossi, Astaritta, Haydn, Paisiello, Piccini, Righini), among them 5 of the *giocoso* type, plus 1 *dramma tragicomico* (*Il convitato di pietra*). 4 reprises (Gazzaniga, Sacchini, Sarti, Salieri), all of *giocoso* character.

1782. 8 premières (Anfossi, 2; Paisiello, 2; Grétry, Haydn, Salieri, Traëtta, 1 each), 5 in the *giocoso* genre, 2 *eroicomico*, 1 translation from French. 4 reprises (Haydn, Paisiello, Piccini, Sacchini), all in the *giocoso* genre.

1783. 6 premières (Cimarosa, 2; Sarti, 2; Guglielmi, Righini, 1 each), 5 in the *giocoso* genre, plus 1 tragedy (*Giulio Sabino*). 4 reprises (Haydn, 2; Anfossi, Paisiello, 1 each), 3 in the *giocoso* genre, 1 *eroicomico*.

1784. 6 premières (Anfossi, Bianchi, Bologna, Cimarosa, Haydn, Sarti—a clear-cut tendency toward enlarging the repertory by including more composers), 3 in the *giocoso* genre, 2 tragedies (among them, Haydn's *Armida* being the favorite of the program), plus 1 *componimento drammatico* (neutral genre). 7 reprises (Sarti, 3; Haydn, 2; Cimarosa, Paisiello, 1 each), 5 in the *giocoso* genre, 1 tragedy, 1 *eroicomico*.

1785. 4 premières (Anfossi, Sarti, Stabingher, Zingarelli), 3 in the

comedy (this antithesis is used by D. J. Grout in his *Short History of Opera*, p. 247) of the 1770's and 1780's tended to adopt the generic term *dramma giocoso*.

giocoso genre, 1 tragedy. 6 reprises (Haydn, 2; Anfossi, Bianchi, Bologna, Sarti, 1 each), 4 in the *giocoso* genre, 2 tragedies.

1786. 8 premières (Cimarosa, 3; Caruso, Righini, Traëtta, Sarti, Zingarelli; 1 each), 5 in the *giocoso* genre, plus 3 tragedies. As a whole, an energetic tendency toward enlarging the repertory is discernible among the premières; especially the relatively high ratio of tragedies is remarkable. 9 reprises (Anfossi, 2; Haydn, 2; Bianchi, Bologna, Gazzaniga, Sarti, Stabingher, 1 each), 7 in the *giocoso* genre, 2 tragedies.

1787. Only 5 premières, perhaps as a reaction to the overstrained program of the previous year (Bianchi, 2; Anfossi, Guglielmi, Paisiello, 1 each), 3 in the *giocoso* genre, 2 tragedies. 9 reprises (Anfossi, 2; Cimarosa, 2; Sarti, 2; Bianchi, Bologna, Haydn, 1 each), 6 in the *giocoso* genre, 3 tragedies. Again the ratio of tragedies is remarkable.

1788. 7 premières (Cimarosa, 2; Bertoni, Fabrizi, Paisiello, Prati, Sarti, 1 each), 4 in the *giocoso* genre, 3 tragedies. 10 reprises (Anfossi, 2; Bianchi, 2; Paisiello, 2; Cimarosa, Guglielmi, Haydn, Bologna, 1 each), 7 in the *giocoso* genre, 3 tragedies.

1789. 6 premières (Anfossi, 2; Cimarosa, 2; Guglielmi, Martin, 1 each), all of them in the *giocoso* genre. 9 reprises (Paisiello, 3; Bianchi, Bertoni, Bologna, Fabrizi, Prati, Sarti, 1 each), 6 of them in the *giocoso* genre, 3 tragedies (a belated reflection of the tendency toward serious drama in 1785–1787).

1790. 4 premières (Cimarosa, 2; Paisiello, 2), all in the *giocoso* genre. 9 reprises (Cimarosa, 2; Paisiello, 2; Bologna, Gassmann, Guglielmi, Martin, Sarti, 1 each), all in the *giocoso* genre, perhaps reflecting the need of gay entertainment for ailing Prince Nicholas.

A short evaluation of the data provided in the chronological lists must keep two special points of interest in mind. First is the importance of Haydn's adaptation work as evidenced in the Italian scores he prepared for performance at Eszterháza. We know of no single instance in operatic history when a composer of Haydn's stature, working through many years as an opera conductor, adjusted so many contemporary composers' operas to his prince's (and probably his own) taste. In the history of musical judgment and creative criticism (a book that still waits to be written) these scores revised by Haydn will provide an important contribution toward our understanding of the classical idiom of Haydn and Mozart. All the pertinent testimony of the Esterházy sources is dealt with in detail in HOK, pp. 177–378 ("Catalogue raisonné der Esterházy-Opernsammlung"), and a short résumé of the principal points discussed there was given in my article "Haydn the Opera Conductor," *Music Review* (1963), pp. 313 ff.[14] A comprehensive idea of Haydn's methods may be indicated by listing some typical features of his changes:

1. In many cases, Haydn considered the orchestration of Italian operas too thin and added, quite often in his own hand, a number of additional parts (mainly oboes and horns).

2. The melodic ardor (*Melodienseligkeit*) of some Italian composers (especially Cimarosa and Anfossi), with its obvious melodic repetitiveness, proved rather tiresome to the mature Haydn; he therefore rigorously cut either entire numbers or portions of them, particularly when there was much repetition of motifs.

3. Haydn tried to set a limit to the pretensions of his Italian singers by simply pruning away empty *colorature;* he cut those places in the original score where the singer would have an opportunity for improvising a cadenza.

4. Haydn took special care of his favorite, Luigia Polzelli (a very mediocre singer and musician), by transposing many arias into a lower key for her sake and by making others more attractive through the addition of new orchestral parts.

5. The tempo of the Italian arias is accelerated by Haydn

[14] That article was prepared and written in 1961, that is before Hárich 62. Accordingly, the chronology of performance statistics (especially that of the repetitions) given there needs to be corrected.

almost everywhere. As an extreme example we quoted an aria from Salieri's *La fiera di Venezia*, where the original *andante maestoso* was changed by Haydn into *allegro vivace*.

6. As compared to his own high standards of differentiation in dynamics and phrasing (shown markedly in his own quartets and symphonies of the 1770's and 1780's), Haydn found in many of the Italian opera scores an obvious lack of dynamic differentiation; accordingly, in order to enhance the expressive and emotional impact of the works he conducted, he often added pointed and sharply contrasting dynamic markings, especially in those operas by Paisiello, Sarti, and Martin which he otherwise found emotionally important.

꽃淡꽃

The other question raised by the study of this Eszterháza repertory is that of the organization of a "repertoire": the selection of pieces for performance at Eszterháza and their popularity as mirrored in the number of performances and repetitions. Here we may observe that historians of opera have not yet paid enough attention to this question of "building up a repertoire." The impressive bibliographical apparatus of Grout's *Short History of Opera* indicates how seldom in current musicological literature this question is treated, notwithstanding the fact that its importance has been emphasized ever since Kretzschmar's *Geschichte der Oper* in 1919. Most of the literature on opera deals with the genre as a product of outstanding (or less outstanding) composers, with relatively little attention paid to opera as a social phenomenon, subject to characteristic changes in public taste and to public demands that are bound to influence, for example, the selection of repertoire and the number of repetitions of certain works and the dropping of others. Of course, there are many perfectly appropriate and pertinent remarks to that point in Grout's great book: page 168 gives some telling statistics on the decline of traditional *tragédie lyrique* in Paris in favor of the new genre of *opéra ballet*; pages 199–200 supply a very enlightening tabulation of the relations between composers and audiences, and the typical attitudes of eighteenth-century audiences; page 246 remarks on the prevailing tendencies within the genre of comic opera—a gradual change from "low-class farce to middle-class comedy."

All this is important and instructive; but I think it could be carried on somewhat farther, if only the necessary statistical data (the number of repetitions in the program) were much more extensively available than they are at present. We know that precise and detailed performance statistics (first performances plus repetitions) can be collected only for certain specified opera houses (like La Scala in Milan) or for such particularly important cities with several opera houses as Venice, Naples, Vienna, London, Paris. Valuable work has already been done in this field by Florimo for Naples, by Wiel for Venice, by Pohl (and recently Anton Bauer) for Vienna, by Desarbres, Prodhomme, and others for Paris, by H. Bolongaro-Crevenna for Munich, by G. Pavan for Florence, by R. A. Mooser for St. Petersburg, by Zabala for Valencia. This work seems impressive at first (especially the magnificent statistics of Wiel for Venice and Florimo for Naples), but it must be noted that most of these very useful chronological surveys have limited themselves to a listing of the first performances, whereas for passing a judgment on public taste and public demands (in other words, just on "opera as a social phenomenon") the number of repetitions is equally important.[15]

But even for the simple listing of first performances, there is a deplorable tendency, especially in recent years, for alphabetical

---

[15] For example, in the biography of Mozart these questions play an important role. Only they can give us a pertinent answer to some burning questions of this kind: Why could not Mozart get a commission for an opera for Italy after 1773? Why not for Paris in 1778? Why not for Vienna between the *Abduction* and *Figaro* (1782–1786)? Why was *Figaro* dropped from the Vienna repertory in 1786 after only a few performances? All these are pertinent questions that reach far beyond an individual biography of Mozart, into the realm of repertoire history.

listings of the data, either by composers' names (as Tintori did for Naples), or by opera titles (as in the third edition [1964] of R. A. Mooser's *Operas, intermezzos etc. . . . joués en Russie durant le 18ᵉ siècle,* and in the important survey by Anton Bauer, *Opern und Operetten in Wien*). Those dictionary-type surveys of the repertoire of a court or a city are very useful in locating the performance of a certain opera, but from the special point of view of repertoire research they are not enough. If we are to establish certain norms for the methodology of operatic repertory history, we must persist in demanding strictly chronological disposition, instead of simple alphabetical listing.[16] The special disadvantages of the alphabetical method are clearly evidenced in the survey of the important Viennese opera repertory provided by Anton Bauer in 1955. As noted in some critical reviews (in *Musikforschung* [1959] and in *Notes* [1956]), there is unnecessary duplication in his title reporting (double listings of Italo-German title pages), which would have disappeared instantly with use of the more appropriate chronological method. Anyone who tries to get a clear picture of the Viennese opera repertory in the years 1740–1790 has to face the lack of completely reliable recent information on this subject; and yet this was the decisive period of the formation of Viennese classical style. Surely it is by no means unimportant to know which operas were attended by Mozart in 1773 or 1781–1791 or by Haydn during his yearly visits to the Austrian capital. The present lack of information on the Viennese repertoire limits the following remarks on the prevailing tendencies within the Eszterháza repertory; our comparison with those prevalent in Vienna, Venice, and Naples will be necessarily of a sketchy nature.

[16] Of course, this objection does not apply at all to O. G. T. Sonneck's magnificent catalogue of the libretto collection at the Library of Congress, Washington, an unparalleled achievement in the field of opera history. But Sonneck had to deal with a tremendous number of librettos of greatly diversified provenience, not with the repertory of a single stage or a single city.

It is remarkable that when Haydn occupied his post with the princes Esterházy in 1761, and fifteen years later when he started to build up a repertory of Italian operas for the princely court, he immediately plunged into the then up-to-date genre of *dramma giocoso* (middle-class comedy with music), completely dismissing at first the traditional genre of *opera seria, à la* Metastasio, which had been the compulsory treat for the princely courts of Munich, Dresden, and even of Vienna up to 1757. We safely may ascribe that tendency toward *dramma giocoso* [17] to Haydn himself, rather than to his prince. During the first five years of Haydn's opera conducting, up to 1780, his repertoire consisted exclusively of the *giocoso* genre, his favorite composers having been, in chronological order of their works appearing on the Eszterháza stage, Dittersdorf, Piccini, Paisiello, Gassmann, Anfossi, Gazzaniga, Guglielmi, Felici, Naumann, Sarti, and Salieri. One distinctive feature of this list is the complete absence of any local limitations, such as were typical of many of the feudal court operas. Haydn proved remarkably reluctant to fill up the Eszterháza repertory with his own operas, as he did in the first period of his activity there, in 1761–1775. His selection of composers and of works testifies to his striving for a comprehensive repertoire, but for the time being always within the limits of the genre of *dramma giocoso*.

From 1781 on, new features appear in Haydn's repertory. First was a tendency to include more and more composers, adding to the above list the names of Astaritta, Righini, Grétry (in Italian translation), Traëtta, Cimarosa (first performed in 1783 and later becoming a favorite of the repertory), Bianchi, Bologna, Stabingher, Zingarelli, Caruso, Bertoni, Fabrizi, Prati, and Martin. The astonishing variety of this repertoire is hardly matched by any other operatic stage in contemporary Italy or

---

[17] The term *opera buffa* was already somewhat antiquated at this time; if it was used at all, for example in Venice, it clearly meant the genre of lower-class farce, as distinguished from the elevated musical comedy, called *dramma giocoso*.

elsewhere. And secondly, an obvious tendency toward including works of more serious character began to appear: in 1781, one *dramma tragicomico* against five *giocoso* pieces; in 1782, two pieces in the new *eroicomico* genre against five *giocoso;* in 1783, one real tragedy (*Giulio Sabino*) against five *giocoso;* 1784, two tragedies (termed *dramma per musica*) plus one *componimento drammatico* against three *giocoso* (thus, exactly half the first performances in that year were of the *seria* or the *semiseria* genre); 1785, one tragedy against three *giocoso;* 1788, three tragedies against four *giocoso;* whereas in 1789 and 1790 only *giocoso*-type operas were performed in Eszterháza. All this shows that in the years from 1782 until 1788 there was a consistent tendency to enrich the traditional *dramma giocoso* repertory of Eszterháza with important works in the serious genre. As composer, Haydn paid tribute to this tendency by choosing for his last Esterházy opera the libretto of *Armida*. Thinking of this choice of his, we may safely suppose that the tendency toward the serious genre represented Haydn's own choice rather than Prince Esterházy's, which perhaps dictated the pure *giocoso* repertory of the earlier years, up to 1781, and again in the last two years, 1789–1790.

Now it seems tempting to look for this same tendency in other contemporary opera-house programs. Let us first have a short look at the nearest place of interest, Vienna. (For the above mentioned reasons I rely mainly on the data of Pohl-Sonnleithner, temporarily dismissing the somewhat shaky evidence in the alphabetical listings of Bauer. At another opportunity I will return to the question of the Vienna repertory in more detail.) Giuseppe Scarlatti is said to have introduced the genre of *opera buffa* to Vienna in 1757. From that date until 1770, the Vienna repertory was a mixture of some popular *buffo* pieces and the traditional serious genre represented by Hasse, Wagenseil, and Gluck. A short tabulation of the tendencies evident in the Vienna repertory for 1770–1790 follows.

From 1770 to 1775 there was an exclusive regime of the *buffo*

genre, including some specimens of lower-class comedy—
burletta or *opera bernesca*, with sixteen (?) first performances
for 1771, eight for 1772, seven for 1773 (including one neutral
genre—*azione teatrale*), eight for 1774, and seven for 1775. In
1776, the performances of the German opera company of Böhm
and Noverre started at Vienna; in addition to their productions,
seven Italian operas were first performed, two among them of
the serious genre (*Daliso e Delmita* by Salieri, *Piramo e Tisbe* by
Rauzzini) and five *giocoso*. In 1777, there were nine first performances: one tragedy (*Armida* by Naumann) against eight
giocoso pieces. The following years, 1778–1782, were the period
of the "Deutsches National Singspiel," finally culminating in
Mozart's *Abduction from the Seraglio* on July 16, 1782. The
first performances of Italian opera in Vienna were interrupted
for those years,[18] when only sporadic performances of Italian
operas are known, as in December 1781, when two serious operas by Gluck (*Alceste* and *Orfeo*) were performed for the
Russian grand duke, and in 1782, which saw productions of two
giocoso works (by Sacchini and Salieri). By April 1783, the
series of Italian opera performances, nearly exclusively of the
giocoso genre, was resumed; it continued until 1790, including
the Vienna performances of Mozart's *Figaro* and *Don Giovanni*.
The pertinent statistics for first performances, according to Pohl,
are: nine in 1783, ten in 1784, eight in 1785, eight in 1786, six in
1787, nine in 1788, six in 1789, and six in 1790, all but one of
which (*Guilio Sabino*, August 1785) belonged to the type of the
giocoso.[19] Taken as a whole, this Vienna repertory between 1770

---

[18] No similar interruption took place at Eszterháza, where a somewhat
analogous phenomenon of German operas was noticeable in the marionette performances of 1773–1778.

[19] Here, again, we have to say that we know Pohl's listings to be
somewhat incomplete; for example, all the performances of French
pieces (partly by Gluck) and those of lower-class comedies (the so
called *Hanswurstiaden*, including Haydn's *Der neue Krumme Teufel*)
are omitted from his lists. But neither of these two genres does in fact
interfere with our special topic here: the statistics of Italian opera.

and 1790 does not excel in any specific way (except perhaps for the sporadic Mozart performances) the repertory conducted by Haydn at Eszterháza. Particularly, serious drama, which, as noticed above, dominated the repertory at Eszterháza during the years 1782–1788, was nearly nonexistent in Vienna. Accordingly, while admitting that Eszterháza relied heavily on Vienna for *giocoso* works, as is evidenced by many Eszterháza scores of Viennese origin, yet in order to explain certain specific tendencies within the Eszterháza repertory we have to look farther. Particularly, the significant trend towards serious drama in the 1780's may perhaps be traced back to some Italian models, especially Naples and Venice.

Haydn may have had fairly precise information about contemporary Venetian repertory from his Eszterháza singers who had come from Venice. To the list of Eszterháza singers published in HOK, pages 168–171, we may add here some information on those among them who came to Eszterháza from previous Venetian operatic service; the years following each name indicate the period of that singer's known employment in Venice: Metilde Bologna-Porta, 1778; Margherita Delicati, 1797–1798; Barbara Ripamonti, 1768, 1775–1776; Barbara Sassi, 1776–1777; Palmira Sassi, 1776–1777, 1779–1782; Anna Zannini, 1754–1755; Giuseppe Amici, 1790–1791; Benedetto Bianchi, 1763–1764, 1781–1782; Prospero Braghetti, 1775–1776; Pietro Gherardi, 1781, 1789; Guglielmo Jermoli, 1774–1775; Giacomo Lambertini, 1762–1763; Pietro Majeroni, 1780–1781, 1795–1796; Paolo Mandini, 1787; Filippo Martinelli, 1788–1799; Vincenzo Moratti, 1760–1762; Bartolomeo Morelli, 1782–1783; Domenico Negri, 1738–1762(?), 1784–1785; Andrea Toti (or Totti), 1776–1777. Thus, more than half of the Eszterháza singers were (earlier or later) connected with Venice.

A general picture of the Venetian repertory must note the fact that there were quite a number of different opera houses performing there at the same time. During the period in question

(1770–1790), there were four or five opera houses whose repertory may be compared to Eszterháza's.

The Teatro San Benedetto was devoted completely to the performance of serious opera, mostly in the traditional genre with Metastasio librettos; a rather modest average of three or four operas a year was performed there. The theatres San Cassiano and San Giovanni Crisostomo were exclusively devoted to the popular lower-class genre of comic opera; *farsa per musica* and *farsa giocosa* were the typical genre titles used at San Cassiano at that time. From about 1775, the genre cultivated by San Cassiano climbed to the middle-class musical comedy, the *dramma giocoso*. Between these two extremes were situated two important opera theatres whose repertory relied mainly on the *dramma giocoso* genre; these, consequently, can be best compared with the Eszterháza repertory. At the Teatro San Moisè the average was about four operas a year. In 1770–1774, 1776, 1779, 1780, 1782–1784, 1786–1790 the theatre presented an all-*giocoso* program, while in the intervening years the program was characteristically interspersed with some specimens of serious musical drama—in 1775, one tragedy (*Didone* by Anfossi) versus four *giocoso*; in 1777, one tragedy, plus one *azione teatrale*, versus four *giocoso*; in 1778, one tragedy and one *dramma eroicomico* (*Il cavaliere errante* by Traëtta, first performance at Eszterháza, 1782) versus four *giocoso*; 1781, one tragedy versus five *giocoso*. This tabulation shows that the turn toward serious drama was effected at San Moisè some years earlier than at Eszterháza and that it had changed the ratio of genres somewhat less than in Haydn's program.

Another Venetian theatre with a mixed program comparable to Eszterháza's was the Teatro San Samuele; it performed an all-*giocoso* program, sometimes with an occasional *opera buffa:* in 1771, two first performances; in 1772, two; 1773, two; 1777, four; 1778, five; 1780, five; 1781, four; 1782, five; 1783, six; 1784, two (in this same year, 1784, the Teatro San Benedetto

came forward with the extraordinary number of five first performances of serious operas, which may have claimed most of the
Venetian public's interest); 1785, two; and 1786, three. In the
remaining years its program was interspersed with some pieces of
serious musical drama—in 1774, one tragedy (*Lucio Silla* by
Anfossi) plus two *scene liriche* versus four *giocoso* pieces; in
1775, one tragedy (*dramma per musica*) versus four *giocoso;* in
1776, one *dramma* versus five *giocoso;* in 1779, one *dramma*
versus three *giocoso;* in 1787, after seven years of pure *giocoso*
programs, one *dramma* (*Pirro* by Paisiello) plus one *dramma
tragicomico* [20] versus two *giocoso;* in 1788, no *giocoso* at all
versus four tragedies—a very significant change (at the same
time three tragedies were first performed at San Benedetto); in
1789, no *giocoso* versus three tragedies (plus four others at San
Benedetto, while in San Moisè the comedies and *giocoso* works
were going on as usual); in 1790, no *giocoso* versus two tragedies
(plus three others in San Benedetto). This tabulation shows that
at San Samuele the turn toward serious musical drama took place
some years later than at San Moisè and at Eszterháza.

As for Naples, the statistical data have been collected and
published by Francesco Florimo, in *La scuola musicale di Napoli,*
Vol. IV (Naples, 1882). Among the four theatres playing operas, the Teatro San Carlo (1740–1799), specialized in the performance of tragedies and cantatas, rather like San Benedetto in
Venice, with an average of three or four first performances a
year. As for the remaining three theatres, two of them, the
Teatro Fiorentini (1706–1818) and the Teatro Nuovo
(1724–1800), played an all-*giocoso* program, with three to five
first performances a year, comparable to Eszterháza especially in
1776–1780. The pieces performed were termed mostly *commedia per musica,* thus avoiding the distinction between *dramma*

---

[20] In the 1780's the specific types of *dramma eroicomico* and *dramma
tragicomico* were much in demand throughout Europe. This may cast a
somewhat new light on the historical background of Mozart's *Don
Giovanni.*

giocoso and *opera buffa;* many of the pieces performed in these two theatres were to appear shortly afterwards on the Eszterháza stage too. Special mention is required for the Teatro del Fondo (1779–1800), whose repertory, with three to six first performances a year, displayed a striking similarity to that of Eszterháza. In the years 1779–1784 it performed an all-*giocoso* program interspersed with some *commedia* and *farsa per musica* pieces, while the years 1785–1790 were marked by a mixture of *dramma giocoso, opera semiseria,* and tragedy: in 1785, one tragedy (Gluck) versus three *semiseria;* 1786, five pieces, all of the *seria* type, with no comedy at all; 1787, one *dramma,* plus one *melodramma,* versus four comedies (this is exactly the ratio of the Eszterháza repertory in the 1780's); 1788, two pieces termed *commedia* versus three termed *dramma* (but the latter are of the *dramma giocoso* type as well; accordingly this is an all-*giocoso* program again); 1789, four first performances, all of the *giocoso* type (notwithstanding one of them being termed *dramma*); 1790, one real drama (*Il sacrifizio di Jefte*) versus four comedies. It must be pointed out that this elastic mixture of comedies and serious dramas is almost identical to the program policy of Haydn in Eszterháza during the 1780's.

This brief comparison has provided, I hope, some factual evidence for the contention that the Esterházy opera theatre under the leadership of Joseph Haydn was an institution of much more than local significance—one of the really important centers for the international cultivation of Italian opera.

Music in the
Works of Fogazzaro

By ROBERT A. HALL, JR.

The Italian novelist and poet Antonio Fogazzaro (1842–1911) made extensive use of music as a topic in his literary productions. In all Fogazzaro's novels and in some of his tales, music is so interwoven with the action and with the emotions of the characters as to constitute an essential part of the story, far more so than in any other nineteenth- or early twentieth-century Italian author. This feature of Fogazzaro's work is mentioned in all the biographies and critical studies on him,[1] and has furnished the material for three articles,[2] none of which goes beyond the level of general appreciation. Some critics have even gone so far as to consider "musicalità" as the major characteristic of Fogazzaro's art.[3] The variety, subtlety, and discrimination with which Fo-

---

[1] Especially those of Lucienne Portier, in her *Antonio Fogazzaro* (Paris, 1937), particularly pp. 420–430, and of Piero Nardi, *Antonio Fogazzaro* (Milan, 1938 and later eds.), *passim*.

[2] Camille Bellaigue, "Fogazzaro musicien," *Le Gaulois*, April 15, 1911; Arturo Pompeati, "Antonio Fogazzaro e la musica," *Il pianoforte*, VI (1925), 213–221; Edouard Maynial, "De Stendhal à Fogazzaro: la poésie de la musique chez un écrivain italien," *Revue de littérature comparée*, XIII (1933), 630–650.

[3] Gaetano Trombatore, *Fogazzaro* (Messina and Milan, 1938), following the suggestions of Karl Vossler, *Letteratura italiana contemporanea*

gazzaro treats music, however, has not been adequately recognized. There is no need for any further discussion of Fogazzaro's general concern with music, but a systematic survey of his treatment of the topic will contribute to a re-appraisal, now long over-due, of his whole achievement. It is therefore my intention here to examine in detail the reflections of Fogazzaro's musical taste in his works, particularly the number of passages into which music enters and the way it enters into them; the relation of music to other themes in the structure and technique of his story-telling; and the significance of music in his outlook on Italian and foreign culture.

Fogazzaro was an ardent music-lover, and his home was the scene of a great deal of music-making.[4] He himself, although not a skilled performer, had at least been exposed to instruction on the piano and played some as an amateur.[5] His father, Mariano, and (at least in the earlier years of their marriage) his wife, Rita, showed considerable ability;[6] their daughter Maria inherited notable skill as a pianist from her mother and from her grandfather Mariano Fogazzaro.[7] A number of professional musicians were among Fogazzaro's closest friends, especially the eccentric Neapolitan cellist Gaetano Braga (who figures, under the name of Lazzaro Chieco, in Fogazzaro's novels *Piccolo mondo moderno* and *Il santo,* and in the short story "Il fiasco del Maestro Chieco");[8] the composer Arrigo Boito;[9] and, later, Giovanni Sgambati.[10]

(Naples, 1916, 1922). Cf. also the (largely erroneous) criticisms of Antonio Piromalli, *Fogazzaro e la critica* (Florence, 1952), in the chapter "La critica del realismo e della musicalità," pp. 29–35.

[4] Nardi, *Fogazzaro,* pp. 75–76, 121–122, 195.

[5] *Ibid.,* pp. 53, 92.   [6] *Ibid.,* pp. 61, 74–75.

[7] *Ibid.,* p. 405; see also Arrigo Boito's letter to Fogazzaro, referring to Maria as "la tua musicista gentile" (*ibid.,* pp. 645–646).

[8] *Ibid.,* pp. 76, 259.   [9] *Ibid.,* pp. 76–78, 645–649.

[10] Who, according to Fogazzaro, received him "like a prince" at Rome (*ibid.,* p. 473).

Fogazzaro's tastes were markedly different from those of his Italian contemporaries. His major preferences were for the German Romantics and for "musica antica," which to him meant that of Italian, French, and German composers of the eighteenth century. It has long been known that such composers as Beethoven, Schumann, Mendelssohn, Pergolesi, and Bach were among his favorites; a sharper focus is afforded by a detailed count of the number of passages in which composers are mentioned (either by name, by their works, or both) in his eight novels and in the six short stories and eight poems in which music is involved. We find the following distribution: Schumann leads the list, with twelve passages; Beethoven and Bellini, ten each; Pergolesi, eight; Bach, seven; Verdi, six; Mendelssohn, five; Clementi, Mozart, and Schubert, four each; Corelli and Meyerbeer, three each; Donizetti, Haydn, Heller, Stradella, Thalberg, and Wagner, two each; and one apiece for Boito, Boccherini, Carafa,[11] Chopin, Rodolphe Kreutzer,[12] Benedetto Marcello, Padre Martini, Saint-Saëns, Tartini, and Weber.

Naturally, the mere number of passages in which a composer is mentioned does not necessarily show Fogazzaro's attitude towards him, favorable or otherwise. The composers whom he mentions most frequently were, we know also from his non-literary writings [13] and his correspondence, his favorites; for

[11] Michele Enrico Carafa (1787–1872), composer of the opera *Le prison d'Edimbourg* (1822), based on Scott's *Heart of Midlothian*. The opera is referred to, without the composer's name, in ch. 4 of *Leila* ("Il pezzo era un'aria manoscritta della vecchia opera buffa *Le prigioni di Edimburgo*"). See George Grove, *Dictionary of Music and Musicians*, ed. Eric Blom, (5th ed.; London, 1954), II, 57.

[12] Rodolphe Kreutzer (1766–1831), whose one-act opéra comique *Jadis et aujourd'hui* (1808) is referred to in the short story "La stria," without the composer's name, as *Allora ed oggi*, "roba antica di cui la Nana neanche aveva udito parlare." See Hugo Riemann, *Opern-Handbuch: Repertorium der dramatisch-musikalischen Litteratur* (Leipzig, 1887), p. 239.

[13] Especially the essay *Il dolore nell'arte* (Milan, 1901); reprinted in his *Discorsi* (Milan, 1905). Cf. below, p. 253.

those less frequently mentioned, we must also take into account the contexts in which they occur in the literary works and Fogazzaro's opinion of them expressed elsewhere. Thus, Verdi is given only passing mention (occasionally with somewhat contemptuous implications), in each of the six passages,[14] whereas Mendelssohn is mentioned favorably in four passages,[15] and an unsympathetic character (Jeanne Dessalle's brother Carlino) makes unfavorable remarks about Mendelssohn in a fifth.[16] Meyerbeer is mentioned at three points in *Malombra*,[17] in all of which he constitutes a major enthusiasm of the insane and *antipatica* heroine Marina. We know from other sources [18] that Wagner's

[14] Marina, the malevolent and insane heroine of *Malombra*, includes Verdi among the operatic composers whose music is the only kind she likes (Pt. I, ch. 5); a superficial student sings some doggerel on geometry to a theme from *I Lombardi alla prima crociata* in *Malombra*, Pt. III, ch. 1; in *Daniele Cortis* (ch. 5) a scratch band plays a fantasia on *I vespri siciliani* at the beginning of a reception at Villa Carré and the "Va, pensier" from *Nabucco* at the end of the reception; a young lieutenant includes *Rigoletto* among the operas on which he improvises in "La stria"; and the composer Bragozzo, at the lecture-concert at Villa Diedo in ch. 5 of *Piccolo mondo moderno*, in the course of a tirade against unappreciative audiences, declares "Altri cinque mi domanderanno se ho suonato Wagner o se ho suonato la *Traviata*." Fogazzaro pronounced a eulogy on Verdi after the latter's death (*Minime* [Milan, 1901], pp. 201–203), a quite conventional piece of post-mortem oratory.

[15] *Il mistero del poeta*, ch. 3; *Piccolo mondo moderno*, ch. 5; "Il fiasco del maestro Chieco."

[16] *Il santo*, ch. 1, where the aesthete Carlino Dessalle "stava appunto per innamorarsi di lei [Noemi d'Arxel], ne aveva avuto una paura enorme," but certain words of hers "venute . . . dopo certa frase, molto borghesemente ammirativa, su quel povero diavolo noioso di Mendelssohn, lo avevano salvato *à jamais*."

[17] Pt. I, ch. 5 (twice), and Pt. IV, ch. 4. On the first and the third mentions, specific reference is made to Marina's playing the "Evocation of the Nuns" and the Siciliana, respectively, from *Robert le Diable*.

[18] E.g. Nardi, *Fogazzaro*, p. 310, referring to an unpublished letter of Fogazzaro's to Ellen Starbuck telling of his disappointment on hearing *Die Meistersinger* at Munich. For that matter, Fogazzaro did not like Boito's *Mefistòfele* at its première in 1868, expressing strong preference for Cimarosa's "musica codina" in the *Matrimonio segreto* (*ibid.*, pp. 77–78).

music did not appeal to Fogazzaro, but of the two references to Wagner in our author's novels, one is neutral, and the other simply refers to a baritone doing a bad job of singing something Wagnerian.[19]

Table 2. Total number of passages mentioning Music

Genre	All passages	Longer episodes
Novels		
Miranda	15	2
Malombra	21	3
Il mistero del poeta	14	2
Daniele Cortis	10	2
Piccolo mondo antico	21	3
Piccolo mondo moderno	10	3
Il santo	15	1
Leila	23	6
Short stories		
"La lira del poeta"	1	
"La stria"	6	1
"Il folletto nello specchio"	1	
"Màlgari"	4	1
"Fedele"	6	1
"Un'idea di Ermes Torranza"	4	1
"Il fiasco del maestro Chieco"	9	1
"R. Schumann (dall'op. 68)"	2	1
Poems		
"Versioni dalla musica"	9	
"Poesie"	2	
Total	173	28

In Fogazzaro's fiction and poetry, a total of 173 passages mention music, distributed as shown in Table 2. The table distinguishes "longer episodes" from other passages; of course the

---

[19] Maestro Bragozzo's remark, in ch. 5 of *Piccolo mondo moderno*, quoted in n. 14 above; and *Il mistero del poeta*, ch. 21, where "un baritono cantò detestabilmente qualche cosa di wagneriano." The same singer is described again later, in ch. 23, as having sung badly, without mention of whose music he sang.

distinction is not sharp, but in general I have considered the "episodes" to be those in which more than a passing mention is made of music and in which, over several pages, an essential step forward is taken in the action of the story, with music playing an important part either in the action or in the background against which the action is set. The short play "La lira del poeta" is included only because its title contains a pun on *lira* "lyre" and "lira (Italian coin)." Fogazzaro wrote seven poems entitled collectively "Versioni dalla musica," in each of which he described a scene or dialogue suggested to him by repeated listening to a given piece of music. In these poems, only two references are made to musical phenomena; I have counted each of the "Versioni" as a passage referring to music, and each of the two references to music just mentioned as such a passage, making nine in all.

The count given in Table 2 includes all references to music, however slight—including similes or metaphors (whose role in Fogazzaro's imagery will be discussed below), but excluding descriptions of the quality of people's voices or of non-musical sounds, no matter how beautiful. For the most part, Fogazzaro's references to music are serious and elevate the tone of his scenes. A fair number, however, of the passages listed in Table 2 (33 out of 173, or nearly a fifth) are humorous, as in the case of Bisata, the player of the *pelittone* (a kind of bass cornet),[20] who seeks Franco Maironi's support for his candidacy for a post in the town band in *Piccolo mondo moderno*. Bisata puts himself forward twice, once to the Marchesa Scremin in chapter 1, introducing himself as "uno che suona il pelittone in *fa bemolle*," and again in chapter 4, where he presents himself to the Commendatore as "quelo che sona el pelittone in *mi*." The humor resides both in the instrument he plays and in his discrepant descriptions of it as in F flat and in E. In the same novel, chapter 6, in answer

[20] This rare instrument was named after its inventor, one Pelitti, a Milanese; cf. Carlo Battisti and Giovanni Alessio, *Dizionario etimologico italiano* (Florence, 1950–1957), IV, 2825.

to a poet's complaint concerning the universal corruption present in modern society, the composer Bragozzo puts in his two cents' worth: "Anche il buon maestro volle dire la sua: se tutte le note musicali volessero essere il *la* perchè il *la* comanda, addio

Table 3. Types of musical activity mentioned

Instrumental		Vocal	
orchestra	1	female:	
band	3	mezzo-soprano	1
dance-orchestra	1	unspecified	9
solo		male	
piano	69	baritone	3
cello	6	unspecified	8
violin	4	unspecified	13
harpsichord	1	duet—female and male	2
spinet	2	chorus	6
organ	6	opera	1
flute	2	organ and song	1
clarinet	2	Total vocal	44
bass cornet (*pelittone*)	2		
trumpet	1		
bassoon	1	Miscellaneous	
guitar	2	music in general (performer not	
lyre	1	specified, or music thought of)	32
duet		concerts in general	1
piano four-hands	5	music-hall singer	
piano and violin	2	("canzonettista")	1
piano and cello	1	compositions by characters	7
harpsichord and cello	1	improvisation	8
Total instrumental	112	Total miscellaneous	49
		Grand total	205

musica!" The whole of the short story "R. Schumann (dall'op. 68)" is a self-satire on Fogazzaro's part (see the detailed discussion below); and all eleven references to the cellist Lazzaro Chieco involve some eccentricity on his part.

Most of Fogazzaro's references to music involve some specific activity, usually performance by one or more characters in the story. Table 3 classifies the types of musical activity involved, subdivided by the source of the music being made (vocal or instrumental), with further subcategories for various miscellaneous phenomena such as mentions of music in general without specification of the performer; compositions by characters in the stories; or improvisation. It will be noted that instrumental performances outnumber vocal by almost three to one, and that—as might be expected from an author with Fogazzaro's musical training and activities—the piano outnumbers all other instruments put together, and its nearest competitors are the cello[21] and the organ with six mentions apiece, piano four-hands with five, and the violin with four. Improvisation is mentioned only eight times, but in *Miranda, Piccolo mondo antico,* and *Leila* it plays an important role in casting light on the psychology of the main characters.

The conditions under which music is performed in Fogazzaro's fiction are almost always domestic; this applies even to the two relatively large gatherings at Jeanne and Carlino Dessalle's home at Villa Diedo in chapters 3 and 6 of *Piccolo mondo moderno.* A band plays twice in chapter 4 of *Daniele Cortis,* at the reception at Villa Carré, and is mentioned once in *Malombra* (Part I, chapter 5) with the casual, humoristic description of the young servant Rico's departure: "Il Rico se ne andò mogio mogio, a guardar gli strumenti della banda di V . . . , che aveva suonato in chiesa, alla brava, fior di polke e di galopp." Although, as we know from his biographers, Fogazzaro himself went to opera-performances reasonably often, attendance at an opera occurs only once, in the early verse-novel *Miranda* ("Il libro di Enrico," I, 19). The only mention of concerts is mildly unfavorable: in *Daniele Cortis* (chapter 10), the old senator Clenezzi admires and is grateful to the heroine Elena, among other reasons, "perchè non gl'infliggeva mai, *rara avis,* nè biglietti di concerti, nè associazioni a opere di autori deputati." The

---

[21] As might be expected from the presence of the eccentric cellist Lazzaro Chieco (Gaetano Braga) in two novels and a short story; see above, p. 221.

organ, as might be expected, occurs in connection with music in church. The six instances of choral singing all take place under solemn circumstances; in *Piccolo mondo antico* (Part III, chapter 2) and *Il santo* (chapter 5), they foreshadow imminent death; in *Leila* (chapter 17), Benedetto's followers sing the "De Profundis" on the boat which is carrying his mortal remains to their last resting-place in Valsolda.

The picture is somewhat different when we turn to the actual compositions which are identifiable from Fogazzaro's mentions of them, either by name or by composer, and to the manner in which they are performed—vocally or instrumentally. Table 4

Table 4. Mentions of compositions by types and manner of rendition

Type of composition	Vocal	Instrumental	Not specified
Church			
Gregorian chant	2		
cantata	2		
Choral (secular)	1		
Opera			
in general	2		2
chorus		1	
aria	13	7	
quartet		1	
ballet		2	
fantasia		2	
Folk-song			
Italian	4	1	
German	4		
Lieder (German)	5		
Piano solo			
sonata movement		4	
folk-dance		1	
suite			
dance-type movement		3	
non-dance movement		5	
other		3	
Violin and piano sonata		2	
Orchestral (incidental music)		1	
Total	34	33	2

classifies the number of mentions given to specific compositions, by types and by the manner of their rendition. Although the total number of mentions of instrumental performances is, as we have just seen, far greater than those of other kinds, the specific pieces mentioned are performed in almost exactly equal measure vocally (thirty-four) and instrumentally (thirty-three). This is because a great many mentions of instrumental performances do not specify the particular composition involved and also because a surprisingly high proportion of the compositions mentioned are operatic arias, mostly from eighteenth- and early nineteenth-century pieces. These are performed, in Fogazzaro's fiction (as they probably were in his own home), in part vocally but also instrumentally—usually, as might be expected, on the piano. This anomaly, in its turn, is due to the fact that Fogazzaro's major music-making characters (especially Marina in *Malombra*, Franco Maironi in *Piccolo mondo antico*, and Marcello Trento and Lelia Camin in *Leila*) are pianists.

Fogazzaro's relation to the opera—which was in his time, as earlier, a dominant feature of Italian musical life—deserves special attention. Italian opera has always alternated passages of dramatic exposition (usually in *recitativo secco*) with arias expressing emotional states. For this reason, Fogazzaro's characters are fond of operatic arias with which they can identify their own feelings and by means of which they can express them, either in song or on the piano. Yet public musical activities—performances of, not only operas, but also symphonies, instrumental trios or quartets, or large choral works—are almost entirely absent from Fogazzaro's fiction. Even Beethoven and Bach appear almost wholly as composers of solos or duets. Fogazzaro's characters, in general, live their inner lives and have their most intense feelings in the privacy of their homes and personal contacts, and their performances of music and their reactions to it follow the same pattern. Fogazzaro's neglect of the opera as an all-pervasive phenomenon in Italian public musical life seems to have been repaid by operatic composers' neglect of his works;

the only opera derived from one of Fogazzaro's works is, so far as I know, Franco Alfano's *Miranda* (1896).

Many of the passages in which music is mentioned are short and the part played in them by music is casual; others are longer and music has great importance in them, either by being a central part of the action (typically, some-one plays or sings and thereby exerts an influence on some-one else) or by furnishing a background either corresponding or contrasting to the emotional tone of the action. In some passages, the music or the making of music serves to characterize; in others, it sets the emotional tone of a scene—the mood of the characters or their relationships to each other. Table 5 lists the twenty-eight most important longer passages and the ways in which music functions in them. In the following discussion, I shall take up these passages, referring to them by the numbers given them in Table 5.

1. In the first scene of the "novella in versi" *Miranda,* the eponymous heroine plays the piano for her mother and an old friend of the family, the village doctor:

> Ed una giovinetta lenta lenta,
> Pensosa in volto, al cembalo venia,[22]
> Correva e ricorrea da un capo all'altro,
> I fragorosi tasti. . . . Si levò ad un tratto
> La suonatrice de' suoi fogli in cerca
> E quei [her mother and the doctor] tacquero; le note
> Ricominciâro furïosamente.
> Forte batteva alla fanciulla il core.
> Le si oscurava il libro, a lor talento
> Vagavano le man' per un pensiero
> Che subito la prese.

Here the musical activity is central to the action, casting light on Miranda's character (slow, dreamy, inclined to lose awareness of

[22] In modern Italian, *pianoforte* is the only normal term for "piano," and *cémbalo* suggests, if anything, *clavicémbalo,* "harpsichord," or else *címbalo,* "czimbalom, dulcimer"; but Fogazzaro, at the time of *Miranda* (1873), was using *cémbalo* for "piano" in his familiar letters, so its use here is not an archaism or an affectation.

Table 5. Rôle played by music in longer episodes

Num-ber	Work	Chapter	Central to action	Back-ground	De-scribes char-acter	Sets emo-tional tone
1	*Miranda*	"La Lettera"	*		*	*
2	*Miranda*	"Il libro d'Enrico"	*		*	*
3	*Malombra*	Pt. I, ch. 3		*	*	
4	*Malombra*	Pt. I, ch. 5	*		*	
5	*Malombra*	Pt. III, ch. 3		*		*
6	*Daniele Cortis*	ch. 11		*		*
7	*Daniele Cortis*	ch. 20	*	*		*
8	*Il mistero del poeta*	ch. 17	*		*	
9	*Il mistero del poeta*	ch. 21		*		*
10	*Piccolo mondo antico*	Pt. I, ch. 2	*		*	*
11	*Piccolo mondo antico*	Pt. II, ch. 2	*			*
12	*Piccolo mondo antico*	Pt. II, ch. 2	*			*
13	*Piccolo mondo moderno*	ch. 3		*		*
14	*Piccolo mondo moderno*	ch. 5	*	*		*
15	*Piccolo mondo moderno*	ch. 7		*		*
16	*Il santo*	ch. 8		*		*
17	*Leila*	ch. 1	*	*	*	*
18	*Leila*	ch. 1		*	*	*
19	*Leila*	ch. 2	*			*
20	*Leila*	ch. 4	*			*
21	*Leila*	ch. 7	*			*
22	*Leila*	ch. 13	*			*
23	"La stria"		*		*	
24	"Màlgari"		*		*	*
25	"Fedele"		*		*	*
26	"Un'idea di Ermes Torranza"		*			*
27	"Il fiasco del maestro Chieco"		*		*	
28	"R. Schumann (dall'op. 68)"		*		*	

the outside world and let her thoughts roam, with her fingers expressing them as she improvises) and also setting the tone of emotional excitement.

2. The hero Enrico, a young poet, the nephew of the doctor, tells how Miranda played for him:

Ella suonava il cembalo e le corde
Raccontavan l'affetto in lor favella
D'uno nell'ombra accanto a lei seduto.
T'ama, dicean tenere, sospira;
Il cor, dicean gravi, gli si frange;
Volgiti a lui, seguivano scherzando;
Se t'ha compresa chiedigli, sorridi;
Sull'agitato sen gli piega il viso,
Finìano dolcemente, attendi e taci,
Quindi sclamar parean tutte quante.
Dicean di rotti accenti e di singhiozzi
Impeto fiero che ogni freno ha vinto,
Virili braccia intorno a lei serrate,
Lo scoppio di due cor, l'uno sull'altro.
A quel modo suonar mai non l'intesi;
Quando levossi, nè lodarla osai.

In the end, neither Enrico nor Miranda declares love for the
other until it is too late; her health gives way, and she dies of a
heart-attack when he finally does avow his love. In this passage
her playing, which is central to the action, seems to Enrico to be
declaring what she does not say in words, and, in addition to
setting a mood of emotional attraction, emphasizes their failure
to speak out, the tragic fault in both of them which frustrates
their love.[23]

3–4. The hero of *Malombra,* a young novelist named Corrado
Silla, has just arrived at the "palazzo" of Count Ormengo on an
unnamed lake in the Brianza region (north of Milan) and is
being taken around by the Count's secretary, a German refugee
named Steinegge:

Quando giunsero in fondo al seno del Palazzo . . . saltò su nel
silenzio il suono chiaro e dolce d'un piano. Rischiarò la notte. Non si
vedeva nulla ma si sentivano le pareti del monte intorno alle note

---

[23] See my "The Poet and His Culture: Fogazzaro's *Miranda*," in
Cesare Barbieri Courier, VIII (1966), ii, 20–22.

limpide, si sentiva, sotto, l'acqua sonora. In quel deserto l'effetto
dello strumento era inesprimibile, pieno di mistero e d'immaginazioni
mondane. Era forse un vecchio strumento stanco, e in città, di
giorno, si sarebbe disprezzata la sua voce un poco fessa e lamente-
vole; pure quanto pensiero esprimeva là nella solitudine buia! Pareva
una voce affaticata, assottigliata dell'anima troppo ardente. La melodia, tutta slanci e languori appassionati, era puntata da un accompagnamento leggiero, carezzevole, con una punta di scherzo.

—Donna Marina—disse Steinegge.

—Ah—sussurrò Silla—che musica è?

—Ma!—rispose Steinegge—pare *Don Giovanni*. Voi sapete: *Vieni
alla finestra*. Suona quasi sempre a quest'ora.

In biblioteca non c'era più lume.

—Il signor conte arrabbia adesso—disse Steinegge.

—Perchè?

—Perchè non ama la musica e quella lo fa apposta.

Silla zittì con le labbra.

—Come suona!—diss'egli.

—Suona come un maligno diavolo che abbia il vino affettuoso—
pronunciò Steinegge.—Vi consiglio di non credere alla sua musica,
signore.

Here the music is acting as a background to the conversation and
serves primarily to cast light on Marina's character, through
Steinegge's reactions to her playing and his description of the
effect it has on her uncle Count Ormengo (who is giving her
board and lodging out of his sense of family duty). Her "music,"
which Steinegge warns Silla not to give credence to, is not only
her playing but also her mad belief that she is the reincarnation
of one Cecilia Varrega, who had been maltreated by her husband, one of Ormengo's ancestors, and that Silla is the reincarnation of Cecilia's lover. Marina, in order to avenge Cecilia, is
directly responsible for Ormengo's death and, when Silla finally
shows signs of turning from her to Steinegge's daughter Edith,
she shoots Silla and commits suicide by fleeing alone in a boat to
a dangerous part of the lake. Throughout the book, Marina's use

of music reflects her wildly romantic, unrestrained, self-centered attitude as reflected especially in the following passage from Part I, chapter 5:

Suonò uno dei suoi pezzi prediletti, la gran scena dell'evocazione delle monache nel *Roberto*. Ella non intendeva, non suonava che musica d'opera.

Suonò come se gli ardori delle peccatrici spettrali fossero entrati in lei più violenti. Alla tentazione dell'amore si fermò, non potè proseguire. Quel foco interno era più forte di lei, la opprimeva, le toglieva il respiro. Chinò la fronte sul leggìo. Pareva che ardesse anche quello. Si alzò in piedi, guardando nel vuoto. La divina musica vibrava ancora nell'aria, le pareva di respirarla, di sentirla nel petto; ne le correva uno spasimo voluttuoso per le braccia.

5. Silla is at an elegant society reception in Milan, where, after a pianist has thundered forth Thalberg's fantasia on Bellini's *Sonnambula* with perfect technique but little feeling ("Dio, come pesta!" says the hostess, Donna Giulia, and "Che eccidio, quel Thalberg!" says another lady, Donna Antonietta), Schumann's "Ich hab' im Traum geweinet" (*Dichterliebe*, no. 13) is rendered by the hostess, in an Italian translation (in the story ascribed to a sentimental "poetuculo," but presumably actually by Fogazzaro):

Intanto donna Giulia cantava con poca voce ma con molta arte un'appassionata musica scritta da Schumann su parole di Heine. . . . Donna Giulia cantava:

> Ho pianto in sogno, ho pianto;
> Ero tradito e sol.

Pareva veramente una musica mista a qualche triste sogno, con le sue prime note insistenti, dolorose. Diceva a Silla come la piova in casa di Edith: "Piangi, il tuo sogno è finito." . . . Derisione, derisione! gli altri erano felici! gli altri avevano l'amore voluttuoso di cui respirava il profumo, l'amore appassionato di cui ascoltava lo slancio nella musica che moriva su verso il cielo, spossato, in un grido:

Balzai dal sonno; il pianto
Pioveami a fiumi ognor.

After the singing is over, one of the ladies asks Silla:

—Dunque?—chiese donna Antonietta a Silla, riassettando il guanto alle sue dita affusolate.—Ha pianto?

—No, perchè non piango mai; ma ho sognato di piangere.

—Malheur à qui n'est pas ému—diss'ella.

The music-making is here in the background and serves chiefly to set the tone for Silla's reactions—of hostility to the superficiality and immorality of upper-class urban society, and sensitivity to emotional stimuli.

6–7. The relation of the hero Daniele Cortis and the heroine Elena (the wife of the corrupt and unworthy Sicilian Baron di Santa Giulia), who are in love but who sacrifice their love to Christian morality and to duty, is epitomized in an aria from Pergolesi's *Olimpiade* (1735). This aria enters into two passages, one a letter from Cortis to Elena (chapter 11), describing its effect on their mutual friend, the old Senator Clenezzi from the Val Brembana (near Bergamo):

Iersera c'è stata in casa S . . . una mezza accademia di musica antica, e donna Laura cantò una arietta del Pergolese che trasse delle vere lagrime al nostro vecchio amico valbrembano. Io scherzai un po', gli dissi che te lo avrei scritto. "Certo" rispose "e le mandi anche l'aria o almeno i versi di Metastasio che valgono, essi soli, tutti i moderni elzeviri." Eccoli come li ho trascritti dalla musica di donna Laura:

Se cerca, se dice
L'amico dov'è?
L'amico infelice,
Rispondi, morì.
Ah no, sì gran duolo
Non darle per me;
Rispondi, ma solo:
Piangendo, partì.

Toward the end of the book (chapter 20), Elena has already resolved that she must accompany her husband in his exile to Yokohama. At an evening party at which both she and Cortis are present, Elena is asked to play and refuses. After another of the young ladies present, a Miss Zirisèla, has played, Elena is asked to sing the Pergolesi aria, but she again refuses; her uncle Count Lao sits at the piano and accompanies old Clenezzi:

Ma Elena non cantava, non aveva mai avuto voce. Lao, ch'era rientrato durante il pezzo della Zirisèla, si pose al piano senza parlare e cominciò a cercarvi il motivo di Pergolese, interrogando Clenezzi con gli occhi.

"Bravo!" esclamò costui. "Bravo! Così!" E si mise a cantare con la sua voce fessa:

<blockquote>
Se cerca, se dice
</blockquote>

Nel dir la frase:

<blockquote>
Ah no, sì gran duolo
Non darle per me
</blockquote>

trovò tanto improvviso vigore che don Bortolo esclamò restando di giuocare: "Bravo, cane!" e fece rider tutti, mentre il senatore continuava imperterrito:

<blockquote>
Rispondi, ma solo:
Piangendo, partì.
</blockquote>

Soltanto Elena non rideva. Chiese di chi fossero le parole. Clenezzi cominciò un panegirico di Metastasio, levando al cielo questi versi tutti sentimento, tutti vezzi, tutti musica anche senza le note divine del Pergolese.

Elena is unwilling to make music, and insists on "sitting it out" with Cortis but refuses to tell even him why she will not play or sing. Her refusals clearly indicate her intense but passive emotion. After the party is over, Fogazzaro diminishes the tension by ending the episode on a slightly humorous note:

In sala non v'era nessuno. Lao, Clenezzi e la contessa Tarquinia eran tornati nella stanza del piano, dove il primo suonava con giovanile

slancio l'aria dell'*Olimpiade,* e Clenezzi ne singhiozzava miserevol-
mente le parole.

8. The unnamed narrator of *Il mistero del poeta,* an Italian
author who meets, falls in love with, and eventually marries a
half-English, half-Italian girl named Violet Yves, only to lose her
by her death on their wedding-night, tells of his visit to Stephan
Topler, the elder brother of Violet's fiancé, in the German town
of Eichstätt:

> Non potrò mai dimenticare la figura del vecchietto curvo che
> portava il suo lungo naso a destra e a sinistra sopra la tastiera, dietro
> al moto composto e agile delle mani. Quelle dita scarne, aggrappate
> come uncini ai tasti, si discorrevan sotto, non parendo quasi muo-
> versi, una musica quieta, leggerissima, serena con qualche punta di
> affetto e di scherzo.
>
> Ogni tanto esclamavo:—Bello!—ed egli rideva muto, suonando;
> poi diceva suonando sempre:—Sa di chi è? Sa di chi è?—Gli nomi-
> navo qualche nostro maestro antico. Rideva, suonava e non rispon-
> deva.
>
> —Toplerus—mi disse quando ebbe finito il pezzo.—Toplerus se-
> nior, organista di villaggio.
>
> Credo di aver interamente conquistato il suo cuore quella sera. La
> sua musica, così bella, non era originale; non riesce difficile a un
> compositore d'ingegno che abbia dimestichezza con le opere dei
> nostri primi classici scrivere in quello stile per modo da ingannar un
> dilettante; ma io, preso così alla sprovveduta, ne rimasi stupefatto.

The narrator becomes, in this way, close friends with "Toplerus
senior." His action in taking Violet away from the quiet, unas-
suming, sickly Toplerus junior becomes thereby all the less acceptable to the reader, until one realizes the cultural symbolism
involved; the Italian intellectual may become friendly with
North Europeans who admire and imitate earlier Italian culture,
but he does not want to relinquish modern Europe (Violet) to
what he sees as a fruitless union with small-town inactivity in a
Protestant environment.

9. Whereas the previous passage involves music-making and

listening by the main personages and serves to characterize them, in the following passage it serves as a background, setting the emotional tone for the narrator's reaction, as an outsider listening in the public square, to German poetry and song coming from within his friends' house:

Entrando nel Rossmarkt udii suonare e cantare. Le finestre di casa Treuberg erano aperte ed i suoni uscivano proprio di là. . . . Un baritono cantò detestabilmente qualche cosa di wagneriano e poi una fresca voce di giovinetta cantò con grazia *Haidenröslein* di Schubert, che avevo già udita canterellare in un mite pomeriggio di novembre, fra le ultime rose della mia collina italiana. Allora la semplice poesia di Goethe, la semplice musica di Schubert con quella loro spensieratezza piena di occulta malinconia, mi avevano stretto il cuore; adesso mi mettevano uno spasimo di dolor geloso, adesso mi torcevo le mani perchè la dolce *Röslein auf der Haide*, la rosetta della landa, si confondeva nel mio segreto con la rosetta mia, con la rosetta della storia amara. . . . Non ressi ad ascoltar la fine e venni via.

10–11. Fogazzaro describes the hero of *Piccolo mondo antico*, Franco Maironi, as he sits at the piano, and uses Franco's improvising as a means of characterizing his nature:

Franco aveva troppe diverse attitudini e inclinazioni, troppa foga, troppa poca vanità e forse anche troppa poca energia di volere per sobbarcarsi a quel noioso metodico lavoro manuale che si richiede a diventar pianisti. [. . .] Franco non avrebbe potuto cimentarsi, nei salotti cittadini, con tanti piccoli dilettanti incapaci d'intendere e d'amare la musica. Tutti o quasi tutti lo avrebbero vinto di agilità e di precisione, avrebbero ottenuto maggiori applausi, quand'anche non fosse riuscito ad alcuno di far cantare il piano, come lo faceva cantar lui, sopra tutto negli adagi di Bellini e di Beethoven, suonando con l'anima nella gola, negli occhi, nei muscoli del viso, nei nervi delle mani che facevan tutt'uno con le corde del piano.

It is generally considered [24] that Fogazzaro's description of Franco in this passage was largely autobiographical—the ama-

[24] E.g. by R. Viola, *Fogazzaro* (Florence, 1939), pp. 144–145.

teurish quality of the playing, the indifference to the physical nature of the sound, and the interpretation of the music in relation to the player's own feelings. In the other major passage of this novel (Part II, chapter 2) involving Franco's improvisation, his wife Luisa defines and develops her relationship to him in the light of his emotions as reflected in his playing:

. . . e Franco, data un'occhiata alla luna che sfavillava allora fuor dal ciglio nero del Bisgnago e giù nell'ondular dell'acqua, si pose a improvvisar sul piano effusioni di dolore ideale, che andavan via per le finestre aperte sulla sonorità profonda del lago. La improvvisazione musicale gli riusciva meglio delle elaborate poesie perchè il suo impetuoso sentire trovava nella musica una espressione più facile e piena, e gli scrupoli, le incertezze, le sfiducie che gli rendevano faticosissimo e lento il lavoro delle parole, non tormentavano, al piano, la sua fantasia. Allora si abbandonava all'estro anima e corpo, vibrava tutto fino ai capelli, i chiari occhi parlanti ridicevan ogni sfumatura della espressione musicale, gli si vedeva sotto le guancie un movimento continuo di parole inarticolate, e le mani, benchè non tanto agili, non tanto sciolte, facevan cantare il piano inesprimibilmente.

Adesso egli passava da un tono all'altro, mettendo il più intenso sforzo intellettuale in questi passaggi, ansando, sviscerando, per così dire, lo strumento con le dieci dita e quasi anche con gli occhi ardenti. S'era messo a suonare sotto l'impressione del chiaro di luna, ma poi, suonando, tristi nuvole gli eran uscite dal fondo del cuore. Conscio di avere sognata, da giovinetto, la gloria e di averne quindi umilmente deposta la speranza, diceva, quasi, a sè stesso con la sua mesta appassionata musica che pure anche in lui v'era qualche lume d'ingegno, qualche calore di creazione veduto solamente da Dio, perchè neppure Luisa mostrava far dell'intelligenza sua quella stima che a lui stesso mancava ma che avrebbe desiderato in lei; neppur Luisa, il cuor del suo cuore! Luisa lodava misuratamente la sua musica e i suoi versi ma non gli aveva detto mai: segui questa via, osa, scrivi, pubblica. Pensava così e suonava nella sala oscura, mettendo in una tenera melodia il lamento del suo cuore, il timido segreto lamento che mai non avrebbe osato mettere in parole. . . .

Luisa venne al piano in punta di piedi, stette ad ascoltar il marito, a sentir la bellezza, la ricchezza, il fuoco di quell'anima ch'era sua e cui ell'apparteneva per sempre. Non aveva mai detto a Franco "segui questa via, scrivi, pubblica" forse anche perchè giustamente pensava, nel suo affetto equilibrato, che non potesse produrre opere superiori alla mediocrità, ma sopratutto perchè sebbene avesse un fine sentimento della poesia e della musica, non faceva grande stima, in fondo, nè dell'una nè dell'altra, non le piaceva che un uomo vi si dedicasse intero, ambiva per suo marito un'azione intellettuale e materiale più virile. Ammirava tuttavia Franco nella sua musica più che se fosse stato un grande maestro; trovava in questa espressione quasi segreta dell'animo suo un che di verginale, di sincero, la luce di uno spirito amante, il più degno di essere amato.

Egli non s'accorse di lei se non quando si sentì sfiorar le spalle da due braccia, si vide pender sul petto le due piccole mani. "No no, suona suona" mormorò Luisa perchè Franco gliele aveva afferrate; ma cercando lui col viso supino, senza rispondere, gli occhi e le labbra di lei, gli diede un bacio e rialzò il viso ripetendo "suona!" Egli trasse giù più forte di prima i due polsi prigionieri, richiamò in silenzio la dolce, dolce bocca; e allora ella si arrese, gli fermò le labbra sulle labbra con un bacio lungo, pieno di consenso, tanto più squisito e ricreante del primo. Poi gli sussurrò ancora: "suona."

Ed egli suonò, felice, una tumultuosa musica trionfale, piena di gioia e di grida. Perchè in quel momento gli pareva di possedere tutta intera l'anima della donna sua mentre tante volte, pure sapendosi amato, credeva di sentire in lei, al di sopra dell'amore, una ragione altera, pacata e fredda, dove i suoi slanci non arrivassero. Luisa gli teneva spesso le mani sul capo e andava di tratto in tratto baciandogli lievemente i capelli. . . . Indovinò adesso che significasse quella effusione musicale di gioia e, commossa, abbracciò Franco, fece tacere il piano d'un colpo.

I have cited virtually all of this long passage because it is the best exemplification of Fogazzaro's ability to interweave the emotional expression of his characters in music with their psychological relationship, in this case Luisa's understanding of her dependence on her husband despite her intellectual superiority to him.

12. Later in Part II, chapter 2, of *Piccolo mondo antico*, Franco and Luisa go out for a boat-ride on the Lake of Lugano,

and she sings a Donizetti aria for him, which Franco (and through him Fogazzaro) interprets as an expression on her part of her desire for a more perfect union in their marriage:

Franco tirò i remi in barca. "Canta" diss'egli.

Luisa non aveva mai studiato il canto ma possedeva una dolce voce di mezzo soprano, un orecchio perfetto e cantava molte arie d'opere imparate da sua madre che aveva udito la Grisi, la Pasta, la Malibran durante l'età d'oro dell'opera italiana.

Cantò l'aria di *Anna Bolena:*

> Al dolce guidami
> Castel natìo

il canto dell'anima, che prima scende e si abbandona a poco a poco, per più dolcezza, all'amore, e poi abbracciata con esso, risale in uno slancio di desiderio verso qualche alto lume lontano che tuttavia manca alla sua felicità piena. Ella cantava e Franco, rapito, fantasticava che aspirasse ad essergli unita pure in quella parte superiore dell'anima che finora gli aveva sottratta; che aspirasse venir guidata da lui, in questa perfetta unione verso la meta dell'ideale suo.

Immediately after Luisa has sung this aria, they are met by friends from the Lake of Como, a lawyer and a man named Pedraglio, who are coming "per far della musica in palese e della politica in segreto"—a good example of the connection that Fogazzaro was able to establish between such apparently disimilar matters as music and politics, through the emotional attachments which his characters have to both at the same time. The friends return with Luisa and Franco to their home and the latter plays a piano-and-bassoon duet with the lawyer. Their neighbor, the Austrian customs-supervisor, sends his wife over, ostensibly to listen to the music, but actually to spy on the Maironis and their visitors. Luisa tells the woman a lot of nonsense, using the music as a blind, and fooling her completely: "Poi, invece di ascoltare la diabolica disputa del piano col fagotto, parlò del Commissario di Porlezza e disse ch'egli aveva l'intenzione di venir a vedere i fiori di don Franco."

13–14. In *Piccolo mondo moderno* there are two extended scenes involving musical performances at receptions at Villa Diedo, the country-house occupied by the esthete Carlino Dessalle and his sister Jeanne. This latter, who is separated from her drunkard husband, is in love with Piero Maironi, the son of Franco and Luisa Maironi of *Piccolo mondo antico;* Piero, however, is married to a woman who is in an insane-asylum. Both the scenes serve as backgrounds for the emotions of Jeanne, as well as for skillful genre-portraits of many minor characters. In the first, Carlino plays the harpsichord (a much rarer instrument in the 1890's than now,[25] and much more specifically identified with "musica antica"), and Lazzaro Chieco the cello, while Jeanne, thinking of Maironi, tries to avoid the unwelcome attentions of others:

Trlin! Trlin! Trlin! Carlino chiama col *clavecin* alla sala di Omero, Jeanne richiama colla voce: "Musica, musica!" Si risponde: musica, musica! Basta, basta!—Tutti corrono alla sala di Omero meno Chieco che cava il violoncello dalla cassa. Poichè stanno per entrare un certo signor Bach, un certo signor Haydn, un certo signor Marcello e altri personaggi in parrucca, spadino, calze di seta e fibbie di brillanti, sia l'accoglienza gaia!

The hearers' thoughts turn to "galanterie," and two of the visiting intellectuals, first a certain Berardini and then the Venetian painter Fusarin, start to pay court to Jeanne during the music:

Infatti Fusarin, preso dalla violenza della musica, teneva su Jeanne gli occhi ardenti, la scongiurava con gli slanci del violoncello. Il *clavecin* parve disadatto a tanta passione. Come poteva Beethoven concepire le sonate senza concepire insieme il pianoforte moderno? Carlino sostenne che la musica di Beethoven aveva creato il pianoforte moderno, come negli organismi non è l'organo che si crea la potenza, è la potenza che crea l'organo.

[25] Notice that Fogazzaro uses the French loan-word *clavecin* for "harpsichord" throughout this scene; although *clavicémbalo* was used in the seventeenth and eighteenth centuries (cf. Battisti and Alessio, *Dizionario etimologico,* II, 977), it was clearly archaic for Fogazzaro and did not come back into use until the twentieth century.

In chapter 5, another gathering at Villa Diedo is entertained
with first a performance on the piano by the composer Bragozzo
and then an illustrated lecture by Carlino; during the first part,
Jeanne is on the terrace with another admirer, a certain Bassanelli, who criticizes Piero Maironi while Bragozzo plays passages
from his unpublished opera, and a "cavalier faceto" relates gossip
concerning events in the household of the Scremin family, Piero's parents-in-law:

A questa placida svolta del racconto si udirono gli eroi del maestro
Bragozzo delirare di passione con lo strepito più indiavolato. [After
Bassanelli has grasped Jeanne's wrist and criticized Piero, he lets go
of her:]
Così dicendo liberò e scosse da sè il polso prigioniero. Nello stesso
momento si udì un sonoro applauso salutar l'ultima battuta dell'opera
di Bragozzo.
"Zitto!" disse Jeanne, quasi atterrita, pallida quanto lui. "Voi siete
un cattivo geloso e niente altro!"

15. Piero's wife has died and he has gone from the hotel where
both were staying; Jeanne visits friends, but goes outside while
listening to the performance of a violinist and pianist. She experi-
ences intense but highly mixed emotions towards herself, Piero
Maironi, and her love for him, and then returns:

Poco prima di quella stessa mezzanotte, Jeanne esce quasi furtiva-
mente dal salotto di villa Cerri dove il maestro e una violinista
fortissima suonano un turbinoso *allegro* che va, per le finestre aperte,
ai boschi e ai prati della montagna. . . .
Il pezzo è finito ed ella si ricompone quanto può, rientra, chiede
distrattamente:
"Che musica è?"
Suo fratello si scandolezza. Come non ha riconosciuto il primo
allegro della *Kreutzersonate?*
"Lo chiamano un *allegro*," soggiunge. "Io lo chiamo un impasto
dei dolori di due anime, quella del piano e quella del violino, dolori
che sono necessari per far nascere una cosa grande."

"Mi pare," osserva timidamente la signora Cerri parlando a Jeanne, "che qualche volta succeda così anche nella vita. Non ti pare?"

Jeanne tace.

There is a clear similarity between Fogazzaro's and Tolstoi's use of the Kreutzer sonata in fiction; however, Fogazzaro could hardly have shared Tolstoi's pessimistic attitude toward the influence of music and his resultant hostility toward it, and it is doubtful whether Fogazzaro was influenced by Tolstoi in this particular mention of the sonata.

16. In *Il santo*, there is only one extended scene in which music plays a role. This novel is concerned mainly with the activities and ultimate death of Piero Maironi after he has become an ascetic (under the name of Benedetto) and an advocate of reform of the Roman church from within. In fact, music drops entirely out of the picture for over half the book, in the central portion dealing with Benedetto's religious activities. Jeanne is in the background, trying to help Benedetto and, toward the end, to save him from the clutches of the police, while he is lying sick unto death in a poor quarter of Rome. Some mutual friends come to visit Jeanne and bring her disturbing news concerning Benedetto, while Chieco and Carlino Dessalle are making music in the next room. There is a strong contrast between the serenity and the cheerfulness of the music and the tragic nature of the news concerning Benedetto. Usually, the emotions of Fogazzaro's characters coincide with the music which he describes them as making or as hearing in the background; in this scene, he uses a somewhat Shakespearean technique of having the music contrast sharply with Jeanne's feelings, and thereby heightens the dramatic tension; at the end, the music stops and Chieco comes out whistling and clapping his hands, indicating, perhaps, the indifference of the outer world to Benedetto's plight and Jeanne's distress.[26]

17. In *Leila*, the old man Marcello Trento, father of Lelia

[26] See Lucienne Portier's detailed discussion, *Fogazzaro*, pp. 424–425.

Camin's dead fiancé Andrea, improvises with his son's picture on the music-rack:

Non era un forte pianista, ma possedeva un'anima di musica. La sua profonda fede religiosa, i suoi affetti, il suo caldo senso di ogni bellezza di arte e di natura, tendevano alla espressione musicale. Venerava Beethoven, non meno di Dante, e, quasi, di San Giovanni Apostolo; Haydn, Mozart e Bach non meno di Giambellino e, quasi, di San Marco, di San Matteo e di San Luca. E, come del Vangelo, così leggeva ogni giorno qualche pagina dei quattro evangelisti della musica. Spesso la sera, nell'ora dei ricordi e del fantasticare, si abbandonava, sul piano, all'estro. Trovando accenti commossi, commovendosi della sua commozione stessa, suonava, suonava, tutto nello sforzo di adeguare la parola musicale al proprio senso interno, dimenticava le cose presenti, il passar del tempo. A faccia levata, a occhi chiusi, egli adesso tentava la tastiera con le grandi mani scarne come il cieco tenta l'aria.

Like Franco Maironi, Marcello incorporates some of Fogazzaro's own characteristics, especially amateurishness of performance combined with intensity of feeling. He improvises first on the theme of the section "Quando corpus morietur" of Pergolesi's *Stabat mater*, thinking of his own death, which he knows is near. His thoughts pass to his deceased son, to his own sins, and to his faith and hopes for a future life, and he plays an impassioned but glad *Miserere*. Lelia and the maid Teresina hear Marcello playing long after the family's accustomed bed-time, and come to see if anything is wrong. Marcello passes to an improvisation on the aria "Sola, furtiva al tempio" from Bellini's *Norma*, which touches Lelia's heart and serves to eliminate some of the hostility she had felt towards him.

This passage is perhaps the best example of Fogazzaro's intimate blending of music and emotional expression. In Table 5, it is the only one of the extended passages marked in all four columns, since the music-making is part of the action (for Marcello) and also serves as background (for Lelia); it helps to characterize Marcello and to set the emotional tone for Lelia's reaction and relationship to him through the dead Andrea and through her own changes in attitude. One of the major changes involved is her attitude towards her own name: Andrea had wished to change it from "Lelia" to "Leila," and Massimo Alberti follows Andrea's lead in this respect. Lelia herself resists the change and only comes to accept it, together with her submission to Massimo's religious and humanitarian ideals, towards the end of the story. Fogazzaro's choice of the name "Leila" for the title of the novel shows his concern with her role primarily as Andrea and, later, Massimo wish to interpret it.

18. Likewise in chapter 1 of *Leila,* but so much farther on as to constitute a separate episode, is the description of the reaction of Andrea's closest friend, Massimo Alberti, who has just arrived. For Marcello, Massimo is a surrogate for his son, and the father hopes that Massimo and Lelia will fall in love and marry. Sitting in his room, Massimo hears the music described in the long passage just discussed. He recognizes the themes, especially that from *Norma,* and thinks it must be Lelia who is playing, though it is actually Marcello improvising. However, Massimo's erroneous deductions concerning the identity of the presumed performer and her state of mind as revealed in the improvisations color his attitude, so that, although the music serves only as a background affecting the emotional level of Massimo's reactions, this passage furnishes the material for a good part of the further development of the story.

19. Lelia suspects that Massimo may be interested in marrying her only to obtain the property that Marcello Trento intends to leave her when he dies. She is therefore cold and unresponsive when Massimo speaks to her in the garden, and again when they are inside the house and she offers to play for him. She plays, from memory, an unspecified piece from Schumann's *Carnaval,* rather unfeelingly. Massimo asks for the aria from *Norma,* but Lelia tries to pick it out on the piano and says she does not know it; he doubts her and is tempted to refer to her having played it the previous night, but refrains from doing so.

Lelia turns the conversation to Piero Maironi ("Benedetto"), whose favorite disciple Massimo had been; later in the same scene, Lelia plays a Heller étude for Marcello, although she tells Massimo she does not like it. The music-making here serves principally as background for the development of the relationship between Massimo and Lelia in the initial stages of the misunderstanding between them.

20. Marcello comes into the drawing-room looking for Lelia but does not find her; he sits at the piano and improvises again on the Pergolesi *Stabat mater*. Lelia enters; as she hears the music, her feelings of antagonism towards Marcello diminish still further, but she is still inhibited by her pride from saying so. Marcello also is inhibited by her presence; he begins to play, from a manuscript copy, an air from Carafa's *Le prison d'Édimbourg*, but, tiring of it, he passes to another of his (and Fogazzaro's) favorite composers:

Buttò via il manoscritto, pose sul leggìo un grosso volume di Clementi, vi cercò certa pagina tutta segnata di annotazioni a matita. Lelia conosceva il volume, non ricordava quella pagina. Il signor Marcello, chino il busto in avanti, aggrappate ai tasti le grandi mani adunche come artigli di falco, fissi gli occhi accesi sulla musica, corrugata la fronte in uno sforzo di lettura e d'interpretazione che gli fremeva nelle mascelle inquiete e persino nei capelli irti, superò sè stesso. Com'ebbe finito, Lelia espresse la sua simpatia per Clementi, prese in mano il volume.

"Povero Clementi!" disse il signor Marcello. "Chi sa dove andrà a finire!"

Ella non capì subito.

Marcello's reference is to what will happen to the book and to his heritage, and, by further implication, to the ideals for which he has lived and which he has seen vanish.

21. After Marcello Trento has died, Lelia visits Donna Fedele Vayla di Brea, a former flame of Marcello's, now an old lady whose friendship extends not only to him but also to Massimo and Lelia. The girl plays for Donna Fedele the only piece

Marcello ever composed, a barcarolle. After Donna Fedele has gone to bed, Lelia goes out intending to commit suicide; she is seen by one Pestagran, a Protestant colporteur of Bibles, who notifies Donna Fedele and causes the latter to go out and rescue Lelia. The emotional background supplied by the music in this passage is therefore seen, in retrospect, to be not only relevant to the quiet presence of Donna Fedele but also a reflection of Lelia's intentions to end her own existence.

22. Before Massimo Alberti leaves to go to Valsolda and compete for a village doctor's post which is open there, he hears Lelia playing "Aveu" from Schumann's *Carnaval;* this piece gives its name to the entire chapter 13, and becomes the emotional corner-stone of their rapprochement and eventual avowal of love for each other. Donna Fedele, in whose house Lelia has remained, gives her a letter of Alberti's to read, in which he recognizes his love for her, saying:

Mi chino, bevo il profumo ch'ella usa e che la carta serba ancora, che mi fa dolere il petto come la divina musica di "Aveu" di Schumann, che, suonata da lei, mi fece dolere in un modo tanto dolce fino alle braccia e ai polsi.

After reading this letter, Lelia comes to a realization of her own love for Massimo; she goes to the drawing-room and plays Schumann's "Aveu":

Passò nel salone, si mise al piano, suonò "Aveu" con un divino impeto, pensando che il piano, se avesse un'anima, a sentirsi sviscerare così, capirebbe; pensando che forse, là nel suo romitaggio lontano, egli sentirebbe qualche cosa vibrare in sè. Le vennero in mente, con un colpo di gioia, versi adattati alla musica di "Aveu" da un amico del signor Marcello:

> "Ah solo un demonio e un angelo il san
> Che pugnan, crudeli, nel fragil mio cor.
> Or vince il più dolce, mi dono in sua man,
> Or scendo a un abisso di fiori e d'orror,
> Or sappi che brucio, che moro di te,

Or tutta mi prendi chè Iddio mi perdè."
Uno solo rispondeva al suo sentimento, ma come ci rispondeva!
Or sappi che brucio, che moro di te.
Suonò il pezzo due, tre volte per quel verso, per quel solo verso.
Poi si alzò dal piano. . . . Ritornò al piano, ne strappò da capo i rotti
accenti della passione delirante.
"Gesù!" pensò Teresina preparando la tavola per il pranzo. "Cossa
gala po?"

After recognizing her love for Massimo, Lelia goes to join him
in Valsolda, where they prepare to spend their lives in humble
service to the poor, and where Maironi-Benedetto's mortal remains are brought to be buried in the cemetery of Oria.[27] The
music of Schumann's "Aveu" and other Romantic songs is repeatedly referred to in the rest of *Leila*, as a background for
their feelings.

23. In the short story "La stria," the "contessina" Nana tries
to play a trick, using a "stria" or Twelfth-Night surprise-party
to bring her boy-friend, a lieutenant of sharp-shooters, to her
house under the pretense that he is her music-teacher. At the
climax of the party, he is asked to play, and he improvises a
string of fantasies on *I Puritani, Rigoletto, Il pirata*, and later on
Boito's *Mefistofele*. The main purpose of the music-making in
this humorous story is to advance the action by showing the
effect of the "maestro's" playing on the company; in the end the
contessina's plans gang agley because the estate-superintendent
Sior Toni takes the supposed music-teacher away and packs him
off to Vicenza.

24. "Màlgari," a story of sixteenth-century Venice, has an
atmosphere like that of a fairy-tale—a noblewoman whose child
has died brings up a foundling (named Margherita but called,
from her childish mispronunciation of the name, Màlgari), but is
told in a dream that if she does not wish to lose her, she must
keep her from all music and poetry. At the end of the story,

[27] For the symbolism of *Leila*, as well as of the preceding three books,
see my "Fogazzaro's Maironi Tetralogy," *Italica*, XLII (1965), 248–259.

after Màlgari has been brought up on the island of Syra and carefully shielded from all contact with poetry or music, she returns to Venice and devotes herself to taking care of the victims of a plague which has just carried off her father:

Ella assistette, fra gli altri, un giovane musicista straniero, venuto dal Nord in Italia per l'arte sua; un povero bello e gentile giovane, che, guarendo, s'innamorò forte di lei e non glielo potè dire perchè ella, sentendo pure confusamente che l'avrebbe amato e che quello non era il tempo di amare, lasciò a un tratto di visitarlo. Cessata la morìa, pensò ancora a lui, e molto, ma non lo vide più.

She is married to the Doge, and on her wedding-trip to the island of Syra, she discovers that one of the sailors is the young Nordic musician. He tells her of a magnificent poem of his father-land (clearly the Kalevala) and recites parts of it to her:

"Mi suoni" diss'ella subito al giovane "mi suoni il canto del vecchio poeta."

Il giovane andò e tolse il suo strumento, un violino italiano. . . . Lo strumento suonò, con tutta l'anima sua di patriota, di artista, e di amante, una musica sublime. I delfini innamorati seguivano la nave, i marinai e gli ufficiali, i servi e i signori accorsero, si affollarono sul ponte ad ascoltare il magico suono senza che il suonatore se ne avvedesse. Quando se ne avvide s'interruppe, volle congedarsi da Màlgari; ma di lei non trovò più che un fazzoletto bagnato di lagrime. . . .

Se di lei solo rimase un fazzoletto bagnato di lagrime, noi sappiam che la perla era fatta di lagrime appunto e dell'anima di un poeta; noi sappiamo cos'ha detto la piccola Nereide malinconica dell'Egeo:

"Io sono del mare, tu sei del cielo."

25. "Fedele," the first tale in the volume of that name, tells of a young woman named Fedele who has become estranged from her father by marrying against his wishes. Fogazzaro tells the story in his own person; the climax is reached at a concert given in a hotel where Fedele's father Zuane, old and blind, plays and then she sings, hoping to soften his heart, the *aria di chiesa* "Pietà, Signore," formerly ascribed to Stradella:

Vorrei poter esprimere la timida dolcezza accorata del suo canto quando incominciò sottovoce:

> Pietà, Signore
> Di me dolente.

. . . Gli occhi miei, tornando lentamente al piano, incontrarono a caso il volto del cieco, mentre la dolce voce saliva con un fremito di passione alle parole:

> Se a te giunge il mio pregar
> Non mi punisca il tuo rigor.

Lo Zuane porgeva il viso accigliato verso la musica, la bocca semi-aperta. A un tratto lo vidi piegarsi a destra, sussurrar qualche cosa a un vicino che gli rispose guardando la Fedele, come se gli parlasse di lei. Ella cantava allora con uno straziante spasimo nella voce:

> Ah! non fia mai che nell'inferno
> Io sia dannata al fuoco eterno.

Fedele breaks down, but Zuane's heart is not softened and the two are not reconciled at the end of the story. The music is an essential part of the action, in that both father and daughter are performers and their final contact and conflict is inextricably interwoven with their music-making; it serves both to characterize them and to set the tone, especially in the correspondence between the "Stradella" aria and Fedele's impassioned but unsuccessful plea.

26. "Un'idea di Ermes Torranza" is, essentially, the trick of an old poet who brings together an estranged couple after his death by telling the young wife, Bianca, to play a certain *romanza* of his at night, alone, in the music-room of her father's house, and her husband, on hearing the music while he waits outside, is to take that as a sign of reconciliation. As Bianca goes into the music-room and prepares to play:

Aperse la romanza per dar una passata all'introduzione, non troppo facile, che avea letto una volta sola. Ma le pagine non volevano stare aperte, si chiudevano tutti i momenti fastidiosamente. Le fermò col ritrattino di Torranza, e suonò, sotto voce, le quindici o venti battute d'introduzione che ricordano molto, in principio, la *Dernière Pensée Musicale* di Weber.

Dio, come parlava quella musica! Che amore, che dolore, che sfiduciato pianto! Entrava nel petto come un irresistibile fiume, lo gonfiava, vi metteva il tormento di sentirne la passione sovrumana senza poterla comprendere. Bianca si alzò con gli occhi bagnati di lagrime, andò ad aprir le imposte della porta che mette in giardino.

The playing of the music has the desired effect, and Bianca and her husband are reunited.

27. "Il fiasco del maestro Chieco" is another humorous tale: Chieco, having met a lady and fallen in love with her, has found that she loves not him, but his friend Cesare, from whom she is estranged. The story, told in the first person by Cesare, is that of a party arranged by Chieco, whose purpose is (although Cesare does not realize it until the end) to bring the estranged lovers back together again. Chieco's wild behavior and his playing, on both cello and piano, are of course present throughout the whole tale; the most extensive characterization is in the passage where Chieco plays excerpts from his as yet incompete opera *The Tempest* for Cesare, who finds it in part too Mendelssohnian but in part very original.

28. "R. Schumann (dall'op. 68)" is a humorous story, an obvious bit of fun which Fogazzaro is poking at his own "Versioni dalla musica." A lady, Donna Valentina, is entertaining some admirers, including a young man, an old gentleman, and the narrator, a poet. She plays a piece of music and then asks each guest to write a description of the scene which it suggests to him. The narrator sees that it is a piece from Schumann's Opus 68, smiles, and goes on to describe its effect:

—Scettico!—diss'ella, sotto voce. E strappò dalle viscere del piano il ripetuto angoscioso gemito che apre quella stupenda pagina di musica e vi ritorna ogni momento.

Aveva una sera felice. Nel *pianissimo* del ritornello, dopo le prime otto battute, mi parve proprio udire il lamento di un'anima.

The old gentleman and the young man describe very romantic scenes, whereas the narrator presents a farrago of nonsense, ending the story thus:

> Questa roba agghiacciò tutti.
> —Scusi—mi disse donna Valentina—cosa L'è venuto in mente?
> —Che vuole?—risposi.—Non capisco la musica. Ho scritto una sciocchezza a caso.
> —Va bene—replicò la dama.—In pena, Lei non avrà il Suo caffè, stasera. O thè con noi, o niente.

That the story is meant as a leg-pull is clear from the nonsensical scene with which the narrator presents Donna Valentina, and also from the subject-matter, Schumann's Opus 68. After all, this latter is the collection "Für die Jugend," none of whose pieces fit the description given; the only one having a *pianissimo* after the first eight bars is number 30, entitled simply "Sehr langsam— molto lento," and a simple little melody which would hardly bear the description given it in the passage just quoted or any of the wildly romantic interpretations placed on it.

In this story, Donna Valentina recognizes that music is "una lingua senza dizionario e senza grammatica da non potersi tradurre lì per lì con sicurezza." Fogazzaro nevertheless, throughout his fiction, treated music as a vehicle for conveying meanings of a wholly emotional type—his characters' loves, sorrows, religious aspirations (especially in *Leila*), and (in the case of Marina in *Malombra*) frustrations and hatreds. Fogazzaro's lecture *Il dolore nell'arte* is often cited in this connection, with his extensive discussion of the first movement of Beethoven's "Moonlight" sonata as a supreme exemplification of the power of music to express feelings beyond the reach of words.[28] Some

---

[28] For the relation between emotional attitudes as expressed in sentence-melody in language and its extension in music on the one hand,

critics, however, have been misled by the fact that Fogazzaro's characters are so frequently both musical and emotional, into considering them as incapable of any other type of behavior—as "affettivi puri," in Raffaele Viola's words.[29] From this misconception has sprung a widespread current view of Fogazzaro as a sentimentalist whose works, with the passing of interest in his religious views after Modernism was condemned in the encyclical *Pascendi* of 1907, and with present-day anti-romantic attitudes, have sunk to the status of mere period pieces of minor value.[30]

It must be pointed out, however, that in the first place not all of Fogazzaro's major characters are musically inclined. Foremost among these are his two reformers, Daniele Cortis in politics and Piero Maironi in religion. There is, in fact, a marked correlation between practicality and absence of music in Fogazzaro's fiction. As we have already mentioned, music is not mentioned at all in the middle third of *Il santo*, when Benedetto-Maironi is in contact with the practical world of peasants, upper-class society, church, and government, in his abortive effort to get across his message that the Church needs reforming. Piero Maironi himself is described at one point as beng so unmusical that "non era capace di metter giù un accordo, sul piano" (Jeanne in *Il santo*, chapter 1).

In the second place, not all of Fogazzaro's musically inclined people are romantically emotional; for instance, the dictatorial Benedictine abbot of *Il santo* (chapters 3 and 4), who expels Benedetto-Maironi from the abbey where he has been a kind of

and in denotational aspects of words and linguistic structure on the other, see my *Introductory Linguistics* (Philadelphia, 1964), ch. 70 and references there given.

[29] Viola, *Fogazzaro*, pp. 1–38.

[30] As shown, for example, by the inclusion of a chapter on Fogazzaro by Antonio Piromalli (one of his major detractors) in *Orientamenti culturali: letteratura italiana—i minori* (Milan, 1962), IV, 2987–3037. I have tried to show the erroneous nature of this judgment in my monograph *Antonio Fogazzaro e la crisi dell'Italia moderna* (Ithaca, 1967).

lay brother, is highly musical, a good performer on the piano, and an admirer of Mozart in the best Fogazzarian manner. A somewhat less disagreeable, but nevertheless rather affected, ridiculous, and unsympathetic character is Carlino Dessalle of *Piccolo mondo moderno* and *Il santo*, a *fin-de-siècle* esthete who is highly musical and shares all of Fogazzaro's enthusiasm for "musica antica." Even in his main characters, there are degrees of musicality: Luisa Maironi and Jeanne Dessalle, to mention only two, are considerably less advanced in their musical understanding and in their reaction to music than are, say, Elena and Lelia. Fogazzaro's sense of humor, which is never far from the surface, also keeps his normal correlation of music and heightened emotion from deliquescing into sentimentality, as in the boating scene (discussed above under number 12) where Luisa sings a Donizetti aria for Franco and immediately thereafter they hear the aria "aped" by the bassoon from their visitors' boat ("s'udì un fagotto scimmiottar l'aria di *Anna Bolena*").

A complete study of Fogazzaro's imagery would require a separate discussion; here, it is enough to say that by far the greater part of his mentions of music fall under the heading of direct description and a remarkably small proportion of them are involved in similes or metaphors. There are only four similes in which something is compared to a musical phenomenon. In two of them, an old instrument is involved: Marina says of herself (*Malombra*, Part I, chapter 2), "Ho i nervi scordati come un pianoforte di collegio," and the deaf old Signora Pasotti's voice is compared to an old spinet: " 'Perdonem, Luisa' diss'ella, con la sua voce velata che pareva venisse da una vecchia spinetta chiusa" (*Piccolo mondo antico*, Part II, chapter 4). In one, a specific composer is mentioned as the source of an emotional effect—"una dolcezza malinconica . . . lo stesso effetto che mi fa qualche volta Mendelssohn" (*Il mistero del poeta*, chapter 2); and in the fourth, the writer of a letter (Elena in *Daniele Cortis*, chapter 11) compares herself to "qualcuno che, avendo perduto una persona cara . . . fugge la musica."

Metaphors involving music are somewhat more frequent; there are fourteen in all: one of general psychology and the others about equally divided between characterizations of scenery (four), of actions (five), and of people (four). Typical of the metaphors involving scenery are those from *Leila* where the environment of Don Aurelio's house is called "una musica di bontà intorno alla povera umile casa dell'uomo di Dio" (chapter 2) or where Massimo says of the mountains of Valsolda ("È musica di Schubert, tutto questo . . . *Der Müller und der Bach*" (chapter 21). Certain actions, particularly conversations, are called by the names of musical activities, general or particular: for example, from *Piccolo mondo moderno*, "La povera marchesa . . . assisteva muta al duetto brillante dell'amica e del Commendatore" (chapter 9), or from "La stria," "cantata almeno in *do*, in *re*, in *mi*, e nei relativi diesis la solita sinfonia, di ritornarsi alla stazione." Sometimes, people are characterized in musical terms, especially in Chieco's rhapsodical description of Donna Antonietta in "Il fiasco del maestro Chieco," primarily as comparable to Bach's music. In one place, a general philosophical consideration is voiced in a metaphor carrying on a direct evaluation of music, where (in *Malombra*, Part IV, chapter 7), just before Marina shoots Silla, she is conversing with the old Commendatore Vezza and the doctor:

—Musica!—diss'ella, sorridendo e guardando il lago.—Quella che vuoi, lago mio! Non è vero, Vezza, che la musica è ipocrita come un vecchio ebreo e ci dice sempre quello che il nostro cuore desidera? Non è per questo che ha tanti amici?

—Marchesina—rispose quegli cercando di fare il disinvolto—fuori di noi non c'è musica, non c'è che un vento. Le corde sono dentro di noi e suonano secondo il tempo che vi fa.

It will be noticed that most of Fogazzaro's imagery involving music has emotional over-tones; the only instances where his metaphors are non-emotional are the five which occur in *Piccolo mondo moderno:* three describing actions, one describing the appearance of the monastery of Praglia (Carlino says of it:

"Praglia è il sogno di un vecchione vergine e santo che . . . si è addormentato al suono di un preludio di Bach," chapter 2), and one characterizing modern esthetes, whom Carlino calls "piccoli concertisti di flauto e clarinetto" in comparison with Goethe and Schiller (chapter 5). This absence of emotion in the *Piccolo mondo moderno* metaphors is part of Fogazzaro's technique in conveying the dryness and emptiness of contemporary upper-class small-town society, in contrast with Piero Maironi's developing religious devotion.

Another type of association is that of a particular piece of music with a person or situation, thus reflecting an aspect of character or of the action. The clearest of these associations in Fogazzaro's fiction is that of Marina, in *Malombra*, with Meyerbeer's *Robert le Diable*, excerpts from which are mentioned in Part I, chapter 5, and in Part IV, chapter 4; in both of these instances the choice of music corresponds to her ungovernable, wayward temperament. There are eight pieces of music involved in this type of association: not only (as might be expected) the Pergolesi aria in *Daniele Cortis*, the Schumann "Ich hab' im Traum geweinet" and the Schubert "Heidenröslein" in *Il mistero del poeta*, and the Pergolesi, Bellini, and Schumann pieces mentioned in the discussion of *Leila*, but also certain pieces whose content seems appropriate for particular occasions. Thus, a fantasia on Verdi's *Vespri siciliani* fits the presence of the Barone di Santa Giulia, Elena's Sicilian husband, at the beginning of chapter 5 of *Daniele Cortis*, and the chorus of exiles from *Nabucco* is played by the band just before Elena leaves at the end of that chapter for her exile in Cefalù. A sardonic comment is provided, in *Malombra*, in Part I, chapter 5, when Marina faints after wondering whether or not she is Cecilia Varrega reincarnated:

e da una barca lontana indugiatasi più delle altre sul lago, veniva il canto spensierato:

> Cossa l'è sta Merica?
> L'è un mazzolin di fiori

> Cattato alla mattina
> Per darlo alla Mariettina
> Che siamo di bandonar.

And of course the best known of all Fogazzaro's associations of songs with people is the repeated use, in *Piccolo mondo antico*, of the song "Ombretta sdegnosa del Mississipì," which her uncle Piero sings to Franco and Luisa's daughter Maria, who, from her pronunciation of the words, becomes known in the story as "Ombretta Pipì."

One of the major obstacles to Italians' willingness to accept Fogazzaro as a great writer has been the extent to which his liking for foreign, especially German, culture was reflected in his works. He was aware of this conflict, and it is referred to several times, beginning with his earliest work of fiction, *Miranda*, in which the heroine is made to say ("Il libro di Miranda," section 9):

> Pareami un tempo barbara favella
> La musica tedesca. Or, se talvolta
> N'apro a caso i volumi e tento il suono
> Entrar mi sembra in una chiesa ignota,
> Di cui nè fin si vede nè principio;
> Vi si sente pregar con tante voci,
> E di tutta le gente inginocchiata
> Si vedono i reconditi pensieri.

Later in the same book ("Il libro di Miranda," section 63) the heroine feels psychological strength coming to her from playing a Neapolitan tarantella set by some German composer:

> Pronta al cembalo m'assisi,
> Sovra le corde docili, possenti,
> Strappai con foga amara una selvaggia
> Tarantella di Napoli dagl'irti
> Nodi e viluppi di tedesche note. [. . .]
> Le ornate lodi e i lusinghier sorrisi
> Non mi turbâr; mutai vita e natura.

Forte voler anche sul male impera;
Guarir mi sento.

That the common people were not as alive to the beauty of such music as Bach's, Fogazzaro was also aware, as shown in the following passage from *Malombra* (Part III, chapter 1), in which the priest Don Innocenzo is telling of a young organist's visit to his church:

Narrava . . . che, la domenica precedente, vi era venuto per caso a suonare l'organo un giovane maestro, il quale avea magistralmente eseguita certa musica di un tedesco, di Bach, gli pareva. Al popolo la musica era piaciuta poco; ma lui n'era ancora imparadisiato.

Fogazzaro's use of music in his fiction is quite individual and peculiar to him. Some other Italian authors of the same period make very little use of it (for example, Verga); others, such as D'Annunzio, use it as an element of show and splendor. For Fogazzaro's characters, reaction to either their own or others' performance of music is a natural accompaniment to heightened emotional sensitivity—one of the ways in which intense longing, primarily but by no means exclusively sexual love, is manifested. The essential role that music plays in all Fogazzaro's major works and in some of his minor ones affords a key to understanding both his importance as a pioneer in bringing turn-of-the-century Italy into contact with modern European culture, and his, we hope, temporary neglect in Fascist and post-Fascist nationalistic and anti-Romantic Italian cultural involution.

The Operatic Novel:
Joyce and D'Annunzio

By ROBERT M. ADAMS

When he sat down, in the late 1880's, at the age of twenty-five or so, to establish himself as his nation's foremost novelist, Gabriele D'Annunzio had in mind a characteristically magnificent scheme. He would write, not one novel, but nine, in three groups of three, to be called romances of the rose, the lily, and the pomegranate. His numerical scheme, so reminiscent of Dante's triplicity, was supplemented by a fruit-and-flower symbolism; the rose, it is fair to guess, represented novels of passion, the lily novels of asceticism and denial, while the pomegranate suggested novels of triumphant ego-affirmation, novels of rebirth invoking the promises of eternity. No doubt fortunately, the grandiose plan remained largely incomplete, the last two categories being represented by but a single novel apiece. *Le vergini delle rocce* stands alone to represent the "lily" program; *Il fuoco* is all that was ever written of the pomegranate. But the romances of the rose, perhaps because they appealed more richly to his imagination, flowered into three books—*Il piacere* (1889), *L'innocente* (1892), and *Trionfo della morte* (1894).[1]

[1] *Il piacere* is a rather lush study of what has become known these days as *la dolce vita;* Andrea Sperelli, rejected by the corrupt and insidious Elena, proceeds after the serpentine fashion of the Vicomte de Valmont to wind himself about the religious innocence of Maria

It is not easy to understand the literary taste which apparently permitted James Joyce to consider the pompous, magniloquent, empty *Il fuoco* as D'Annunzio's fictional masterpiece (Stanislaus Joyce, *My Brother's Keeper* [New York, 1958], p. 147). *Trionfo della morte* had aroused D'Annunzio's special devotion; though he was a fatally fluent composer, he worked five years over this novel, deepening and intensifying it as, unfortunately, he did with too few of his other productions. His theme was the slow, almost eventless disintegration of a personality; his protagonist was young, sufficiently gifted, sufficiently attractive, and quite sufficiently wealthy; he was in full possession of an adored and endlessly seductive mistress. Yet an unbroken chain of "states of consciousness" was to lead Giorgio Aurispa fatally, and in the end avidly, to a blind wrestle of love and hate atop a precipice from which he and his entangled mistress Ippolita must ineluctably, despairingly, triumphantly fall. *Trionfo della morte* was as free as any of D'Annunzio's other stories from the laborious logic of a developing plot. But it had, unlike most of the others, a sustained inner tension, an undercurrent of destructive violence tugging at the fragile structure of reason—which still lend it immense dramatic power. *Il fuoco* preaches, and at artless length; *Trionfo della morte* dramatizes. Particularly in the figure of Ippolita, goddess of love and death by whom Giorgio is helplessly hypnotized, forces are at work which could not have failed to appeal to Joyce's imagination. The very architecture of the book's emotions, with a vortex of hysterical anxiety hidden just beneath a cool social surface, must have appealed to the future author of *Ulysses;* by contrast, the emotions of *Il fuoco* are all on the verbal surface and open for display. In the conven-

---

Ferres; in the end his pursuit of sensual pleasure becomes moral torment. *L'innocente* appears to be a more artless first-person retelling of the pure, forgiving woman and the profligate, dishonest, self-torturing male, until, halfway through the novel, Tullio discovers that his immaculate Giuliana is pregnant. The rest of the novel studies his reactions to cuckoldry, which culminate in the murder of the innocent bastard.

tional derogatory sense, they are theatrical. Joyce may have admired the pompous Nietzschean arrogance of *Il fuoco;* but for the fictional path he himself was to tread, the *Trionfo* was a more valuable precursor.

D'Annunzio was useful to Joyce not only by example but by precept; and his most explicit precepts were attached specifically to the *Trionfo.* In dedicating this violent, opulent volume to the painter Francesco Paolo Michetti (as he had already dedicated to the same friend *Il piacere*),[2] D'Annunzio laid down an impressive program for himself and for the modern novel; and this pronunciamento was so richly suggestive in itself, and so broadly applicable to the future fictions of Joyce, that no apologies are needed for translating it here:

To Francesco Paolo Michetti

I place your name before this book as well, which you particularly preferred above all, O Master of the Monks; before this book which I have written for you with special deliberation amid the retreats of strict art and silence.

When the last page was completed, you experienced along with me that sudden, deceitful joy over which, later, the spring dusk spreads so pure a veil of melancholy. And you experienced along with me regret for those already remote evenings when you used to come to my distant cell, and when, in the vast silence of the convent,

---

[2] I am indebted to my colleague Gian-Paolo Biasin for pointing out to me an early version of certain ideas and phrases of D'Annunzio's dedication in a three-part article on "La morale di Emilio Zola" first published in the *Tribuna* of July 1893 and reprinted in *Pagine disperse* (Rome, 1913), pp. 555–572. In fact, D'Annunzio's early journalism is rich in indications and insights which would find place in his later novels. Three articles on Wagner, inspired by Nietzsche (*Pagine disperse,* pp. 572–588), provide the core of the great discussion in *Trionfo della morte;* the scene of public auction which so tellingly concludes *Il piacere* first appears in a Roman chronicle of *mondanités* (*Pagine disperse,* pp. 126–129). Though it is only a coincidence, the sort of brief, enigmatic sketch which D'Annunzio collected under the heading "Grotteschi e rabeschi" has a good deal in common with the Joycean short story.

while our favorite beverage smoked in its cups, and the warmth of our thoughts seemed to rise through the air, I read aloud to you my latest writings. Dear to me was that time of truce, and greatly did I look forward to it, after the bitter struggle of each day. The loftiest joy to which a devoted artist can aspire today—is it not that of uncovering the still-virgin and secret work to one who is his equal, *one who understands everything?*

We had often talked together of an ideal book of modern prose, which—while being rich in its tones and rhythms like a poem, combining in its style the most diverse energies of the written word—might bring into harmony all the multiplicities of knowledge and all the multiplicities of enigma; which might mingle the precisions of science with the seductions of the dream; which might seem, not to imitate, but to *continue* Nature; and, free from the shackles of the story, might carry within itself, created with all the means available to literary art, the particular vitality—sensual, sentimental, and intellectual—of a human existence located at the very center of the universal cosmic life.

You will find this idea reflected (alas, too palely, perhaps!) in this work when you consider the whole book in its unity.

Here is just a single *dramatis persona*, and here is represented—with all the power of the artistic instrument at my disposal—his particular vision of the universe; or, to put it better, since man is, according to the words of your divine kinsman Leonardo, a "model of the world," here is represented *his universe*. The interplay of actions and reactions between his individual sensibility and exterior things takes place against a background woven out of direct observations. His feelings, ideas, tastes, and habits do not vary according to the events of some particular adventure, developed from page to page with the aid of a logic more or less strict; rather, they present the principal quality of every organic life, consisting of an exact equilibrium between what is variable and what is fixed, between the constant forms and the forms which are adventitious, fugitive, and illogical. A sensation, an intuition, an initial idea, appear on the first page and continue to develop, according to the laws which govern such phenomena, through an innumerable forest of varied symbols which for a single comprehensive and clearsighted soul are all correspondent. From the vain bitterness of those words spoken on the bench of the Pincio to the ferocious struggle by night on the brink of the precipice, the *persona* feels, thinks, and responds through a perpetual succession of states of consciousness—a wakeful conscience indeed. In a word, you will not find here the continuity of a well-laid plot, but rather the continuity of an individual existence manifesting itself according to its triple nature over a limited period of time.

You will find, above all—though I may perhaps seem to hope that the effort I have made, to render the inner life in its richness and diversity, will have a value surpassing that of pure esthetic representation—you will find, above all, the resolve to make a work of beauty and poetry, a plastic and symphonic prose, rich in imagery and music.

To contribute generously toward the establishment in Italy of a *modern* prose for narrative and descriptive uses—that is my most lasting ambition.

The greater number of our narrative and descriptive writers never make use, for all their needs, of more than a few hundred common words; they ignore completely the most lively, rich, and vital element of our mother tongue, which some dare to accuse of poverty and even of stupidity. The vocabulary adopted by most of these authors comprises dubious vocables, inexact, linguistically corrupt, mottled and distorted by the vulgar usage which has destroyed their original meaning or changed it, and so constrained them to express senses different from, or even opposed to, the real one. And these vocables are hung together in sentences, nearly all of the same length, ill-organized, unrhythmic, and answering in no way to the ideal movement of the things they try to image forth.

Our native tongue, on the other hand, is the joy and the root-energy of the painstaking artist who knows it, penetrates it, and explores within it those treasures slowly accumulated from century to century, some of them continually turned over and renewed, others covered only by a layer of bark, still others hidden in the occult depths, full of marvels still unknown, capable of intoxicating the next explorer.

This tongue, sprung from the thick Latin trunk with a rich growth of innumerable flexible twigs, never resists a will which has enough strength and dexterity to twist and weave it into graceful garlands and sinuous wreaths.

Or, to forego figurative speech, I will say the Italian tongue has no reason to envy, and nothing to borrow from, any other European language, not only for the representation of the whole exterior world of modern times, but for the world of those "states of mind," the most complicated and rarefied into which analysts have ventured ever since the study of the human psyche was begun. And the psychologists, particularly they (since it seems that the new Italian novelists lean toward this science), the psychologists particularly have, to express their introspections, a vocabulary of incomparable richness, capable of fixing on a page with graphic precision the subtlest fugitive ripples of sentiment, down even to the uncoercible dream. And at the same time, along with these surpassingly exact symbols, they have musical elements so various and so effective as to be capable of rivaling the great Wagnerian orchestra in suggesting what only music can suggest to the modern mind.

Certainly in these very recent writers none of the characteristics are manifested which distinguish the peasant tradition in the novel —a tradition too remote and too alien from the present state of general consciousness. The ancient novelists of our tongue represented actions; none was ever curious about motives. Caught up in the intrigues of adventures either joyous or melancholy, they all defined their task as the creation of a frankly sensual life, leaving to cloistered monks the task of composing treatises on the nature of the soul.

If then the new psychologists want to relate to their spiritual ancestors, they should rediscover the ascetics, the casuists, the popularizers of sermons, homilies, and soliloquies; they should communicate with Frate da Scarperìa, with Bono Giamboni, with Catherine of Siena, with Giordano da Ripalta, with Cavalca and Passavanti; they should earnestly study themselves in the Mirrors of the Cross, ramble pensively through the Gardens of Consolation, and patiently frequent the company of Origen alternately with that of Saint Bernard.

Neither need they step outside the good ages to find examples of beautiful musical prose. Our greatest craftsmen in words have inherited from Latin eloquence the study of rhythms. In Rome verbal music was spoken and written; first spread abroad through the air from rostra, then enclosed by means of symbols in a book. As Marcus Tullius Cicero modulated his periods, almost in the manner of a singer, to produce within his hearers a vehement impulse, so Titus Livy in his *Decades* rivaled the poets in his metrical effects that he might resound Roman magnanimity through those deeds which he was called on to describe. Both knew that words, besides their intellectual significance, have a suggestive and emotional power in their compounded sounds.

Master that he was of the new tongue, Boccaccio was neither ignorant nor neglectful of this skill; occasionally he made use of a quite learned ear to vary the cadences of his exuberant sentences, to express better languid feminine blandishments or softnesses of amorous revery. Through the limpid and voluble speech of Firenzuola there flowed sometimes the melody of the brooks which slope through quiet hills down to the Bisenzio. And certainly Annibal Caro, before setting pen to paper, paused to hear, prolonging their resonance within him, those special words with which his two shepherds would mingle lascivious ingenuities in that secret and cavernous gulf lit only by the moon.

You will, then, rediscover, O Master of the Monks, in this prose which I have written for you, an occasional exact image, a noble rhythm. I have carried this prose within me for a lustrum, always enriching and compressing it. As the painters of those ancient *Triumphs of Death* invoked the fugitive graces of Life, so I in this *Triumph* have several times

celebrated the rich rituals
of tones, of colors, and of forms.

I have diffused light, music, and perfume over the griefs and distresses of him who is about to die; about his agony I have invoked the most malicious Appearances; I have spread a carpet of many colors beneath his vagrant feet. Before the eyes of the dying man, a beautiful and voluptuous woman, *terribilis ut castrorum acies ordinata*, raised against a great mystery of greenish-blue waters sprinkled with red sails, bites into and slowly savors the flesh of a ripe fruit, while from the corners of her greedy mouth the juice drips down over her chin like liquid honey.

And in other pages I have also collected for you, O Master of the Monks, the most ancient poetry of our race: that poetry which you first understood and loved forever. Here are the images of the joy and the sorrow of our race, beneath a sky invoked with savage faith, upon an earth labored over with the patience of centuries. The dying man sometimes feels passing through the air about him the breath of the sacred springtime; and, reaching after fresh strength, invoking an intercessor to grant him life, recalls the dedicated colony of fresh and warlike youths whom a monstrous bull of singular beauty conducted to the distant Adriatic. But as the Numidian king Syphax and the last of the kings of Macedon, Perseus the cruel, perished within the cyclopean walls of Alba de' Marsi, so the tragic descendant of Demetrio Aurispa perishes here in his tatters of alien purple and exile and prison. May peace be his, in the shadow of the mountain, forever!

We, O Master of the Monks, remain to listen for the voice of the magnanimous Zarathustra; and prepare in our art, with secure confidence, the advent of the Ubermensch, the Superman.

G. d'A.

From the Convent of Santa Maria Maggiore,
calends of April 1894

At first glance, the most striking aspect of D'Annunzio's program is the abandonment of plot, in the sense of a particular sequence of exterior happenings developed more or less logically from a beginning through a middle to an end. And it is true that what we casually call "nothing" keeps happening throughout *Trionfo della morte*. D'Annunzio has made the aimless nothings of exterior inaction precisely the strongest and most dramatic counterpoint of his inexorable inner story. He has not merely abandoned plot, he has made positive, active use of the reader's expectation of plot, as a desire to be disappointed. (The device is by no means unique to D'Annunzio; something of the same technique appears in writers like Huysmans and Maeterlinck, and of course it will rise to spectacular heights in the work of Proust. One might speculate that so long as the exterior world appeared almost static, a mobile plot was accepted as entertainment, diversion; in the modern world, where change seems to be out of control and motion is incessant, the most spectacular thing a story can do is stand still.) External circumstance thus becomes the material, not for an action, but for an anti-action; the overpowering mastery of psychological obsession is rendered precisely by the tug of unrepresented immobility against the obvious needs, of the reader outside the story, of the characters within it, for Something To Happen.

When the story is not stretched out like a string, it may be arranged in numerous interesting patterns—for example, in the form of a circle. *Trionfo della morte* opens with Giorgio Aurispa and Ippolita seated on a bench in the Pincio looking out over Rome; they are disturbed by a shout, investigate, and discover to their horror a crowd gathered about the stained street where a man has flung himself off the cliff. Periodically, through the novel, the image of Uncle Demetrio Aurispa appears before Giorgio, as he was in the last days before his suicide; and the two streams of imagery flow together in Giorgio's final, fatal leap from another cliff, with Ippolita in his arms. The devices of thematic repetition, of recollection and recapitulation, thus tend to replace those of progressive narration. Thematic repetition implies a pre-existing pattern for the novel's action; the motion of the fiction does not so much exploit a freedom or develop an assumption as discover a presupposition—the pattern proposed by D'Annunzio is akin to that known to students of Ibsen as "retrospective exposition," in which a minor step forward in time and action leads to a major reassessment of the action's predicates. In traditional romance, the adventurous hero makes, undoes, and remakes his destiny afresh on every page; the supreme question is, What will he do next? Not only does the D'Annunzio hero look inward and back; he is fulfilling a destiny which has already been spelled out, if only he can read the writing. He is a reader who deciphers the signatures of things, even as the reader deciphers him. Reality is diaphanous; the adventure of the hero is to look through it, and to allow himself to be looked through; both processes are aided by the example of other works of art. What the explication of *Hamlet* is to *Ulysses*, the account of *Tristan und Isolde* is to *Trionfo della morte;* through a Wagnerian glass darkly the hero looks to intuit the laws of existence which are exemplifying themselves silently, ineluctably, in his own being. Life is a forest of symbols, which Art does not imitate so much as continue; it must be explored not just unidirectionally, but through a complex crisscross of simultaneous interrelationships and juxtapositions—through the ineluctable modality of the visible rather than of the audible. The novel must take on, in the full sense, spatial dimensions, and hence be seen, like an artifact, outside time, in the simultaneous tension of its particulars. Of particular interest to Joyce must have been D'Annunzio's acceptance of new psychologies, new manners of analyzing "states of consciousness"—which should yet take their inspiration from old monkish students of the human conscience, doctors, and casuists, and guides to the bewildered.

Finally, D'Annunzio proposes a prose style as richly wrought as a poem, making use of the full resources of the language, and marshalling them so that they "answer to the ideal movement of the things they try to image forth." This ideal of prose which not only names but imitates the action it describes, which is impregnated with the secret emotional life of the viewer, could not have been more congenial to James Joyce; it is precisely the major difference between the prose of *Stephen Hero* and that of the finished *Portrait* as well as *Ulysses.* For this new mode of prose Joyce could have found ample inspiration in *Il piacere* and *Trionfo della morte*—not so much in *L'innocente*, which is rather gauchely first-person confessional, or in *Il fuoco*, which is "plastic" in the Ciceronian, or windbag, sense. An instance of D'Annunzio's prose at its unobtrusive, insinuating best may be

worth another extended quote—which, as we are concerned
with stylistics, had better be in the original:

Era il pomeriggio. Egli esplorava il sentiero tortuoso che ora saliva
ora scendeva andando verso la punta della Penna, lungo il mare.
Guardava davanti a sè, intorno a sè, con una curiosità sempre vigile,
quasi con uno sforzo d'attenzione, come se volesse comprendere un
qualche oscuro pensiero espresso dalle semplici apparenze o impa-
dronirsi d'un qualche inafferrabile segreto.

In un seno del colle litoraneo l'acqua d'un ruscello, derivata in una
specie di esiguo acquedotto composto di tronchi scavati e sorretto
da altri tronchi morti, attraversava la cavità dall'uno all'altro ciglio.
Altri rigagnoli erano guidati da tegole concave nel terreno fertile ove
prosperavano le verzure; e qua e là, su i rigagnoli luccicanti e
mormoranti, certe piante di bei fiori violetti s'inchinavano con una
grazia leggera. Tutte quelle cose umili parevano avere una vita
profonda.

E l'acqua soverchia scorreva, discendava per la china verso la
spiaggia ghiaiosa; passava sotto un piccolo ponte. All'ombra dell'arco
alcune donne lavavano le tele; e i loro gesti si vedevano riflessi
nell'acqua come in uno specchio mobile. Su la ghiaia le tele erano
spiegate al sole, candidissime. Lungo il binario camminava un uomo
scalzo, portando le sue scarpe in mano penzoloni. Una donna esciva
dalla casa del guardiano e gettava con un atto rapido qualche avanzo
da un canestro. Due fanciulle, cariche di tele, correvano ridendo a
gara. Una vecchia sospendeva a una canna una matassa tinta di
turchino.

Andando, nella terra tagliata, che faceva da argine al sentiero,
minute conchiglie biancheggiavano, esili radici agitate dall'aura pal-
pitavano. Era ancora visibile il segno della zappa che aveva tagliato la
terra fulva. Da un dirupo pendeva un gruppo di radici morte, con
una leggerezza di spoglie serpentine.

Più in là sorgeva una grande casa colonica portando alla sommità
del tetto un fiore d'argilla. Una scala esterna saliva a una loggia
coperta. Due donne in cima della scala filavano; e le ròcche splende-
vano al sole come d'oro. S'udiva strepitare il telaio. Si scorgeva per
una finestra una tessitrice, e il suo gesto ritmico nel lanciare le spole.
Nell'aia contigua stava coricato un bove grigio, enorme; che scoteva

le orecchie e la coda placidamente ma incessantemente contro gli insetti molesti. Le galline intorno razzolavano.

Poco oltre, un altro ruscello attraversava il cammino. Rideva: tutto crespo, ilare, vivido, limpido.

Poco oltre, presso un'altra casa, un orto folto di allòri taceva recinto. I fusti sottili e diritti sorgevano immobili, coronati dalla fronda lucente. E uno di quegli allòri, il più robusto, era tutto avviluppato da una gran vitalba amorosa che vinceva il fogliame severo con la mollezza dei suoi fiori nivei, con la freschezza del suo profumo nuziale. Sotto, la terra pareva smossa di fresco. Da un angolo una croce nera spandeva sul chiuso, nel silenzio, quasi la rassegnata tristezza che regna in un camposanto. In fondo alla viottola si scorgeva una scala, metà nel sole, metà nell'ombra, saliente a una porta socchiusa che proteggevano due rami d'ulivo benedetto sospesi su l'architrave rustico. Su l'ultimo gradino inferiore un vecchio seduto dormiva, a capo scoperto, col mento sul petto, con le mani posate su le ginocchia; e il sole stava per toccare la fronte venerabile. Giù per la porta socchiusa scendevano, a conciliare quel sonno senile, il rumore eguale d'una culla agitata, la cadenza eguale d'una cantilena sommessa.

Tutte quelle cose umili parevano avere una vita profonda. (*Trionfo della morte* [Milan, 1907], pp. 189–191.)

The passage sets up, as it were, a quiet ground bass of insight into natural things; repeating the sentence which reassures us that these humble things seemed to have a deep life of their own, and reinforcing it with careful particularities, the prose promises to remove us from the feverish mind of the tormented lover, insisting upon lowliness and the quiet continuity of objects. But Nature is not merely imitated, it is gradually extended till it penetrates the mind of the beholder with overtones of his own condition. The ground, compounded of tangled roots and shells, seems an intricate battlefield of life and death—and the dried roots, hanging off a crag, have the special quality of dead, abandoned life which is summarized in the snake's shed skin. The three spinning females may make us think, though without any special emphasis, of the three fates; while the enormous gray ox (his grayness wonderfully qualifying his oxiness with a sense of the drab) and the old man sleeping the sleep of senility to the sound of the lullaby serve as subdued emblems of torpid humanity. Most splashy and explicit, of course, is the climactic image of the loving clematis swarming over the laurel bush, conquering that "severe" foliage with the "softness of its snowy flowers, the freshness of its nuptial perfume." When we find a black cross set up nearby, the sense of Grand Guignol is not far from oppressive. Yet the passage as a whole is not marked out as spectacularly or obtrusively "symbolic"; most of the symbolism walks hand in hand with, and shelters itself behind, a meticulous surface realism. The careful reader will find a good many more symbolic overtones than I have troubled to indicate; but he will find them chiefly by probing behind the screen of represented things, perhaps only after he has sensed the whole book's pattern and progression, then turned back to this passage to seek out symbolic echoes. Thus the book makes clear its expectation of being read backwards as well as forwards, with the eye of an active analyst as well as of a passive entertainee. Finally, the richness and multiplicity of D'Annunzio's representational commitment calls for a word. His sentences are nervous, mobile, and responsive. They respond, first, to the object seen or sensed—as in the "altro ruscello" which "rideva, tutto crespo, ilare, vivido, limpido," in such striking contrast to the first one. But they are also responsive to the mind which is imagined as receiving and qualifying all these impressions—an anxious, placatory mind, which is seeking from nature one sort of peace and receiving from it terrible, half-perceived intimations of another. The mind of Giorgio Aurispa moves in cycles of centrifugal hope and ever-tightening despair; and because the alternations are unmotivated or motivated from outside the scale of represented reality, one has a sense of the mind's utter helplessness in the grip of vast impersonal powers. His thought expands, each time a little more anxiously, into an area of hope, then clamps shut, each time a little more tightly, on the sweet assurance of despair. Thus a

major effect of the book is achieved by repetition—not development, but mechanical return.

❧

Now in all these details D'Annunzio's novel finds intimate
parallels with the technique which Joyce first put to proof in the
Portrait. The abandonment of consecutive plot is not immediately apparent, for the sections are arranged in almost unbroken
chronological order.[3] But the consecutive plot has been broken
by a series of massive temporal discontinuities into a series of
vignettes and counterpointed scenes. A controlling principle in
relating these scenes is symbolic analogy. Stephen Dedalus,
crouching under the table and reciting a poem about "Pull out
his eyes, / Apologise, / Apologise, / Pull out his eyes," can be
seen in retrospect to have foreshadowed the tussle with Heron
and his cronies over Lord Byron and the demand to "admit"
(page 86) as well as the climactic "I will not serve" of page 281.
In the same way the succession of dimly perceived and altogether voiceless girls who wander through Stephen Dedalus'
self-absorbed consciousness gather slowly toward definition as
emblems of an anti-Ireland and an antireligion—batlike souls
they are, waking to consciousness of self in darkness and secrecy
and loneliness (pages 213, 259, 280), over whose imaginations
Stephen wants to cast his shadow. (The half-submerged image
here is of a warlock surrounded by his satellite conventicle of
witches, bound to him in sin, shame, and Luciferian pride.) So
too with the almost obsessive imagery of birds, which multiplies
and thickens toward the end of the book like the gathering of
migratory flocks, portentous and enigmatic. These repetitions,
no doubt about it, are more incremental in feeling than those in

[3] See a provisional outline of time relationships within the *Portrait* in
my *James Joyce: Common Sense and Beyond* (New York, 1966), App. I.
All references to the *Portrait* itself in this article are to the old Modern
Library edition, for reasons specified in the foreword of the book. The
other editions of Joyce's works referred to in this article are *Critical
Works* (London, 1959) and *Ulysses* (New York, 1934).

D'Annunzio's novel; the *Portrait* grows forward in time as *Trionfo della morte* does not. Yet it is not simply temporal development; rather the forward pattern of the *Portrait*, like the backward pattern of the *Trionfo*, is conditioned by an alternating cycle of contraction and expansion. Joyce introduces it first under the image of the moon:

Nothing stirred within his soul but a cold and cruel and loveless lust. His childhood was dead or lost and with it his soul capable of simple joys and he was drifting amid life like the barren shell of the moon.

> *"Art thou pale for weariness*
> *Of climbing heaven and gazing on the earth,*
> *Wandering companionless? . . ."*

He repeated to himself the lines of Shelley's fragment. Its alternation of sad human ineffectualness wtih vast inhuman cycles of activity chilled him, and he forgot his own human and ineffectual grieving (page 108).

The pattern of alternation is clear from then on; Stephen's extravagance with the exhibition money is explicitly an effort "to dam up, by rules of conduct and active interests and new filial relations, the powerful recurrence of the tide within him" (page 110), and the collapse of this dam, in his adventure among the whores, leads by direct revulsion to the long trauma of the retreat, and the short-lived effort at an artificial sanctity. And this whole process is summarized in metaphor, at the beginning of section 3, where a passage of personal introspection is superimposed on the waxing and waning of an equation in a scribbler, likened at third hand to a peacock's tail. The vast inhuman cycles of activity appear in this vision as the birth and death of stars, glowing and disappearing like the indices of the equation; they encounter in turn the equation of Stephen's soul, "going forth to experience, unfolding itself sin by sin, spreading abroad the balefire of its burning stars, and folding back upon itself, fading slowly, quenching its own lights and fires. They were quenched: and the cold darkness filled chaos" (page 116). This vision of the soul going forth to sin and experience, folding back upon itself, and coming to final rest only in the chill indifference of self-knowledge, encompasses after a fashion the entire book; [4] and it sharply qualifies that impression of it as a triumphant progress toward artistic freedom and fulfillment which simplistic readers sometimes bring away from the *Portrait*. In fact, Joyce's book, no less than D'Annunzio's, ends with a leap into the dark. Stephen Dedalus when he takes flight from Ireland knows, if not where he is going, at least what he is cutting himself off from; and the first section of *Ulysses* ticks off these alienations almost automatically—from church, from family, from country, from women, from language, from the traditions of his race and culture. But what has he found instead? His vocation, of course. But it would be in a stale Romantic tradition to have artistic creation represented as a soaring flight into the intense inane in pursuit of AE's "formless spiritual essences" (*Ulysses*, page 183). Joyce did not believe in flight of this sort; his art is a wrestle with the material, an act of incarnation—his essential subject is Ireland seen as fleshly men and women. If the term "epiphany" has any value at all in connection with Joyce's work, it is in calling attention to the translucence of the object, its capacity for embodying a meaning without forfeiting its thinginess. Joyce could never be permanently happy with a view of art which did not root its feet, at least some of the time, in the mud. The ending of the *Portrait* thus represents Stephen Dedalus, not at an ideal terminus, but at one momentary phase, the expansive phase, of his development; it will be followed by the "cold indifferent knowledge of himself" (*Portrait*, page 117) which speaks so powerfully in the first scenes of *Ulysses*. The real terminus of this development is the little black dot, at the end of "Ithaca,"

---

[4] It grows out of an earlier set of alternations—the train going through tunnels and open spaces alternately, the alternation of school and vacation, and the alternation of noise and silence caused by covering and uncovering one's ears in the refectory: "Term, vacation; tunnel, out; noise, stop" (p. 13).

down which the conscious mind of Joyce disappears into a visionary world—after which all flight is inward flight. But if we read the ending of the *Portrait* as the pausing on its outer arc of a pendulum which still has a swing to make the other way, the structure of Joyce's novel may be thought more closely related to that of *Trionfo della morte*, because more ironically limited, than at first glance appears.

A last area of influence from D'Annunzio to the *Portrait* has to do with imitative prose. Both authors shared a fondness for the purple patch and the plastic period; but the quality in question is what Joyce called elsewhere "an admirable adjustment of style and narrative" (*Critical Works*, page 122), a conscious imitation of the motion of consciousness, whether lyrical or merely contaminated. For example, in D'Annunzio's book, several layers and segments of experience often impinge on Giorgio Aurispa's mind simultaneously; through the repetition of thematic phrases and the mingling of different time levels, one gets the sense of a mind in vortex, at the mercy of its own superstitions and affinities. Early in the *Portrait* the same dreamlike interfusion of disparates can be seen in little:

The face and the voice went away. Sorry because he was afraid. Afraid that it was some disease. Canker was a disease of plants and cancer one of animals: or another different. That was a long time ago then out on the playgrounds in the evening light, creeping from point to point on the fringe of his line, a heavy bird flying low through the grey light. Leicester Abbey lit up. Wolsey died there. The abbots buried him themselves (*Portrait*, page 19).

Almost all these phrases have a previous record of usage in the *Portrait;* they flow together here, overrunning coherent grammar, as the little boy's mind fades into its memories. They prepare too for the dreamlike repetitions of the later sections—the imagined interlude of incestuous affection lying behind the grotesque little dwarf in the library, John Alphonsus Mulrennan's conversation with the red-eyed old man, and the actual dreams recorded in Stephen's diary. A deliberate loosening of logical structure is apparent in the last pages of the *Portrait;* images stream together, the story elements fade, language itself takes control. In allowing factual description to merge imperceptibly with symbolic representation and both to fade into a deep visionary insight, Joyce was treading paths down which D'Annunzio had passed before him. That he was not aware of his heraldic precursor seems in the highest degree improbable.

I don't suppose we need imagine Joyce sitting down to study D'Annunzio, and then conscientiously retiring to his work-desk in order to imitate him. Some authors may operate that way on special occasions, but Joyce was never a plodding follower. He roamed the fields of literature and subliterature, taking what he wanted and applying it when and where occasion offered. His view of the recent history of fiction envisioned a tide advancing "from Flaubert through Jacobsen to D'Annunzio" (*Critical Works,* page 71), and his own destiny was clearly to advance that tide still further. His acquaintance with D'Annunzio's work dated back, after all, at least a decade before he began work on the *Portrait* as we now know it, and two decades before its completion. We may estimate the ripening process, the increasing compression of materials and economy of effects, from comparison of the *Portrait* as finally finished with the surviving fragments of *Stephen Hero.* Such a transformation of one's entire artistic approach does not occur in isolation, or as a result of any single impulse; Joyce had to metamorphose himself and his whole conception of fiction in order to convert the ugly duckling of *Stephen Hero* into the glittering, angled *Portrait.* But in the process of this transformation it does not seem open to question that Gabriele D'Annunzio, both by precept and example, played a major role; and if he did so, *Trionfo della morte* must have been the vehicle of his influence. Paradoxically, but in all seriousness, it is a pretty good proof of these assertions that Joyce never mentions the book. He was more likely to talk about books and people whom he despised than about those from whom he drew practical and immediate inspiration; he was not eager to challenge indiscriminate comparisons. But the relationship with D'Annunzio was both intimate, long-lasting, and curiously prophetic—as a volume from Joyce's private library, now at the University of Buffalo, may serve to remind us. The volume is *Notturno;* it was written by D'Annunzio in hospital during the long pain-filled months after he lost an eye in aerial combat during World War I. It is a despairing, stripped, and painfully accurate record of a mind struggling in darkness, not just for sight but for vision. Joyce in his own unending struggles against blindness during the twenties and thirties evidently called once more for courage on the precursor who many years before had helped him to draw his own *Portrait.*

❧❧

The failure of Gabriele D'Annunzio as a novelist lay altogether in the unforeseeable collapse of his middle and later career. Looking upon *Trionfo della morte* as the work of a young man barely entering his thirties, one can scarcely imagine a more impressive exordium in the art of fiction. But the path trod by the later Joyce was one on which his only major novelistic predecessor was Flaubert; D'Annunzio turned back after his one unalloyed triumph, and the marks of regression are on *Il fuoco* —as we have seen. The prose is no longer ingeniously imitative, or not to such a degree; its aim is to be plastic, "fine," Chateaubriandesque. It is as if Joyce, after the radical experimentation of the later *Portrait,* had turned toward a fictional style founded more frankly on Newman. In fact the adventures of *Ulysses* into mindlessness or the universal mind (odd but authentic equivalents!) follow the grand example of *Bouvard et Pécuchet.* The *Wake* deepens and elaborates this bent, with incomparable consistency and complexity, but works from premises already laid down in *Ulysses*—as *Ulysses* itself derives straight from the attitudes worked out in the *Portrait* and *Dubliners.* Joyce's career develops in a magnificently straight, consecutive, inflexible line; that of D'Annunzio wavers, breaks, turns back on itself; hence their sharp divergence. But in following out his own premises, Joyce was also following out some of D'Annunzio's.

As Joyce finally came to conceive it, the novel is not merely a new and more complicated sort of story; it is a global and ultimately a cosmic construct—a continuation of Nature, not an imitation of it. That Bloom is not just Bloom, but Noman, a sun-god, a wandering star, a wandering Jew, Sinbad the Sailor, and fifty other historico-mythologic-folkloric-religious-imaginary analogues suggests a dimension for Joyce's later novels which D'Annunzio perhaps conceived but never tried to realize. Not so, however, the author of *Bouvard et Pécuchet*, a book which resembles the *Wake* most strikingly in accepting practically everything within its globe, and yet "representing" in the conventional fictional sense practically nothing. Like animated cartoon figures, Bouvard and Pécuchet rummage insatiably through the fields of human knowledge; they neither age nor learn nor progress toward any particular condition, they merely deepen the state they were "given." And simultaneously that state, of absolute inanity, expands through the cosmos and becomes, like the rhythm of Joyce's Brunonian opposites, forever quarreling and identifying, quarreling and identifying, the music of the spheres. Emancipated from the world of events and consequences, given the multiple freedoms of elastic space and simultaneous time, Joyce's last work, like Flaubert's, provides nothing less than a substitute cosmos in the form of fiction, a book which consists of its own style, "un livre sur rien." In this stage, Joyce's fiction has far transcended the dimensions of D'Annunzio; yet it does not cease to aspire, as D'Annunzio and Newman and Pater had taught it to do, after the condition of music.

This never-forgotten lesson provides a point of differentiation on which late Joyce stands quite free of Flaubert. *Bouvard et Pécuchet* is written in the very prose of prose; it cultivates an antistyle, in which the quality of a catalogue, all of whose separate multiple items add up ineluctably to a total value of zero, is imitated in deliberate effects of monotony and flat plod. The *Wake*, on the other hand, not only ripples and lilts and sings; it is musical in the formality of its structuring, the complexity of its inner relationships, and, above all, in the directness of its action on the reader's consciousness. Like music, it does not discourse on a limited number of specific referents, but offers itself to response as a multiplex, infinitely divisible, infinitely multiple *thing*. Music, one supposes, does not properly act on the mind through translation into a set of equivalent concepts or images; it is not reducible to anything except itself. No more does the reading of *Wake*prose act through evocation of characters, scenes, or ideas. Characters, scenes, and ideas are intermittently present, but the continuum they provide is so often violated or neglected that we cannot dwell in it for long with any satisfaction.

In effect, what Joyce found in his last fiction was a richly sufficient voice for D'Annunzio's "exact equilibrium between what is variable and what is fixed, between the constant forms and the forms which are adventitious, fugitive, and illogical." Every sentence in the *Wake* is a conflict, every structure contains its own destruction. The result is an order of music very different from D'Annunzio's—more richly harmonic, more sharply dissonant on occasion, always more complex. But music it always is—not just metaphorically, not in the sense of honeyed, rhythmic phrasing; it is language plucked, wrung, scraped, or hammered percussively, language which works on us, not wholly through its reference to something else, but also through its own internal push-and-pull of continual conflict and conciliation.

At the end of "Byzantium" and "Among School Children," Yeats figures forth a certain reconcilement of sense and intellect, of blood and images, under the metaphor of a dance. They are famous and properly admired passages; yet one may be excused for finding them both a little grandiose and facile. The reconciling metaphor of the dance comes in a shade too pat; it is easy to invoke as conclusive-inconclusive image, but hard to make operative as an answer to the serious problems raised by the poems. By contrast, Joyce involved his verbal music more actively in the creation and working-out of his novel's energies; he sensed the inarticulate ground bass of mood-underlying-speech as a part of the artist's whole given, an inescapable woof in the seamless web of human experience. It has been my contention that D'Annunzio did something to trigger Joyce's early interest in multiplying the artistic applications of which language is capable—in using it to represent deeply layered "states of mind." But behind the intermediate figure of D'Annunzio, it is impossible to overlook the looming shape of Richard Wagner, the supreme master of all the arts, the great poet-dramatist-musician of the nineteenth century. In his final development of notions which D'Annunzio helped stir to life in him, Joyce worked, by a commodious vicus of recirculation, back to D'Annunzio's great predecessor and patron saint. Joyce is, no less than D'Annunzio, Wagner's spiritual child—in token of which, *Tristan und Isolde* lives quite as fully in *Finnegans Wake* as in *Trionfo della morte*, and not much less reverently, either. The roundabouts, crosscurrents, and metamorphoses of intellectual influence in late-nineteenth-century European culture could scarcely find a more explicit paradigm.

Index